T0321465

BALFOUR AND WEIZMANN

Balfour and Weizmann

*The Zionist, the Zealot and the
Emergence of Israel*

Geoffrey Lewis

continuum

Continuum UK, The Tower Building, 11 York Road, London SE1 7NX
Continuum US, 80 Maiden Lane, Suite 704, New York, NY 10038

www.continuumbooks.com

Copyright © Geoffrey Lewis 2009

First published 2009

British Library Cataloguing-in-Publication Data
A catalogue record for this book is available from the British Library.

ISBN 978 1 84725 040 7

Typeset by Pindar NZ, Auckland, New Zealand

Contents

Maps and Illustrations

Maps

Maps drawn by David Appleyard

Illustrations

Acknowledgements

I must thank first the friends who have generously made their knowledge and views available to me and, the Balfour Declaration being a subject on which there are as many opinions as there are people ready to give them, who have not hesitated to tell me what they really think. Of these, I would particularly like to thank Owen Chadwick, Damian Collins, Alexander and Amira Goehr and Harry Levinson. I am very grateful also to Charles Elliott for reading my manuscript and giving me the benefit of his unerring critical judgement.

I owe a debt of gratitude to the writers and scholars who have gone before: Leonard Stein, whose *Balfour Declaration* remains the best account of the extraordinary episode and is a model of thorough research, fair-mindedness and subtlety; Elie Kedourie, scrupulous scholar of the Arab viewpoint; the editors of the twenty-three volumes of Weizmann's letters, whose commentaries and footnotes provide all the answers to the questions which arise in the reader's mind; Isaiah Berlin, whose thirty-page sketch of Weizmann in *Personal Impressions* gives the most discerning portrait of all; and Chaim Weizmann himself whose autobiography, *Trial and Error*, is a wonderfully vivid account of his heroic pilgrimage through life.

I thank the many archivists who have helped me in the quiet and courteous way that archivists always have: at the National Archives at Kew, the National Archives of Scotland in Edinburgh, the British Library, the House of Lords Record Office, the libraries of Cambridge University and Pembroke College, Cambridge, the John Rylands Library at Manchester University and the Brynmor Library at Hull University; and in Israel, Merav Segal at the archives of the Weizmann Institute at Rehovot, and the staff of the Central Zionist Archives in Jerusalem.

I must record my thanks to the following for permission to quote extracts from the following papers: for the quotation in Chapter 7 from the remarkable letters passing between Yusuf Ziya al-Khalidi and Theodor Herzl in 1899, the

Central Zionist Archives in Jerusalem; for extracts from the papers of Sir Ronald
Storrs, the Master and Fellows of Pembroke College, Cambridge; for extracts
from C. P. Scott's diaries, the University Librarian and Director, The John Rylands
University Library, Manchester; for extracts from the Lloyd George papers, the
Archives Officer, the Parliamentary Archives, Houses of Parliament; for extracts
from the papers of Sir Mark Sykes in the archive of the Sykes Family of Sledmere,
the Archivist of the Hull University Archives, Brynmor Jones Library; for extracts
from the papers of the Kerr family, Marquises of Lothian, the Archivist of the
National Archives of Scotland; for extracts from the papers of the Balfour family
of Whittingehame, East Lothian deposited in the National Archives of Scotland,
A. M. Brander, Esq.

Finally, I thank Robin Baird-Smith, a most sympathetic and knowledgeable
editor and one of the dwindling band of publishers who makes an author his
friend, and his devoted and resourceful staff at Continuum.

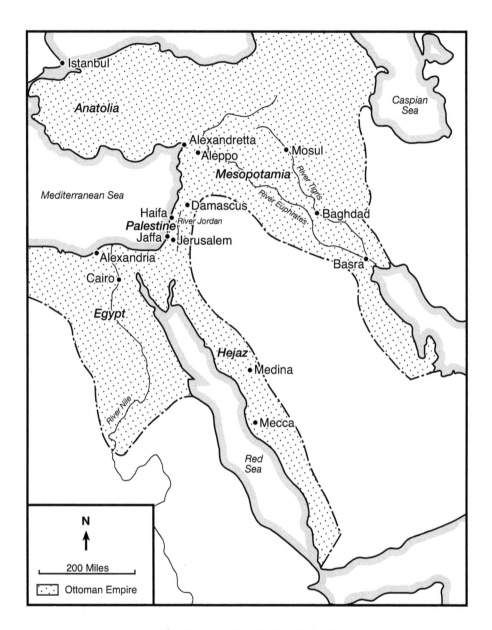

1. The Ottoman Empire in Asia in 1914

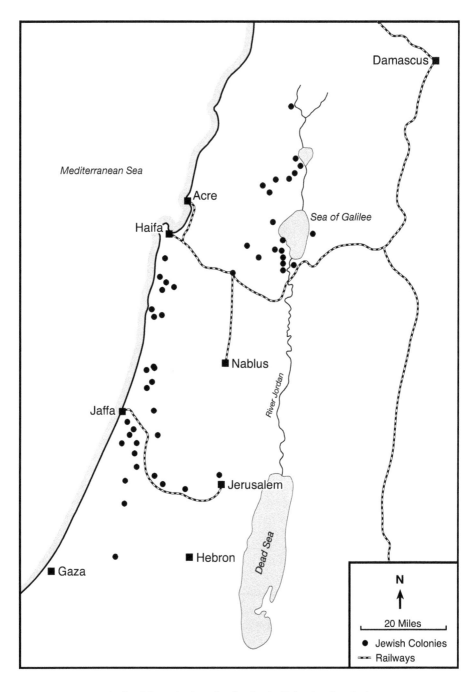

2. Jewish agricultural colonies in Palestine in 1914

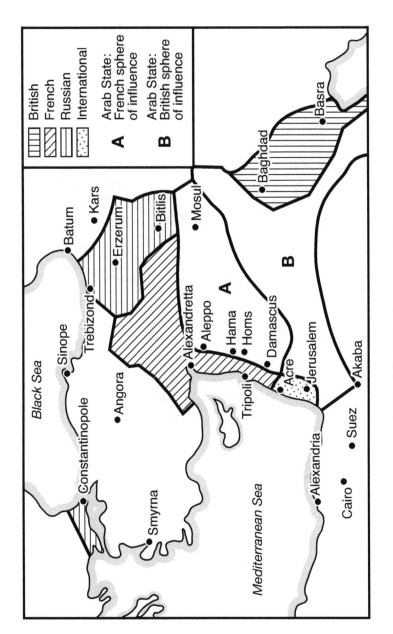

3. The Sykes–Picot Agreement, 1916

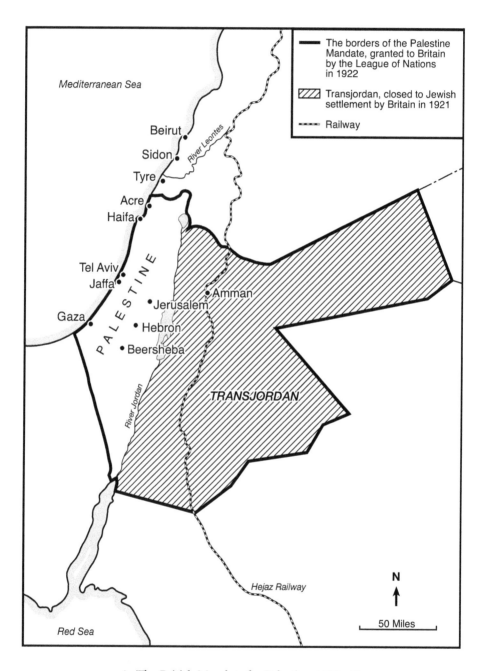

4. The British Mandate for Palestine, 1922–48

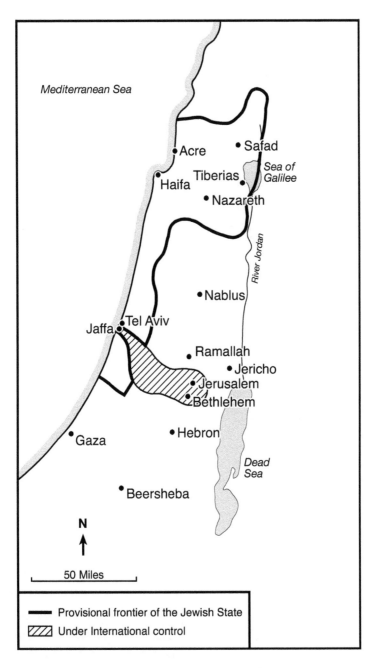

5. Provisional frontier for a Jewish State proposed by the Peel Commission in its plan for partitioning Palestine, 1937

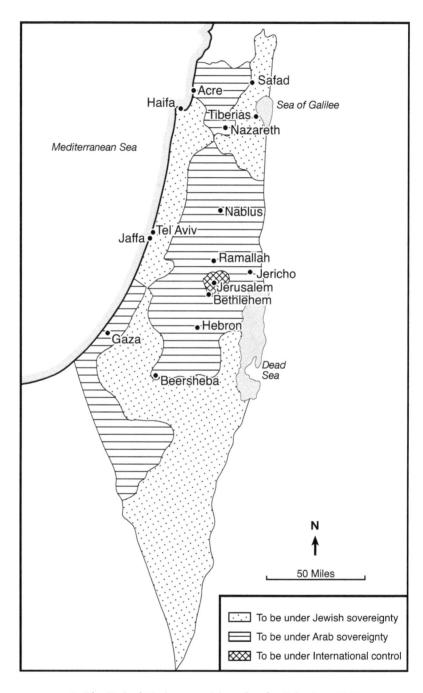

6. The United Nations partition plan for Palestine, 1947

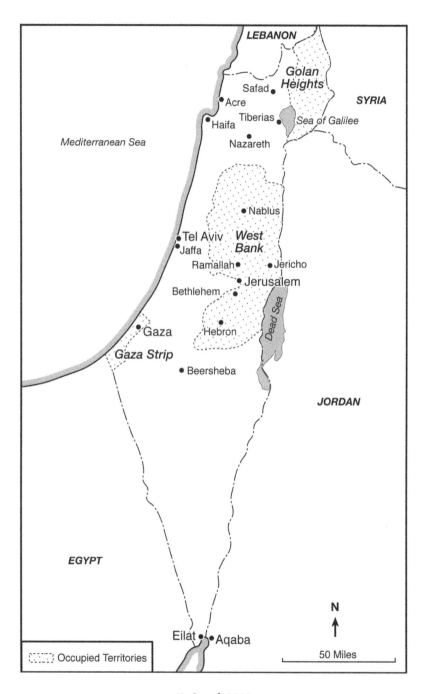

7. Israel, 2009

for Christine,
my wife

Jew and Arab

Well into the fourth year of the First World War, in November 1917, the British government did an extraordinary thing. It authorized Arthur Balfour, Foreign Secretary and Tory elder statesman, to write to Lord Rothschild, the most potent name in Engish Jewry, informing him that the government was in favour of establishing a national home for the Jews in Palestine. This was the Balfour Declaration. It was cast in understated terms and had been weakened by the drafting of many hands. It stated that the civil and religious rights of other communities in Palestine were not to be prejudiced. But its message to the world was unmistakable: the British cabinet was lending its authority to the return after nearly two thousand years of the Jews to the Holy Land.

Why should the British do such a thing? For it set off, as the government should have foreseen, a new enmity between Jew and Arab which has grown ever since in bitterness and violence. Any answer to this question must have regard, among many things, to the history of the Jews and Arabs in Palestine.

THE JEWS

At a time when myth and tradition cannot be disentangled from historical fact, Semitic tribes coming from the deserts of Arabia reached the east coast of the Mediterranean. One tribe claimed descent from Abraham of Ur and became known as Israelites from his grandson, Jacob, or Israel, the man who, according to the mysterious and provocative metaphor, wrestled with God. The Israelites went south to Egypt where they were later held in slavery by the Pharaohs until their leader, Moses, roused them to liberty and led them back across the Red Sea to the promised land of Canaan (Palestine). Their God had made a covenant with them that they should have Canaan as an everlasting possession. By 1100 BC they were established in the hill country there. They were distinguished from the people inhabiting the coast – Phoenicians or Philistines, from whom the word 'Palestine' is derived – by the peculiarity of their religious beliefs. By contrast with the idolatrous polytheism of the ancient world, the Israelites believed in one invisible God who had given them a set of Commandments as a basic code to live by.

By the time of King David and his son Solomon, at the beginning of the first millennium before the Christian era, the small nation of Israelites were the most powerful people in the eastern Mediterranean between the Egyptian and Assyrian Empires. Their chief city was Jerusalem. Here Solomon built his Temple to the glory of his people's God.

In the early sixth century BC, Jerusalem was sacked by Nebuchadnezzar, emperor of the Babylonian empire, and most of the people were removed to Babylon. But their captivity, although harsh, was short. The Persians soon occupied Babylon and permitted the Jews to go back to Jerusalem. During the next period of three centuries or so, the Jews again flourished and produced works of literature which are today an integral part of the civilization of the western world. Their law, known as the *Torah*, was refined into a binding and detailed code of religious observance and social behaviour.

The arrival of Hellenism in the Middle East marked the next attempt to force the Jews to abandon their religion and to adopt instead the worship of alien gods. They revolted under the leadership of the Maccabees, and by 150 BC they had recovered their independence over an area as great as in the time of David and Solomon.

The expanding might of the Roman Empire then reached the eastern shores of the Mediterranean. In 63 BC Pompey stormed Jerusalem and put an end to the independent Jewish state until the foundation of modern Israel. The history of the Jews in Palestine, a country barely the size of Wales, thus ended until the twentieth century, is one of the great stories of civilized man. Its gifts of a highly developed ethical code, a conception of one God, immortal, invisible and wise beyond the comprehension of man, and the timeless works of poetry and prose in which it was given expression, are as much part of the European cultural heritage as the legacies of ancient Greece and Rome.

THE ARABS

Palestine remained under Roman and then Byzantine rule for six hundred years until it suffered yet another conquest. The Arabs broke out of the Arabian desert, just as their Semitic cousins, the Jews, had done centuries earlier and began a career of conquest as extraordinary as that of Alexander or Rome. Arab power eventually extended from Spain in a great crescent along the southern rim of the Mediterranean as far as the Indus in the east, and the central Asian steppes in the north. Moslem Pakistan in the east and the Moslem central Asian republics now mark the boundaries of the great Arab conquests.

The inspiration for this great conquest was the rise of Islam, the third and last monotheistic religion, in the seventh century AD. All three, Islam, Judaism and Christianity, had their origins in the narrow lands between the eastern seaboard of the Mediterranean and the Persian Gulf. They are close in other senses than their geographical origins. Moslems claim descent from Abraham whom they revere as the first Moslem. They are thus cousins to the Jews. Moslems accept the teachings of the Jewish *Torah* and the Christian Gospels. They believe that Islam is the perfection of the religion revealed to Abraham and, later, to other prophets including Jesus; but, they consider, both Jew and Christian have gone astray from the true faith. However, Moslems hold adherents to Judaism and Christianity in higher esteem than pagans and unbelievers, and for centuries allowed them to practise their own religions in Islamic lands.

In the great expansion of Islam, Palestine played little part. There was no great Islamic city in Palestine to rival the wealth and refinement of Baghdad, Alexandria or Granada. But on the same high place in Jerusalem where Solomon's Temple had stood is the magnificent Mosque known as the Dome of the Rock. This is the third sacred site of Islam with Mecca, where the Prophet was born, and Medina, where he lies in his tomb. Here, on the high platform in Jerusalem, known to the Jews as the Temple Mount and the Moslems as *Haram es Sharif*, is the place where Moslems believe that the Prophet took flight to the heavens on his supernatural steed with a human face.

In the course of three or four hundred years, the vast Arab empire began to disintegrate. The Middle East was exposed first to the invasion in the eleventh century of the Seljuk Turks (the Turkish dynasty who ruled between the eleventh and thirteenth centuries), and then to periodic invasions from Christian Europe by the Crusaders. After further depredations at the hands of Mongol raiders under Tamerlain, it reverted to Moslem rule. In 1517, the same year that Martin Luther launched the Protestant revolution in Europe, Palestine was conquered, with Syria and Egypt, by the Ottoman Turks (the Turkish dynasty founded by Osman I at the beginning of the fourteenth century). Those lands remained under Turkish sovereignty until the First World War.

In the eighteen centuries that had passed since the Roman conquest, Palestine was virtually left aside by history. Indeed, 'Palestine' was not a country recognized by cartographers: on the map it was part of Syria. The 1911 edition of the *Encyclopaedia Britannica* describes it as a 'geographical name of rather loose application'. The Hebrews, it says, have preserved an indication of the north-and-south limits in the proverbial expression 'from Dan to Beersheba'.

However, the genius of the place was and is spiritual. It remained sacred for Moslems for having in Jerusalem one of the three Holy Places of Islam, for Christians as the place of the Incarnation and the founding of their religion, and for Jews the imperishable memory of Zion. No event disturbed the poor rocky landscape except the less-than-wholly-noble Crusades. The Arabs who lived there eked out an impoverished existence. But it was their home.

THE DIASPORA

The Romans destroyed Israel in Palestine. The country became virtually a Roman province. But the national spirit of the Jews was strong. The unrest culminated in a general rising in AD 64, which was put down only after years of fighting. In AD 70, Titus sacked Jerusalem and destroyed the Temple, the last citadel to be taken. His triumphal arch, built with Jewish slave labour, can be seen today in the Forum at Rome, ornamented with the *menorah*, or branched candlestick, and other symbols of the Judaic religion. But the Jews were not finally crushed by Titus. They rose again in AD 115 and 132. Rome determined to make a final end to Jewish resistance. In 135 Jerusalem was destroyed and its site ploughed up. Many Jews were put to death or carried off as slaves. The remainder were dispersed to the four winds and forbidden to return to Jerusalem. Jewish history ceased to be the history of Palestine. But the fate of the people continued to be inextricably linked to the country which they call 'Eretz Israel', the Promised Land of Israel.

Some few Jews had remained in Palestine through the centuries of Moslem occupation. For others the Diaspora, or Dispersion, had begun long before the disaster of the Roman destruction. There was a community in Baghdad which had been there since the exile to Babylon. There was another ancient community in Egypt. The Jews of these communities were completely 'assimilated', except for their religion. They spoke and wrote Arabic or, in the case of the community in Egypt, Greek, and adopted Arab or Greek names. The community in Alexandria translated the Old Testament into Greek in the third century BC. Their translation is known as the Septuagint because tradition ascribes the work to seventy-two Jewish translators working on the island of Pharos.

After the final destruction of Jerusalem in 135, waves of Jewish emigration swelled the Baghdad and Egyptian communities. They reached Syria and the Yemen, Italy and Greece. They followed the advance of the Arab empire along the North African coast and into Spain. Relations between Moslem and Jew were for the most part harmonious. Like the Jewish communities in Baghdad and Egypt, the Spanish Jews, or *Sephardim*, accepted assimilation in everything but religion. With that exception, they contributed to every aspect of Islamic life and culture.

The source of anti-Semitism, from which Jews can hardly be separated in the mind, was not Islam but Christianity. Jews had penetrated into Italy and Gaul, and with the fall of the Roman Empire, into Germany and England. Everywhere in Christendom they found themselves under disabilities. They were penned off as an alien people and social inferiors. This ill feeling intensified in the time of the Crusades. It became as pious to kill a Jew as a Saracen. If that were virtuous where the Crusaders found them in the Middle East, it was equally so in England or France. So the Church gave sanction to torture, expropriation, deportation and murder. Behind all this lay the guilt of the Crucifixion.

In the Middle Ages, and beyond, Jews could not own land. They became an urban people. Their work was as middlemen or, especially, moneylenders because the prohibition against usury in the Middle Ages prevented Christians from lending at interest. They were expelled from England in 1290 and only readmitted by Cromwell. In the Spain of the Counter-Reformation, they were hunted down by the Inquisition and, if they refused to convert to Christianity, they were burned as heretics. In 1492, those that refused to bow the knee were expelled. That set off another wave of migration, this time eastwards. Many of the refugees from Spain found shelter in the Turkish empire and they settled in the Balkans, Egypt, Baghdad, Aleppo or Constantinople. There was an important Sephardic community in Salonika. Although the Jews, being unbelievers, were regarded as inferiors by Moslems, those living under the protection of the Turks were free to worship their God according to their own practices.

In western Europe Jews who were not expelled were kept apart and confined to a 'ghetto'. Many of those who were treated in this way in Germany, together with those expelled from France and England, moved to the eastern fringes of developed Europe: Russia, Lithuania, Poland, Romania, Hungary. This move-ment gained momentum until eventually more than half the world's Jews were gathered in those countries.

In face of all these centuries of persecution, it is a source of wonder that the Jews of the Diaspora survived at all. Numbering perhaps four million in the early days of dispersion, they were reduced to one and a half million by 1700. But they had not been eliminated. What Judaism had lost in numbers it had gained in intensity.

Such a closed world of confinement and fear could not last indefinitely. Unless those conditions changed, the Jews must have ceased to exist as a distinct people. The change came with the eighteenth-century Enlightenment. The spirit of reason and tolerance swept Europe. The ideas of the French Revolution of liberty, equality and fraternity meant that there could be no restrictions which differentiated one man from another. Jews were freed from all disabilities in the United States in 1787 and in France in 1791. The expanding Napoleonic empire brought the same freedom in Holland, Germany and Italy. In England the Jews had to wait longer. The first English Jewish member of parliament, a Rothschild, took his seat in the House of Commons only in 1858.

But with these new-found freedoms came a dilemma which would split Jewry. In 1791, during a debate in the French Convention, the Marquis de Clermont-Tonnerre drew a distinction which precisely expressed the dilemma: 'The Jews must be refused everything as a separate nation, and be granted everything as individuals.' Jewish nationalism, Jewish separateness, preserved as sacred during centuries of wandering and contumely, was the price to be paid for emancipation.

The Enlightenment affected Jewry as it affected Christendom. The founder of the *Haskala*, as the Jewish enlightenment was called, was the eighteenth-century philosopher Moses Mendelssohn. He wanted to end what he called the 'narrow labyrinth of ritual' and the superstition and fear which was crippling life in the ghetto. His movement captured the imagination of the young, but it was violently denounced by Orthodox Jews and Rabbis who recognized the threat that secular education and rationalism posed to traditional faith.

Many Jews left their homes for the cities of Germany and Austria, leaving behind the conservative religious communities in which they had been brought up. They wanted to escape the ghetto of the mind as well as the place. These conservative sects seemed to them to observe for observance's sake and to cling to their formalities for fear of losing hold of the past. There were myriad rules of worship, hygiene, diet and dress. They had been preserved through the centuries to keep alive the hopes and destiny of a scattered people. But many of the rules were more suited to the hot climate of Palestine than the countries to which their wanderings had brought them. Intermarriage was strictly forbidden. Since the law laid down that Jewishness passed through the female line, a girl who 'married out' was liable to be disowned by her family or even pronounced ritually dead.

It is not surprising that to some Jews living in countries where there were no disabilities all this should seem outworn and unnecessary, even distasteful. They would choose instead to become as like non-Jews as they could and assimilate; or choose other alternatives such as humanism or communism.

But in eastern Europe, there was rarely any freedom to choose. At the beginning of the eighteenth century Poland-Lithuania was the relatively safe haven for the greatest concentration of Jews in the world. By the end of the century it had been broken up and divided among its predatory neighbours, Russia, Prussia and the Habsburg Empire of Austria-Hungary. Jews who found themselves living in the Russian empire were in the main confined to the 'Pale of Settlement', a great tract of country that was nothing but a huge ghetto. The humiliating laws of the Pale, introduced by Catherine the Great in 1791, were not rigorously enforced by the Tsars until 1881 when Alexander II was assassinated. His son, Alexander III, succeeded him and at once resolved to govern 'in the strength and truth of autocratic power'. Fearsome waves of *pogroms*, a Russian word meaning round-up or lynching, began. The riff-raff set fire to Jewish villages and murdered indiscriminately. These massacres were connived at, or even instigated, by the Tsarist government. They provoked yet another mass migration. In the thirty years between 1880 and 1910, more than two million Jews fled from Russia to the United States, Britain, South Africa and other havens. The great majority went to America, where the Jewish population was transformed from a quarter of a million to more than two million. In Britain until 1880, the Jewish community formed a small, compact and comfortable minority. It was then changed dramatically. The immigrant Russian Jews were poor aliens and the old-established Jewish families felt for the first time that their safety and ease were under threat.

In the grievous history of anti-Semitism, race now began to play a more significant part than religion. A Jew was to be identified by his blood – who his family were – rather than by the God whom he worshipped. Hatred was fuelled by conspiracy theories of Jewish power and money. The fear was given pseudo-academic respectability by nineteenth-century writers like the Englishman Houston Stewart Chamberlain (1855–1927), who lived in Germany and fell under the spell of Richard Wagner's music and philosophy. Like Wagner he held that the Jews were an element foreign to everything that Europe had been and was called to become. Anti-Semitism of this sort appeared in the late nineteenth-century Russia of the pogroms. It also emerged in the Balkans, Austria, Germany, Romania, Hungary and the France of the Dreyfus case.

The flood of Jewish refugees pouring westward to the United States and Britain was swollen by the new impetus given to anti-Semitism. Yiddish, the language of the Jewish Pale, was heard in the streets of Whitechapel, and the local Magistrates' Court had to have a Yiddish-speaking interpreter. 30,000 census forms for the British census of 1911 were printed in Yiddish. Britain, thought by the refugees to be an asylum as secure and tolerant as the United States, brought in its first controls on immigration. The Aliens Bill was introduced into the House of Commons by the Prime Minister, Arthur Balfour.

2

The Dream of Zion

By the Balfour Declaration Britain intended that a foreign element should be interposed in an Arab land. The nature of that element was European, predominantly Russian. Palestine had been Arab since the seventh century, and the Jews had not lived there, except in insignificant numbers, for almost two thousand years. In 1917 there were perhaps 90,000 Jews and 700,000 Arabs in Palestine – a proportion of eight to one.[1] Approaching the matter for the first time, one could be forgiven for thinking that the British government was putting forward a hopeless proposition or a foolish dream. It was in fact the triumph of an idea over all principle and reason. That idea was Zionism.

The dream of the Jews to return to Zion is as old as the Diaspora. Its wellspring is the establishment of a Hebrew nation in the Promised Land of the ancient Hebrews. The Hebrew word, *Tsiyon*, means a hill and is a biblical name for Jerusalem, connoting the spiritual centre of the Jewish people. Ever since the Romans, with characteristic thoroughness and finality, broke up and scattered the Jewish nation, the Jews have dreamed of the Land. The dream is incorporeal. There is no monument to represent it, only an idea to carry in their minds and to pass from generation to generation. The Hebrew Testament and Prayer Book are full of references to the Return. Each year the Passover is celebrated not by the veneration of an artefact, not even in the synagogue, but at home. Each year the story of the deliverance from exile is told by question and answer and through a symbolic meal. Each year the prayers include the plea, 'Next year in Jerusalem'. The pious are therefore constantly reminded of it. But for all Jews, the land of Israel has a powerful significance, a tidal pull, which they cannot deny in their hearts. It is why, against all odds and during the centuries of the Diaspora, even in the most terrible times of oppression, the hope of Jews to redeem their lives by the return to Zion was kept alive as a sacred flame.

Nowhere was this felt more strongly than in the Russian Empire of the Tsars.

In the Pale of Settlement, where Chaim Weizmann, who with Arthur Balfour are the two principals of this book, was born, extremes of piety and even mysticism were to be found in the conservative sects of Judaism. Here the secular and the religious were virtually fused, as in the Christendom of the Middle Ages, and all learning was pious learning. Religious life was devoted to the study of the sacred texts. The faith was not assertive or evangelical, but quietist, as in life the Jews of the Pale accepted their fate with resignation. But inside the Pale it was not necessary to belong to one of the conservative sects to feel the same longing for freedom.

This urge for freedom faded among the assimilated Jews of the west. In the eyes of the Jews of eastern Europe, their 'enlightened' brothers in the west had repudiated their history and traditions and had come to despise everything that made them conscious of belonging to an eternal people. A letter from Weizmann to a sympathizer, Mrs James de Rothschild, written in 1914, makes clear the gulf between the Jews of the east and west.

> You were so kind in letting me talk to you about our hopes and aspirations. I would like you to realise that the six million of Russian Jews who suffer daily in an atmosphere of lawlessness are not frightened for their bodies, they can bear heroically physical torture, but what they want is freedom, Jewish freedom, not merely 'rights' for which one has to *beg* the Russian government, but a Jewish *pied à terre*, a spot in the world where we can be masters of our own destiny And in this respect we, the 'beggars' from the East, are freer men and women than our 'happy' co-religionists in the West, who have lost the taste for Jewish freedom, who don't believe in it, and who have exchanged this freedom for the 'meat-pots of Egypt'.[2]

The series of pogroms or massacres of Jews that began in the 1880s in Russia and elsewhere in eastern Europe changed the character of Zionism. Until then the longing for Zion had not taken a political form. It was, with few exceptions, an idea of Jerusalem as a centre of prayer and Jewish culture, and settlements on a small scale. It stood for a Jewish national revival. Its aim was to create a new home, not so much for physical as for spiritual life. Now it was all to change under the impulse of repression and danger in Russia; and with the coming of new prophets.

In 1862 Moses Hess, a German Jew, published *Rome and Jerusalem*, advocating a Jewish state in Palestine. A more powerful appeal under the title of

Self-Emancipation: An Admonition to his Brethren by a Russian Jew appeared in 1882, written by Leon Pinsker, a Russian physician. Jews, he wrote, were an object of bewilderment and hatred in the countries in which they had settled. Pinsker painted a lurid picture of his people.

> This ghostly apparition of a people without unity or organisation, without land or other bond of union, no longer alive, and yet moving among the living – this eerie form scarcely paralleled in history, unlike anything that preceded or followed it, could not fail to make a strange and peculiar impression upon the imagination of the nations.[3]

He considered that anti-Semitism was a psychosis which was incurable while the Diaspora lasted. The only cure was for the Jewish people to find their own land where they could be masters of their own fate.

The start of the Russian pogroms in 1881 meant that the overriding need for Jews was safety of life and limb. Their thoughts began to turn to a national refuge in Palestine. Groups began to form in eastern Europe for the purpose of establishing settlements piecemeal in Palestine. These societies were known as *Choveve Zion* (Lovers of Zion). Under their auspices a trickle of settlers moved to Palestine during the fifteen years before the setting up of the Zionist Organization in 1897. The numbers were only a tiny fraction of those who chose the easier options of New York or London. In 1885 the Turkish government prohibited all foreigners from acquiring or holding land within the empire and forbade further Jewish settlements in Palestine. Only the venality of the Ottoman officials made settlements possible – and a grant of money from Baron Edmond de Rothschild. But scratching a living from the unforgiving desert rock of Palestine compared poorly with sanctuary in the United States or Britain. The Lovers of Zion were the pioneers but they were an inchoate group. Jewish Zionism awaited a political leader and an organization.

It had only to wait a few years for the coming of Theodor Herzl. A man of commanding presence and a compelling speaker, Herzl looked like an Assyrian King with his deep black beard. He was born in Budapest in 1860 and grew up in a time when things went well for Hungarian Jews, particularly the well-to-do like his own family. There was little in his upbringing or circumstances to inspire devotion to things Jewish. But that is not to say that his family background was devout by mere convention. The customs and festivals of Judaism were observed in the Herzl household and the young Theodor accompanied his father to the synagogue every Friday evening and Saturday morning. When he was eighteen he moved with his family to Vienna and studied for the law, but he left the legal profession as soon as he could to devote himself to literature and travel. He wrote plays, short stories and articles for newspapers. The fiction and plays were not successful but he acquired some reputation in the art of the *feuilleton*, a short evanescent newspaper piece enjoying popularity at the time. He began to write for the *Neue Freie Presse*, the most influential newspaper in the Austro-Hungarian empire, and in 1890 he was appointed the Paris correspondent of that paper. It marked the end of his attempt at a career as an independent man of letters. He was then thirty-one.

By this time he had begun to think out the 'Jewish question' for himself. It is sometimes said – indeed he said it himself – that it was the Dreyfus case which made him write 'The Jewish State'. But it seems that it was not so. He had written the pamphlet before the 'case' became the notorious 'Affair'.

In November 1894 Captain Alfred Dreyfus, a Jewish officer in the French army, was arrested and charged with high treason for betraying military secrets to the Germans. He was found guilty by a court martial and sentenced to military degradation and perpetual solitary confinement on Devil's Island. Many, including Herzl, were convinced that he was the innocent victim of the anti-Semitic hysteria which was then gripping France. The principal document on which Dreyfus was convicted was ultimately proved to be a forgery, but it was not until June 1899 that he was allowed to return to France, and 1906 before he was reinstated with his former rank of Captain. In the intervening years France was riven and shaken by the Affair.

Herzl reported the trial for the *Neue Freie Presse* and he was present at the public degradation ceremony in which Dreyfus' epaulettes and buttons were literally torn from his tunic, and his sabre and scabbard broken. He heard the mob howling 'Death to the traitor, death to the Jews'. He said that it was the Dreyfus case that had made him a Zionist, but that was a foreshortening of the real story for dramatic effect.[4]

His diaries, which cover the period from June 1895 to May 1904, begin with an account of how he came to the Zionist idea. There is no word of Dreyfus in that account. But the Affair epitomizes in one example his experiences of anti-Semitism and his view of the Jewish future. If such things could happen in modern, civilized France a century after the Declaration of Human Rights, the Jews had better look to themselves for salvation in a land of their own.

In the opening section of the diaries, he says that he first began to concern himself with the Jewish question when in 1881 or 1882 he came across a book by the German philosopher, Eugen Dühring, which preached a straight racist war against the Jews. Dühring's view of the Jewish question was that it was not a matter of religion or culture or even social behaviour – but simply of blood. Then in September 1895 Herzl was in Vienna for the City Council elections. All the vacant seats were won by the virulently anti-Semitic Christian Socialist Party led by Karl Lüger. Herzl was standing in the crowd when Lüger suddenly appeared. A man next to Herzl said with loving fervour, but softly, 'That is our Leader'. 'More than all the declamation and abuse', Herzl wrote afterwards, 'these few words told me how deeply anti-Semitism is rooted in the heart of the people'. Lüger, a brilliant demagogue, was elected Burgomaster and his party passed resolutions boycotting Jewish merchants and confiscating Jewish property. Like Dühring he was a forerunner of Hitler and his National Socialists. 'In the course of the succeeding years', Herzl confided in his diaries, 'the question gnawed and tugged at me, it tormented me and rendered me profoundly unhappy.'[5]

He found the same thing in the Paris of the Dreyfus case where the writings of the anti-Semitic journalist Edouard Drumont were enjoying an unhealthy popularity. He realized the futility of trying to 'combat' anti-Semitism. It could not be fought by pamphlets, still less by giving the Jews rights or privileges. He saw the Jewish question, at bottom, as a question of anti-Semitism, and wrote about it with the candour that was one of his most engaging characteristics.

> I understand what anti-Semitism is about. We Jews have maintained ourselves, even if through no fault of our own, as a foreign body among the different nations. In the Ghetto, we have taken on a number of anti-social characteristics. Our character has been damaged through oppression and must be repaired through some other sort of pressure. As a matter of fact, anti-Semitism is a consequence of the emancipation of the Jews. The peoples about us who lack an historical understanding – in a word, all of them – do not see us as a historical product, as a victim of earlier, crueller, and still more narrow-minded times.[6]

Herzl published *The Jewish State* in 1896. It was little more than a pamphlet in length. The Jews were a single people, it proclaimed, not a miscellaneous collection of communities. They must be recognized by the family of nations as a member and be granted sovereignty over some part of the globe large enough to satisfy the rightful requirements of a nation. His was essentially a political and a secular conception. He did not necessarily advocate Palestine (he canvassed Argentina as an alternative) although he acknowledged that the Jews' historic home would 'attract our people with a marvellous potency'.

Herzl was a western Jew who knew at first hand only those countries in which Jews sought to make their lives and habits as similar as possible to their gentile neighbours. He knew very little of the Jews of the Russian Pale where Zionism had been nursed and nurtured. He had no knowledge of what had earlier been written by Hess, Pinsker and others on the subject of the return of the Jews to Palestine. And yet, in spite of the differences of background, he had reached the same conclusions.

The Jewish State was published in Vienna. English and French translations followed rapidly. Although it contained nothing new, it said it in a new way. It was addressed to the emperor, sultan, statesman and the wealthy as much as to the common reader, and it was written by an experienced journalist. It was an immediate sensation and it polarized opinion among Jewry. It was lauded on one hand and attacked on the other with equal passion. Herzl was to some a prophet who was bringing salvation to his people, while to others his prophecies were false and his utterances those of a demagogue.

The supporters were concentrated in Eastern Europe. The assimilated Jews of the West felt *The Jewish State* was dangerous and threatening to their own position. The book had exposed the ambiguities of their position and undermined their optimistic delusions as much as the Dreyfus Affair. On the other hand conservative Rabbis considered that the book was a blasphemous contradiction of the messianic doctrine of Judaism that the millennium would come only when the entire Jewish congregation could reassemble in the land of Israel in perfect peace and freedom.

Herzl's supporters thought this the dried-up parchment of traditional Judaism, irrelevant to the harsh realities of the late nineteenth-century world. Another group influenced by Ahad Ha'am preached that these old doctrines must have new life breathed into them. They considered that settlements in Palestine would be of little use if they were not accompanied by spiritual regeneration. One institution of higher learning in Palestine, declared Ahad Ha'am, irradiating the Diaspora, was worth more than ten agricultural settlements. Fault lines appeared in Zionism whose depth and seriousness were not apparent until later.

It was a fundamental of Herzl's thinking that the foundation of the Jewish state should have the legitimacy of international law. His object was to obtain the consent of the Sultan of Turkey whose empire included Palestine. He travelled about trying to enlist support for that object. The reactions varied from the friendly to the sceptical, but nowhere was any practical help forthcoming. But if his diplomacy was a failure he succeeded in making Zionism and its founder well-known in the Chancelleries of Europe.

The diplomacy also provoked opposition. Herzl appeared to his critics to believe that the Jewish state could be created by the intervention of saviours from outside Zionism. Like the god out of the machine, the Sultan, the Kaiser, the British parliament or even the Pope could by a masterstroke bring about the Return to Zion. Chaim Weizmann and the Zionists who thought as he did considered that diplomacy by itself was futile: Israel could only be created anew by gradual colonization and hard work on the ground.

Meanwhile Herzl concluded that, diplomacy having failed at any rate for the time being, he must gather together a congress of the whole Jewish people. It would, he thought, have the double objective of mobilizing Jewry and inducing the political powers to take Zionism more seriously.[7] The first Zionist Congress opened in Basle on August 27, 1897. More than two hundred delegates from all parts of the world were there, representing every shade of Jewish opinion. When he opened the Congress, many who were present were seeing Herzl for the first time. He appeared before them as a majestic figure, a prophet-like presence from an Oriental land. The Congress was an immediate success and would be repeated every year. It was a lodestone for the scattered fragments of the Jewish people and the necessary first step towards the formation of a Jewish nation which could take its place in the international community.

The Congress settled a constitution for the newly born World Zionist Organization. There was to be an executive (the 'Smaller Actions Committee') charged with the day-to-day conduct of Zionist affairs, and a general council (the 'Greater Actions Committee') to whom the Smaller Actions Committee was responsible and which represented all countries where there was a Zionist Organization. The first Congress promulgated the so-called Basle Programme or manifesto, whose opening statement read: 'The aim of Zionism is to create for the Jewish people a home in Palestine secured by public law.' The key to Herzl's thinking lay in the last four words: 'secured by public law'. The Jewish state would be a modern nation state legitimized by a charter granted by the Sultan and formally recognized by the great powers.

Herzl was to see only five more annual Congresses in his lifetime. He established the Jewish National Fund, to provide finance for the purchase of land in Palestine, and the Jewish Colonial Trust, to act as the financial instrument of the movement. He died in 1904 aged only forty-four, the first Jewish statesman produced by his people in almost two millennia. By then he had become a legend in his lifetime. He had met European sovereigns and their ministers, treating with them as equals. And this in the teeth of the opposition of factions of his own uniquely argumentative people.

The fourth Zionist Congress in 1900 was held in London. By then Herzl felt that he could carry negotiations with the Sultan no further, and it was time to look to England for help. In his inaugural address he voiced a sentiment which was to be heard again: 'England, with her eyes roaming over all the seas, will understand us and our aims. From this place the Zionist idea will take a still further and higher flight: of this we may be sure.'[8] England, with its long tradition of individual liberty and its independent belief in the return of the Jews to Jerusalem, seemed to be naturally cast in the role of sponsor of Zionism.

There was a belief in England, as old as the seventeenth century, that the Jews must return to the Holy Land. Only then would the millennium come and the prophecies of Isaiah be fulfilled. These beliefs were Protestant beliefs and were one of the consequences of the English Reformation which had been accomplished by the end of Elizabeth's reign. 'No greater moral change ever passed over a nation', wrote J. R. Green in his *Short History of the English People*,

> than passed over England during the years which parted the middle of the reign of Elizabeth from the meeting of the Long Parliament. England became the people of a book, and that book was the Bible. It was as yet the one English book which was familiar

to every Englishman: it was read in churches and at home and everywhere its words, as they fell on ears which custom had not deadened, kindled a startling enthusiasm.

The prime mover in this revolution was the Puritan. His faith was a grim matter of 'thou shalt' and 'thou shalt not'. He thought of the Old and New Testaments alike as directly inspired by God. Every moral precept and human sentiment they contained became a divine command and a rule for living. A bigoted, plain-dressing, sober-sided killjoy though he may appear in a backward look, his influence can hardly be overstated.

The Puritans found a parallel between their own fortunes and those of the ancient Israelites. They were persecuted and were sustained by the hope of Canaan. All forms of ceremony, ornament and earthly beauty were to them as idolatrous as graven images were to the Jews. They took heart from 'the belief that the English people were the chosen of God, distinguished among the nations of the earth by the signal mercies they had received at His hands'.[9] ('Chosen', not in the sense of being preferred above all others, but of being called to receive and propagate the Law. The 'choice' of the Jews, as of the Puritans, carried with it the obligation to act as God's servants in establishing His Kingdom throughout the world and to be a light to lighten the gentiles.) For the Puritans, too, 'the Old Testament became a book of the Wars of the Lord. Their God was the Jehovah of Hosts who would help them smite Philistines and Amalekites hip and thigh.'[10] When Cromwell's Ironsides went into battle they carried Bibles and sang the psalms of David as songs of encouragement and triumph.

There was also a new vision of Palestine. It had been revered as the Holy Land for its Christian associations. For the Puritans it became associated with the Jews to whom a divine promise had been made, and repeated time without number in the Old Testament, that they would one day return to their ancient home.

Gerrard Winstanley was a Leveller and communistic thinker whose plan for Utopia carried with it the abolition of all titles and all private property. He was a member of one of the extreme sects that proliferated in the Puritan Age. His writings were typical of those who believed in the Return of the Jews to Zion, as *The True Levellers' Standard* (1649) makes clear. 'It is shewed us,' he wrote, 'that all the Prophecies, Visions and Revelations of Scriptures, of Prophets and Apostles, concerning the calling of the Jews, the Restauration of Israel, and the making of that People, the Inheritors of the whole earth, doth all seat themselves in this work of making the Earth a Common Treasury.'

It was not only the Levellers and others who inhabited the lunatic fringe of religion and politics who considered that the Return of the Jews was a necessary precursor to the millennium. The view was widely shared by those who made Cromwell's revolution. The Puritans wanted the Jews to be readmitted to England, from where they had been banished since 1290, so that the ingathering in Zion could take place from all countries. The Book of Deuteronomy (28:64) was precise that the Diaspora must be extended to all countries: 'The Lord shall scatter thee among all peoples from one end of the earth even unto the other.' Then, when the Jews were restored to their ancient inheritance, the Puritan believed, they would be converted to Christianity. More of this surprising argument would be heard in the nineteenth century.

Cromwell himself wanted to see the Jews readmitted to England. Apart from his strong inclination towards religious tolerance, he thought the Jewish merchants could help to finance his wars. In spite of difficulties and objections Cromwell had his way and the Jews came back to England while he was Lord Protector.

After lying dormant during the eighteenth century there was a revival of interest in the Return in nineteenth-century England, particularly among the Evangelicals. A mystique grew, which never altogether disappeared, that Britain had been chosen by God to bring back the Jews to the Holy Land. In the early years of the nineteenth century, there was a confluence between British political interests in the Middle East and religious enthusiasm for the Return of the Jews. The rivalry between Britain and France in the region had been a constant since the time of Napoleon; and it was later to form an important part of the background to the events leading to the Balfour Declaration. In 1840–1 there was a dispute in Syria between the two imperial powers. Britain took the side of the Ottoman empire while France supported the insurrectionary, Mohammed Ali.

The Syrian crisis fired the imagination of the Evangelicals for the Return of the Jews to Palestine. The surge of enthusiasm was taken up by Palmerston. He pressed his ambassador in Constantinople, Lord Ponsonby, with the argument that the Ottomans' interests in many countries could be benefited if the Jews were permitted to return to Palestine under the protection and sanction of the Sultan, telling him: 'The Jews are a sort of Free Mason fraternity whose goodwill would be useful to the Sultan.' Palmerston's emphasis on Jewish wealth and influence is striking. Although the evidence for it was slender, British ministers continued to be impressed by what they thought Jewry could achieve for its friends and benefactors. This consideration, too, was to reappear in the formation of British policy on Palestine in 1916 and 1917.

The force and importance of the Evangelical movement in British public opinion was considerable. In 1840, Lady Palmerston, who was in a position to know, wrote to a friend: 'We have on our side the fanatical and religious elements, and you know what a following they have in this country. They are absolutely determined that Jerusalem and the whole of Palestine shall be reserved for the Jews to return to; this is their only longing.'[11] Palmerston himself acquired first-hand knowledge of the Evangelical mind when Lord Ashley, later the seventh Earl of Shaftesbury and the greatest social reformer of the Victorian age, became his step-son-in-law. Ashley was an Evangelical of demonic energy. He held all his beliefs with tenacity and fervour, and one of them was that the Jews must be restored to their ancient home, in accord with biblical prophecy, so that they could be converted to Christianity.

In August 1840, Ashley dined alone with Palmerston and propounded a scheme for the establishment of an Anglican bishopric at Jerusalem. He recorded in his diary that it seemed to strike the great Foreign Secretary's fancy, and he commented: 'Palmerston has already been chosen by God as an instrument of good to His ancient people'.[12] Palmerston would have been startled to hear that his foreign policy was divinely inspired, but nonetheless his own views coincided with those of his son-in-law, albeit for other reasons. Ashley's scheme for an Anglican bishopric at Jerusalem had as one of its main purposes the conversion of the Jews once they had regained their inheritance. It did not seem to occur to him that there was not the slightest basis for the idea that the Jews would wish to be converted to Christianity en masse, or that they could even conceive that this was the real purpose of restoring them to Zion.

The Times joined the supporters of the Return in August 1840. The editor's view was that it was not only Jews but Christians also whose minds were turning towards Palestine and who were interesting themselves in 'a reconstruction of the Jewish state'. 'The Jews', the editorial declared significantly, 'although bereft of their temple, their city and their country, have never ceased to be a nation.'

Nothing concrete came of the Evangelicals' enthusiasm for the Return. Writers, however, continued to agitate the Jewish question and to press on the conscience of English liberal minds. Benjamin Disraeli, himself the archetypal assimilated Jew, published his romantic novel *Tancred, or The New Crusade* in 1847. The book sets out to vindicate the claims and destinies of his own Jewish race. In it, a young nobleman, Tancred Montacute, refuses a seat in Parliament and goes instead to the Holy Land to seek to discover God's purposes. He falls in love with a beautiful Jewess and offers her his hand, but at this critical moment his horrified parents appear.

Thirty years later, George Eliot published her novel *Daniel Deronda* (1876), a more serious novel about Zionism. In the romantic plot the heroine, Gwendolen Harleth who is married to the cruel and selfish Grandcourt, falls under the influence of Deronda who, it is gradually revealed, is a Jew. Grandcourt dies and Gwendolen becomes completely dependent on Deronda. Her hopes turn to despair when Deronda decides to devote his life not to her but to the cause of a national home for the Jewish people. The book was widely read. In 1895, as he was writing *The Jewish State*, Herzl noted: 'Must read *Daniel Deronda*'; and when he was discussing his idea with the Chief Rabbi of France, the Rabbi remarked, 'That is the idea of *Daniel Deronda*.'[13]

George Eliot was extraordinarily sensitive to everything that was stirring. In the case of Zionism, she anticipated by twenty years the movement started by Herzl. She was also a formidable campaigner. In a letter written at the time of the publication of *Daniel Deronda*, she confessed to her friend Harriet Beecher Stowe that she had felt urged to treat the Jewish characters 'with such sympathy and understanding as my nature and knowledge could attain to . . . precisely because I felt that the usual attitude of Christians towards Jews is – I hardly know whether to say more impious or more stupid when viewed in the light of their professed principles'. She continued:

> Can anything be more disgusting than to hear people called 'educated' making small jokes about eating ham, and showing themselves empty of any real knowledge as to the relation of their own social and religious life to the history of the people they think themselves witty in insulting? They hardly know that Christ was a Jew.[14]

Conscientious interest in the Jewish question was aroused again in England by the plight of the Russian Jews in the 1880s, and the flood of refugees seeking asylum. The theme of the Return of the Jews to their ancient inheritance in Palestine had never been altogether lost in England since the seventeenth century, and now, at the end of the nineteenth, it received an unexpected fillip from the surge of British imperialism in Africa and the Near East. It was to prove an unlooked-for bonus for Zionism.

3

Arthur Balfour

To contemporary observers Balfour was a detached figure, languid and rather cold. He saw a great deal of life from afar, said Ramsay MacDonald. According to Winston Churchill, he glided upon the surface of life. When he has gone there will be nothing left but the scent on a handkerchief, said Lloyd George. These observations, which could be multiplied, betray a baffled inability to understand the essential character of Arthur James Balfour. It was one of the most elusive of his day.

Balfour was born in 1848. When he came of age he was one of the richest and best-connected young men in the kingdom. The family seat was at Whittingehame, the grandest pile for miles around, built by Robert Smirke, the architect of the British Museum, in the farming country of East Lothian at the foot of the Lammermoor hills. His mother, Lady Blanche Cecil, was sister of Robert Cecil, the future third Marquis of Salisbury, whose massive presence as Prime Minister personified the self-confidence of late-Victorian England. She had been a favourite of the old Duke of Wellington, who gave her a copy of the map of the field of Waterloo he had made the day before the battle. The Duke was Arthur's godfather and he was named after him.

Arthur was eldest son of a family of eight children. Lady Blanche wore herself out in childbirth and in nursing her sick husband. He died in 1856, too early for Arthur to remember anything of him. The bereavement left her having to act as lone parent and teacher to her young family. Although she died when Arthur was only twenty-four and she forty-seven, she was the single most important influence on his young life, as his uncle Salisbury was over his later political life. Salisbury was his nephew's patron and political mentor. *Punch* called Balfour 'Prince Arthur' and the phrase 'Bob's your uncle' went into the language. But, according to Balfour himself, his mother's influence was deeper and more far-reaching. He wrote that her children's debt to her was incalculable, and when he acknowledged what he owed to many statesmen, philosophers and friends, he added, 'all my debts to them, compute them how you will, are as nothing to what I owe her love, her teaching and her example'.

She was a formidably strong woman of courage and principle, who inspired her children, apparently without effort, to try to please her and win her praise. Her eldest daughter, Evelyn, used to leave reading a book which seemed to be turning in a direction she thought her mother would disapprove of. It was as if a warning light went on in her head. Lady Blanche belonged to the evangelical wing of Anglicanism. She gave her son his dour and inveterate dislike of the Roman Catholic faith, and she had too the evangelicals' high seriousness and dissatisfaction with herself.

Lady Blanche's intellectual attainments were impressive. As a child of eleven, she made a précis of Clarendon's *History of the Rebellion*. She read French novels to her children, omitting passages that she thought harmful and adding text of her own seamlessly as she went along. Her alternating moods of austerity, conversational sparkle and helpless laughter provided a wonderful start to life for the young Balfours – if they were up to it. Not all were, but Arthur certainly was. Jane Mercer was a nursery maid at Whittingehame. She was devoted to Lady Blanche and retained the clearest recollection of her fifty years after her death. 'She is like a force about me now', she said. Asked whether Arthur had something of her power, she admitted that he did, 'more than any of the rest of you'.[1]

Balfour went away to board when he was eleven and the headmaster of his preparatory school in Hertfordshire, the Rev. C. G. Chittenden, told Lady Blanche that her son's conversation was 'much more like that of an intelligent boy of eighteen than that of a boy of twelve'. Balfour later told his niece, Blanche Dugdale, that philosophy had been continuously in his mind, and that even before Eton he began 'muddling about with those ideas'. He remembered Chittenden as an excellent teacher, clear, interesting and kindly. 'He was very ready to to answer questions about things in general, asked by an inquisitive and doubtless tiresome pupil.' It must have been on Sunday afternoon walks with Chittenden that Balfour began 'muddling about' with philosophical ideas; and he acknowledged that he owed more to him than to any other teacher of his boyhood.[2]

At Eton, neither the school nor he made much impression on each other. He was only middling in the classroom, and had no apparent desire to do more.

Balfour was temperamentally lazy and ill-equipped by physique to take part in the savage competition which was universal on the playing fields of private schools. He was not robust and was easily tired. In any case he was repelled by the philistine heartiness of those whose god was sport.

By contrast he thrived at Cambridge. It was intellectually exciting and had none of the tiresome compulsions of school. He was a fellow-commoner of Trinity, a privileged status which gave the right to dine at High Table with the dons. His feeble health and energy vanished as if it had never been and he rapidly made close and durable friendships.

His interest in philosophy continued and philosophical speculations and writings preoccupied him on and off for the rest of his life. It provided intellectual stimulus and it delighted and invigorated him. All his life it gave him solace when he needed to escape from the din of the political world. There were times when he simply wanted peace and quiet. The constitutional crisis of 1911 over the House of Lords made Balfour thoroughly weary of the strain of holding the Unionist party together. When the crisis was at its height he retired from the fray to Bad Gastein and told a woman friend that he was trying to forget politics amid the cataracts and pines, and was writing an article about philosophy.[3] And when earlier, in 1898, he met Cosima Wagner, the composer's widow, at Bayreuth, she was lost in admiration for his ability to withdraw from the daily round of affairs to contemplate eternal questions.

> It seems to me [she wrote in her suffocating way] the prerogative of England that her greatest statesmen have the gift of contemplation and find their recreation from the hard practical questions in ascending the summits of Idealism, from whence, no doubt, they return with larger views and deeper solicitude for all the cares which lie at their charge.[4]

Balfour left Cambridge with a second-class degree, which he described characteristically as 'an unimportant episode', and spent some years drifting about, thinking of devoting his life to philosophical speculation. The practical, admonitory voice of Lady Blanche intervened. 'Do it if you like', she said, 'but remember if you do, you will have nothing to write about by the time you are forty.'[5] At the age of twenty-two he bought a fine London house at 4 Carlton Gardens, overlooking the Mall and St James's Park, and two years later, on the death of Lady Blanche, he became the master of Whittingehame and the family estates in Scotland.

He became friendly with the Gladstones. Gladstone's wife was a Lyttelton, a tribe famous for their exploits in cricket and tennis. The two families formed a clan. Their exuberance and boisterous life were new to Balfour, whose home was overshadowed by his mother's illness and death. The warm atmosphere of Hagley, the Lyttelton home in Worcestershire, supplied something which was missing in his life. 'Spencer [Lyttelton]', wrote one of his sisters

> brought Arthur Balfour to Hagley in the summer of 1870, feeling sure he would be liked by us all. Mary Gladstone was there too. Both she and May played on the piano as much as possible, and AJB sat wherever there was music going on. I remember being amused at my brother Neville saying: 'I don't know that I like this friend of Spencer's – he seems to do nothing but hang about the girls.' I told him it was the music he was enjoying first and foremost.[6]

She may have been mistaken, for he came as near as he ever did to falling in love – with May Lyttelton. Balfour enjoyed feminine company and was at ease with women. He had graceful manners and was a good listener. But a serious relationship was another matter. Balfour's courtship of May Lyttelton was hesitant. In 1875, when it seems that Balfour was at last on the point of proposing, she suddenly succumbed to typhoid fever, lay for some weeks between life and death, and eventually died. He was devastated and lapsed into a condition of despair.

He never married. Early in the 1880s he formed an attachment, whose real depth, at any rate on his side, is not clear, to Mary Wyndham, later Lady Elcho. But after May Lyttelton's death, he never committed himself without reserve to any woman, and her death was the only occasion when he gave way to unrestrained grief. His niece, Blanche Dugdale, considered that the view that he was cold at heart was ludicrous; but, she said, he loathed displays of emotion: 'fundamentally he was afraid of emotion – it was one of the few things of which he was afraid – and this coloured his reception of it in other people on all ordinary occasions'.[7] This opinion is probably as near the truth as it is possible to come about the emotional core of this elusive man. Mrs Dugdale remarked that in addition to 'the discomfort of stirred-up feelings', Balfour objected very much to the waste of energy involved. 'Energy was something to be husbanded and harnessed to produce results.'

He certainly practised what he preached and never fell into the temptation to overtax his energies. In 1874 his uncle Salisbury persuaded him to stand for the Hertford constituency, which was near enough to Hatfield to come under Salisbury's influence and which had fallen vacant. Although he had no experience of public speaking and apparently no interest in politics, he had gained his uncle's confidence and won the seat. He did not speak in the House for two years. The tendency to withdraw was characteristic.

Salisbury patiently groomed him. As Foreign Secretary, he took his nephew to the Congress of Berlin in 1878, where Balfour saw Disraeli, Bismarck and the other great figures of European diplomacy at close quarters. In this political education Balfour was uniquely fortunate, for Salisbury confided in his young nephew completely. He told him, for example, that 'Dizzy was entirely misunderstood out of doors'. As a politician, Salisbury said, Disraeli was exceedingly short-sighted, though very clear-sighted. 'He neither could, nor would, look far ahead or attempt to balance remote possibilities; though he rapidly detected the difficulties of the immediate situation, and found the easiest, if not the best, solution for them.'[8] Having thus educated his nephew and within a short time of taking power after the defeat of Gladstone's first Home Rule Bill in 1886, Salisbury gave him the most severe test possible by sending him to Dublin as Chief Secretary. Ireland was ablaze with agrarian outrage, fuelled by the frustration of having a separate parliament of its own dashed from its grasp. The Irish Nationalists thought that they had been sent a weakling to govern them; but Balfour justified his uncle's confidence and proved his toughness. His political career was made in Ireland.

No one, except perhaps Salisbury himself, could have foreseen it. Balfour at this stage was the butt of cartoonists. *Punch* portrayed him lolling nearly prone on the benches of the House of Commons. He was the delicate product of Cambridge culture drifting languidly from one country house to another. It was absurd to think of him as Prime Minister. If that was beyond foresight, at least as unpredictable was his sudden conversion to Zionism in 1906.

Balfour's attitude to Jews was equivocal. He had the casual prejudice of his time and his class and he shrank from the 'anti-social characteristics' which Herzl thought the Jews had acquired in the ghetto. In 1899 Balfour told Mary Elcho about a dinner party. 'I believe the Hebrews were in an actual majority – and though I have no prejudices against the race (quite the contrary) I begin to understand the point of view of those who object to alien immigration!' And then in 1911, writing to the same correspondent, he told her that the Jewish 'eager interest in all things of the mind instead of attracting half repels. It all seems so much on the surface.'[9]

These were instinctive reactions. But the jibe about alien immigration was unfortunate. It fell to Balfour to deal with a surge of anti-Semitism in the first years of the twentieth century caused by the influx of refugee Russian Jews. The refugees were congregated in the East End of London where they were working as sweated labour in the tailoring, shoemaking and similar trades. There was pressure on the government from the trade unions to protect the livelihood of their members whose work, it was claimed, was being taken from them by the immigrants; and from a group of 'hard right' anti-immigration Conservative members.[10]

In March 1902 Salisbury appointed a Royal Commission on alien immigration. The Commission received much dubious evidence denouncing the Jewish immigrants for their greed, immorality and insanitary habits in an overcrowded environment. The Commission's report in 1903 recommended restrictions on immigration and the power to deport 'undesirable aliens'.[11] Although the report speaks of immigration generally, the 'undesirable aliens' were in fact the east European Jews. Among the members of the Commission there was a powerful dissent from Sir Kenelm Digby, an under-Secretary at the Home Office, in which Lord Rothschild concurred. The minority considered that no new controls on immigration were necessary.

By the time the Commission reported in 1903 Balfour had succeeded his uncle Salisbury as Prime Minister. The report showed that, according to the 1901 census, the population of the United Kingdom was forty-one million, of which some 300,000 were aliens and 95,000 were Russians and Poles. There were shown to be 42,000 Russians and Poles living in Stepney, the area of greatest concentration. The increase in numbers of all aliens in the twenty years from 1881 to 1901 was about 150,000.[12] In 1904 Balfour, ignoring the minority's closely argued objections, brought in a Bill adopting the recommendations of the majority of the Commission. His handling of the immigration question is worth examining as it casts light on his attitude to Jews.

The Bill violated the traditional policy of admitting anyone, without fear or favour, who might seek asylum in Britain. It was probably unnecessary, having regard to the relatively small numbers of Russians and Poles revealed by the report, and it was fairly criticized on the ground that, although expressed as a general control over immigration, it was in fact aimed at the refugee Jews. A stronger Prime Minister than Balfour might not have yielded to the pressure.

The Bill ran into a storm of opposition led by Winston Churchill who had only recently crossed the floor of the House and joined the Liberals. A filibuster in committee resulted in only three lines of the Bill being dealt with in six days and the government was forced to withdraw the Bill. A new Bill was introduced in 1905 which, with a different procedure being adopted in committee, was passed into law in August of that year.

Although the history of the legislation does not show Balfour in a favourable light, it is unfair to ascribe anti-Semitism to him on this account. He himself protested against the charge and told the House of Commons that he could not imagine anything more disastrous than that the Bill or any speech in the House should be linked with 'the bigotry, the oppression, the hatred of the Jewish race has too often met with in foreign countries'.[13] *The Jewish Chronicle* was only one voice among many who thought Balfour's protestations unconvincing. The editor asked how in one breath the Prime Minister could bemoan the tarnish on the name of Christianity left by the persecution of Jews, and in the next breath refuse asylum to Jewish refugees fleeing for their lives.[14]

Balfour thought it his elementary duty to do anything he could to mitigate the disfiguring evil of anti-Semitism. But at the same time he felt that the influx of Jews into Britain must be checked. The heart of the problem was the unwillingness of Jews to integrate fully. He told the House of Commons that a state of things could easily be imagined in which it would not be to the advantage of the civilization of the country that there should be an immense body of persons who, however patriotic, able and industrious, however much they threw themselves into the national life, still by their own action remained a people apart, and not merely held a religion differing from the vast majority of their fellow-countrymen, but only intermarried among themselves.[15]

Jewish separateness was the subject of a letter written by Balfour in July 1905 at the time of the Aliens Bill. He wrote to Sir Frederick Milner MP, in response to one of Milner's constituents whose letter, Balfour said, exhibited 'a very curious misapprehension of my attitude'. Anti-Semitism, he told Milner, was the cause of the most abominable crimes wherever it had prevailed. The Jews were not only a most gifted race but had proved themselves ready and anxious to take part in the national and civic life of the countries where they were settled. But from his point of view it was an undoubted disadvantage that they did not intermarry with the rest of the population, not because he did not like Jews but because he admired them; their rigid separation from their fellow-countrymen was a misfortune for the country. 'If they think it wrong, I do not of course complain of their obeying what they hold to be a binding law; but I must be permitted, from my own point of view, to regret their decision.'[16]

The difficulty of squaring that circle must have been evident to Balfour. For if the Jews were to preserve the qualities which he so admired they had to maintain a separate community. And if they intermarried, as he wished they would, they would in time assuredly lose their separate identity, and with it, those self-same qualities. What then should be their place in a gentile society?

There is an element of mystery about Balfour's attachment to Zionism. A number of possible explanations have been put forward without a great deal of plausibility. It has been said that he inherited a deep knowledge and love of the Old Testament from his mother; that his sympathy was aroused by the situation of small nations derived from his upbringing in Scotland and from his experience as Chief Secretary of Ireland where he had the responsibility of governing a subject nation; that he was moved by philanthropy, or alternatively by Christian guilt, in wanting to do something tangible for the Jews. None of these reasons really rings true, or fits with what is known of Balfour's disposition and character. All are contrary to the dominant strain of sceptical detachment which is observable throughout his public life.

Notwithstanding his scepticism, he had a speculative mind. In Isaiah Berlin's phrase, he was a connoisseur of ideas. That was probably the real appeal of Zionism. Its intellectual attraction was derived from Balfour's ideas about 'race' and nationality. Balfour's concept of race had nothing to do with racial purity – a theory which he dismissed as nonsense. 'There is no such thing in these islands as a man of pure descent from any race whatever', he once said. 'Race' meant loyalty to common traditions, customs, habits, ways of looking at the world. 'Britishness' or membership of the British race was not limited to the United Kingdom, but subsisted wherever men were joined by bonds of sentiment and understanding which made war between them unthinkable.[17] But Jews were subject to two loyalties and, so long as they maintained a distinct community within British society, they could not give the same loyalty to Britain as a gentile. Zionism helped to resolve the dilemma of double allegiance: it gave Jews a choice which they were free to make.

It also had the appeal of idealism. 'No man who is incapable of idealism', Balfour said, 'is capable either of understanding the Zionist movement or effectually contributing to its consummation.'[18] Zionism might eliminate the age-long curse of anti-Semitism, or at least help to do so. It could, he thought, mitigate the miseries created for western civilization by the presence in its midst of a body 'which it too long regarded as alien, even hostile, but which it was equally unable to expel or absorb.'[19] He once remarked to Harold Nicolson that the Jews

> have many material aptitudes, a wide spiritual foundation, but only one idea. That idea is to return to Zion. By depriving them of that idea the world has diminished their virtue and stimulated their defects. If we can help them to attain their ideal, we shall restore to them their dignity. Upon the basis of that dignity their intelligence will cease to be merely acquisitive and will become creative. The New Jerusalem will become a centre of intelligence: and Judaea an asylum for the oppressed.[20]

When in 1919 Balfour met Justice Brandeis, the great judge and American Zionist, they had a discussion about Zionism which showed something of the views of both men. Brandeis said that every Jew was potentially an intellectual and an idealist: the problem was one of direction of those qualities. Many Russian Jews had become revolutionaries. The same men could have found 'constructive channels for expression' in the United States. Some had done so and were already making 'positive contributions to civilisation'. Balfour interrupted him to agree emphatically: 'Of course, these are the reasons that make you and me such ardent Zionists.'[21] Brandeis was talking as an American and Balfour as a Briton. For both Zionism was a force for good, but it was also a cause which should be taken up on grounds of expediency. It could act as a lightning conductor.

Balfour's colleagues in the cabinet, Lloyd George and Milner particularly, supported Zionism and the policy of the Balfour Declaration for mixed motives, but the dominant consideration for them was the geographical importance of Palestine in post-war British aims. Balfour's approach was different. He opposed any extension of Britain's responsibilities in the Near East, indeed any post-war imperialist expansion at all. He thought Zionism and a British Palestine were issues which barely touched, and was an ardent supporter of the first and opponent of the second. He did not think it right that, even as a temporary measure, Britain should undertake the sole responsibility for and become the sole sovereign power in Palestine. As late as March 1917, only months before the Balfour Declaration, Chaim Weizmann found that he 'did not see the importance of the Zionist claim from the British point of view'. A year earlier, he had told Weizmann that he strongly objected to strategic or other opportunist considerations being brought forward as an argument for assuming responsibility for Palestine. Indeed, he thought that were England to become responsible, she would be suspected of seeking territorial aggrandizement and would 'never be given credit for undertaking idealistic responsibility'.[22]

Unhappily, Balfour was blind to the rapid growth of Arab nationalism. It may have been that the impact Zionism made on him prevented him from facing the issue squarely; or he may have simply assumed, as his cabinet colleagues did, that the Palestinian Arabs were of little account and could be ignored in planning for the future of the Middle East. In 1917 Arabs outnumbered Jews in Palestine by about eight to one. If consulted, there is no shadow of doubt that the Arabs would have given an anti-Jewish verdict. It is almost embarrassing to read Balfour's arguments on this subject. He said that there was only 'technical ingenuity' in the contention that Palestine was the Arabs' home and that they constituted a large majority there. The post-war peace was intended to be based on self-determination. Very well: let all the Jews of the world vote, not only those in Palestine, and regardless of whether they were Zionists and whether or not they wished to live in Palestine. 'I do not think that Zionism will hurt the Arabs', he wrote in 1919, 'but they will never say they want it.' He continued to believe it in face of mounting evidence against it.[23]

Balfour came to think that the Jewish case for a homeland in Palestine was wholly exceptional and fell outside the normal rules. In an unusually emotional plea he told the House of Lords in 1922 that the ground which chiefly moved him was that 'we may send a message to every land where the Jewish race has been scattered, a message which will tell them that Christendom is not oblivious of their faith, is not unmindful of the service they have rendered to the great religions of the world . . . and that we desire to the best of our ability to give them the opportunity of developing, in peace and quietness, under British rule, those great gifts which hitherto they have been compelled . . . only to bring to fruition in countries which know not their language, and belong not to their race.'

The experiment might fail. He did not deny it was an adventure, but were we never to have adventures?[24]

4

Chaim Weizmann

Chaim Weizmann bore little resemblance to the popular image of the Jew. He looked something like his contemporary, Lenin, with his small, regular features and straight nose. He was of middle height, with broad shoulders and upright carriage. He radiated confidence and dignity. Sir Harold Nicolson, who saw a good deal of him, once said, 'I sometimes wonder whether his fellow-Jews realise how deeply he impressed us gentiles by his heroic, his Maccabean quality.'

He was the most potent advocate Zionism ever had. He was adroit, sure-footed and resourceful with an instinctive gift for diplomacy which was uncanny – for he had no means of learning the trade. His exposition was lucid and compelling, and his charm of manner captivated those whom he wished to seduce, especially British statesmen. He knew what the other man most wanted to hear, but he would not flatter.

He possessed the power to fire the imagination of his listeners with a sort of mystical belief in the destiny of his people and the significance of its survival. He created a nation out of floating fragments and he spoke as tribune for an inarticulate people. He burned with zeal and at the same time was a man of compromise and moderation. He believed it essential to take sides, and he did not hide his contempt for the purist, the Utopianist, the political monk and the pallid neutral.

He did not find it easy to work in harness with others. He did not cultivate friendships for short-run political advantage. He could seem aloof. His biting wit might appear arrogant. He did not undervalue himself and was every bit as confident in his cause and in himself as he seemed. This could blind him to the hopes and fears of others with whom he had to deal – Arabs and those who made the Arab cause their own, anti-Semites of every stripe, assimilated Jews and the Zionists with whom he disagreed. He was not a humble man and he did not suffer fools gladly. His rages were terrible. His favourite word of dismissal was

'Bilge!' But in the last analysis, he was so convinced that what he was doing was right that he was a man at peace with himself.

He wished to make his nation happy as well as free. Isaiah Berlin tells a story of the old philosopher, Hermann Cohen, whom a Zionist was trying to convince of the merits of his cause. 'Oho!', said Cohen, 'So the gang now wants to be happy, does it?' Berlin comments that that was exactly what Weizmann wanted, and he could see nothing unworthy in it.[1]

Chaim Weizmann's origins and family life were as different from those of Arthur Balfour as is within reach of the imagination. Each might have thought the other came from one of the more remote planets. Weizmann was born on 17 November 1874 in the little town of Motol in the Pripet marshes. It is now in Belarus, but then it was in the Pale of Settlement, the area of the Russian empire to which Jews had been confined since the time of Catherine the Great. Motol was on the bank of a little river, a flat, mournful country of forests and lakes. In the summer it was dusty, in winter a world of snow and ice, and in spring and autumn impassable with mud.

His was a lower-middle-class family, more fortunate than many but still poor. His father, Ozer Weizmann, had fallen in love with Rachel Tchermerinsky and married her when he was sixteen and she just under fourteen. She bore him fifteen children of whom twelve survived childhood. She had her first child at seventeen and her last at forty-seven. Somehow this large family was fed, clothed and shod out of an annual income which Chaim estimated at the equivalent of three hundred dollars.

Ozer Weizmann cut and hauled timber and had it floated down by canal and river to the Baltic at Danzig. His working year was governed by the Jewish festivals. After the feast of Tabernacles in November, he disappeared into the forest to fell timber. He was home in the spring for Passover, after which he left home again to supervise the despatch of the rafts down river. He was back for the great autumn festivals of the New Year and the Day of Atonement. During his absences he completely lost touch with his family, living in the forest and surviving as best he could. He employed year by year a number of gentile peasants. Relations between the Jews and the peasants were friendly but they could barely understand each other across the barrier of language. The Jews spoke little Russian and the peasants no Yiddish.

The Jewish communities in the Pale – half the Jewish population of the world – were closed and steeped in tradition. It went without saying that all were religiously observant. One of Chaim's recurrent and vivid memories is of his father standing before the Ark in the synagogue and leading the congregation in prayer. He describes in his autobiography, *Trial and Error*, how Zionist ideas and aspirations were already awake in his early childhood, and how in his first memories his father was moving towards becoming a Zionist.

Ozer worried about the future of his children and wanted to give them the best education possible in their straitened circumstances. Like all Jewish boys, Chaim went to *Cheder* (a school devoted exclusively to religious instruction) at the age of four. The *Cheder* was a noisy, squalid one-room school which was also the teacher's home. Chaim did not relish a diet of religion only, but he was fortunate enough to have a teacher who shared his young view that it was not possible to live by the Talmud alone. This teacher, Shlomo Sokolovsky, smuggled in secular textbooks in Hebrew on natural sciences. Here he encountered chemistry for the first time.

It seems that even before he left *Cheder* at eleven, he had an understanding of Zionism at which one can only wonder. In the summer of 1885, he wrote a letter to Sokolovsky, declaring that he had decided never to throw off Judaism or the Hebrew language, or listen to those who said that one could become a doctor only by casting off religious faith. He enclosed one of his ideas about *Choveve Zion*, the 'Lovers of Zion' which he described as a lofty and elevated idea.

> Because by this we can rescue our exiled, oppressed brethren who are scattered in all corners of the world and have no place where to put up their tents, and all will attack us and the Jew is a burden on all the nations and on all the Kings of Europe in general and on the King of Russia in particular . . . Let us carry our banner to Zion and return to our first mother upon whose knees we were born – For why should we look to the Kings of Europe for compassion that they should take pity upon us and give us a resting place? In vain! All have decided: the Jew must die, but England will nevertheless have mercy upon us. In conclusion to Zion! – Jews – to Zion! Let us go.[2]

By the time this extraordinary letter was written, these ideas were the common currency of discussion in Jewish homes in eastern Europe. An intelligent boy of eleven could have been expected to be familiar with them. In the Pale there was a picture of England as a humane and liberal country. But this is more. It seems to be a conviction that it was England who would help the Jews back to Palestine, an idea which was to possess Chaim Weizmann all his life until the last, disillusioning phase.

When he was eleven in 1886 he went to high school in Pinsk, the largest town in the district. The number of Jewish children who could enter high schools in the Russian empire was limited to ten per cent. In the universities the limit was three or four per cent. The atmosphere was heavy with disaster for the Jews. The first pogroms had taken place in 1881. They had not reached Motol, but the shock was felt all through the Pale. Chaim Weizmann went to Pinsk with his elder brother, Feivel, and they lodged at first with some friends. Then Chaim was received into a wealthy family where he supervised the homework of the sons. For this, he received his board and lodging and a fee to cover his school books. He did well at Pinsk. The science master noticed him and persuaded him to specialize in chemistry.

In 1892 he matriculated with the highest marks in all subjects except drawing. His natural course would have been to go to a Russian university, particularly as he could by now speak Russian. But the narrow gate through which the restricted numbers of Jewish students had to pass made his chances slight. Moreover, his pride made him recoil from any form of assimilation with Russia. As he said, to go to a Russian university would very likely have involved him in chicanery, deception and humiliation.[3] He determined to go to Germany to continue his studies.

A Jew who wanted to leave the Russian empire had to pay a large sum for a passport. If he could not afford the fee he had to rely on his wits. Weizmann travelled on one of his father's rafts to the Baltic as a raft-worker. In this guise he did not need a passport. As soon as the raft crossed the German frontier he jumped ship. He used his last coins to take the long train journey to Pfungstadt, near Darmstadt in the west of Germany, where he had a contact in a Jewish school. In this new world of cleanliness and order, he could earn enough as a junior teacher in Hebrew and Russian at the school to continue his studies in chemistry at Darmstadt Polytechnic. He imagined that he could get by in Germany with Yiddish, but it turned out to be nearly incomprehensible to the Germans.

The headmaster of the school at Pfungstadt was one Dr Barness. He was a pious Jew of a stuffy orthodoxy and smugness with which Weizmann was unfamiliar.

Barness was completely assimilated and described himself as 'a German of the Mosaic persuasion'. He was naturally aware of the anti-Semitism around him in Germany, but he considered that with a little patience and enlightenment, these ignorant prejudices would vanish. Weizmann had never met anybody like him. It infuriated him and permanently coloured his opinion of a certain sort of assimilated German Jew.

After two terms at Darmstadt, in 1893 he moved to Berlin and continued his studies in Charlottenburg. Berlin was a world away from provincial Darmstadt and Weizmann immediately found himself in a large circle of Russian Jewish students. Colonies of students, predominantly Jewish men and women, were a feature of western European cities at this time. Exiled from their homes in Russia by persecution and intellectual starvation, they belonged in the main to the middle classes and were from homes that were liberal-minded and ambitious for their children. The students were vague about where their future lay, but they were anything but vague in their opinions. In Berlin they met in cafés or small hotels in and around Alexanderplatz where beer and sausages could sometimes be had on credit. They talked endlessly, mostly about the Return to Palestine. They were Zionists before the word had come into use. They were violently opposed to assimilating, which they thought of as abandoning their heritage and merging into the background, if possible making themselves indistinguishable from the gentiles around them.

The students' acknowledged master and the philosopher of the movement was Asher Ginzberg, known by his pen-name of 'Ahad Ha'am'(One of the People). Born near Kiev in 1856 he was the foremost Hebrew writer of his day and the originator and leading advocate of 'spiritual Zionism'. He taught that there could be no salvation for the Jewish people except by being restored to freedom and creative life in the land of its heritage. This did not mean that all Jewry was to go at once to Palestine. The ancient land, in his conception, was to be a spiritual centre from which freedom would flow out to a still-dispersed Jewry. Ahad Ha'am despised the slavery that was called emancipation but which in reality was the price of assimilation. His essay 'Slavery in Freedom', on the evils resulting from assimilation, was published in 1891 and became a text for the émigré colonies of Russo-Jewish students. Weizmann was greatly influenced by the essay and other writings of Ahad Ha'am. The older man became his friend and mentor.

In 1896 Theodor Herzl published *The Jewish State*. The incendiary pamphlet came like a bolt out of a clear blue sky, but it contained nothing new for the young students of Berlin. Chaim Weizmann welcomed it because it confirmed his own views about the false hopes of the assimilated. He also welcomed Herzl as a charismatic leader and carried his picture with him everywhere. He wrote to tell him so: 'This is the picture which is ever in our mind's eye and which we always carry and shall carry in our hearts.'[4]

But Herzl's view that the Jewish state should be created by the grant of a charter from the Sultan or by the sponsorship of one or more of the powers was a sticking point and a source of difference. Weizmann and his friends thought it impracticable. For them, as for their prophet Ahad Ha'am, the Return would come through the gradual colonization of Palestine and accompanied by the spiritual re-invigoration of Jewry. They began to diverge from their leader.

Weizmann finished his third year in Berlin in 1897. He went home to see his family that summer and received a mandate from the community at Pinsk to represent them at the first Zionist Congress in Basle in August of that year. But to his intense regret he could not attend. He had made a discovery in dyestuff chemistry and his professor thought he could sell it. He introduced Weizmann to a friend who had a dyeing plant in Moscow. The prospect of making a little money and relieving his father of the continuing burden of supporting him was irresistible. But it was dangerous for a Jew to travel in Russia outside the Pale without the right permits, which he could not afford. He had to dodge the police to avoid arrest. These difficulties detained him and he could not get to the Congress in time.

That summer he decided to leave Berlin to take his fourth year in Freiburg in Switzerland. He would then, in 1899, submit his thesis for his doctorate. Freiburg was less than an hour away from Berne where there was another colony of Russian Jewish students. Switzerland was then also the home of another sort of Russian émigré, the revolutionary Socialists Lenin, Plekhanov, Trotsky and their followers. The Socialists and the Zionists were rival fishers for souls; and they held each other in contempt. Weizmann particularly resented the arrogant Trotsky's attitude to Zionists. The fact that Trotsky was himself a Jew made matters worse. '*They* could not understand why a Russian Jew should want to be anything but a Russian', Weizmann wrote of the Socialists. '*They* stamped as unworthy, as intellectually backward, as chauvinistic and immoral, the desire of any Jew to concern himself with the sufferings and destiny of Jewry.'[5]

Weizmann and his friends decided to challenge the Socialists in debate. It required moral courage. He was a young unknown of twenty-six, while Plekhanov, Lenin and Trotsky, although not yet world figures, were already famous. The meeting took place in a beer hall in Berne in 1901 and lasted for three days and two nights. In the end, when the resolutions were put, the Zionists were found to have won. Weizmann, who debated with Plekhanov, was cock-a-hoop about the victory. He wrote to a Berlin friend about it.

> Mr Plekhanov was debunked and routed and retreated in the most ignominious manner ... I was in the seventh heaven at having knocked out *Balaam*. I had been looking for an opportunity to come to grips with Mr P for a long time. I doubt whether I shall ever again be in such spirits as I was that evening. We had an almost sleepless night afterwards.[6]

Weizmann relished the fight and he flayed the heretics who could not or would not accept the truth about Zionism. He wrote to the same friend about a member of the *Bund*, the Jewish revolutionary labour organization and another band of unbelievers.

> Davidson has been propounding his critique of Zionism here ... He argued that Zionism leads to slavery, to the attachment of Jews to capitalism, and he denied the very existence of Jewish cultural creative power ... A smell of corpses and of death pervaded his whole speech. It was a dirge sung out of tune ... He is a vanquished, subdued Jew.[7]

It was about this time in Geneva that Weizmann first met Vera Chatzman who was to become his wife. She was eighteen at the time and was in Geneva to pursue her medical studies. She was born in Rostov-on-Don of Jewish parents. Her father had served in the imperial Russian army during the Crimean war, and as a result obtained permission to live outside the Pale. The Don valley was described by her as 'hard-riding, prosperous Cossack territory'; and despite the usual quotas and restrictions, Rostov was remarkably free from 'the wilder and more vulgar Jew-baiting and anti-Semitism which prevailed in other parts of Russia'. She described the impression he made on her at that first meeting.

> I was sitting at a table with a group of young fellow-students at a well-scrubbed deal table eating my meal, when a tall, impressive man, with a fine imposing head which was almost bald despite his comparative youth – he was only twenty-seven at this time

– walked in and, standing with one foot on a chair, began to talk to someone. He was pale, dedicated, very frail yet serene, with a faint ironic gleam in his eyes, mingled with deep and affecting sadness.[8]

She knew next to nothing of Zionism until she met Weizmann. He was seven years older and already a junior teacher. He quickly fell in love with her and became her patient instructor in the cause which was to be his life.

During the years in Switzerland Weizmann was searching for the best way to realise the dream of Zionism. His mentor was Ahad Ha'am but he did not blindly follow him. Weizmann actively assisted in the preparations for the first Zionist Congress in 1897 and, although he was compelled to miss it, he attended the subsequent Congresses regularly. Ahad Ha'am, on the other hand, would have nothing to do with Congresses or Herzl's diplomacy, remarking dismissively that 'the salvation of Israel will be achieved by prophets and not by diplomats'. Weizmann was not prepared to give unquestioning support to Herzl either. He considered that Herzl's obsession with diplomacy and a political solution was not sufficient. It was just as necessary to bring the Jewish masses out of their torpor and make themselves conscious of their heritage and their potential. As early as 1901 he and a group of friends conceived the idea of a Hebrew University in Palestine, a project dear to his heart at which he worked steadily until the university was finally inaugurated.

In these years Weizmann was only a minor figure in the Zionist movement and felt powerless to influence its direction. The movement seemed to be stagnant and riven by faction. The debates were endless and mostly fruitless. His letters to Vera Chatzman are eloquent of his frustration and of how much he was already relying on her. 'Verunechka, my darling,' he wrote in July 1901, 'I so much want you to be here, to be able to talk to you. I feel so wretched; something is stifling me, choking me, and I cannot get rid of a nightmare that torments me . . . Everywhere, among those that are dear to us, there prevails such a feeling of disappointment, such a terrible mood . . .'[9]

But his mood had changed when he wrote to her again in September. He was once more buoyed up by hope. 'May the young shoots now appearing on the old time-worn trunk grow into a mighty tree in the shade of which the Wandering Jew may seek repose . . . Israel is awaiting its children – and they are coming, they are returning, and may the coming years be a festival of reunion, a festival of the return of him who has been lost.'[10]

Few foresaw that within a year or two the movement was to be shaken to its core by the unexpected results of Herzl's diplomatic efforts.

5

'Uganda'

Theodor Herzl was convinced from the outset that, if he was to succeed in his campaign for a Jewish state in Palestine, he must have the consent of the Sultan of Turkey. The new state must have the legitimacy and the recognition which could only be conferred by the sovereign power. He therefore began to travel the Courts of Europe even before the publication of *The Jewish State* in February 1896. It was a frock-coated and silk-hatted diplomacy conducted with stately decorum, and it failed wholly to achieve its object. But by the time of Herzl's death in 1904, his name was known everywhere it mattered. When he saw the Kaiser in 1898 he noted with satisfaction that his three years' work had made 'the obscure word "Zionism" a *terme reçu* that fell naturally from the lips of the German emperor'.[1]

His first venture into the labyrinthine Court of the Sultan was in May 1896. The plan was to offer twenty million Turkish pounds in exchange for Palestine. The money, Herzl vainly hoped, could be raised with the help of the Rothschilds and other Jewish financiers and philanthropists and would go to relieve the Sultan of the debilitating burden of his funded debt. He was received with studied courtesy but he could penetrate the Court no further than the Grand Vizier. The Sultan was not yet disposed to see him. Herzl's next idea was that he should try to recruit the Kaiser, who prided himself on his warm relations with the Sultan.

At the first Zionist Congress in 1897, Herzl's diplomatic campaign was confirmed by the Congress. It was formally decided that the home for the Jewish people should be in Palestine and that it should be founded in 'public law'. The following year the Kaiser was to make an opportune visit to Turkey and a religious pilgrimage to the Holy Land. Herzl managed to arrange to be received by the German emperor in Constantinople and again in Jerusalem. The occasions were more remarkable for the exotic splendour of the Kaiser's military uniforms (a dark Hussar uniform for Constantinople and a grey outfit with turban and riding whip for Jerusalem) than for the results of the meetings. After promising overtures through diplomatic channels, the Kaiser merely said that the plan called for further study and discussion. He permitted himself the observation that 'the land needs, above all, water and shade'.

Herzl finally penetrated the diplomatic defences guarding the Sultan. He passed the procession of eunuchs, princesses, pashas, dignitaries, sycophants and lackeys and reached the Presence in May 1901. '*Der Herr* stood before me exactly as I had pictured him: small, thin, with great hooked nose, full dyed beard, a weak quavering voice.' He assured Herzl that he was and always had been a friend of the Jews. Indeed he relied mainly on the Moslems and Jews and had not the same confidence in his other subjects. Herzl observed that the thorn in the Sultan's side was the imperial debt: if that could be removed Turkey would develop new strength. The Sultan sighed and smiled. It was his exalted predecessors who had acquired the thorn, and he had been concerning himself with it ever since his glorious reign began. Herzl said he believed he could help – but the first condition was absolute secrecy. '*Der Herr* raised his eyes to heaven, placed his hand upon his breast, and murmured, "Secret, secret!"' The talk began to wander and became inconsequential. After two hours Herzl was exhausted and the Sultan found nothing more to say. When Herzl took his leave the Sultan once more assured him that he was a friend of the Jews and would give them lasting protection if they sought refuge in his lands. On reflecting afterwards Herzl concluded that the Sultan was a weak, craven but good-natured man. 'I believe him to be neither clever nor cruel, but a profoundly unhappy prisoner in whose name a thieving, infamous, scoundrelly camarilla perpetrate the vilest abominations.'[2]

The frontal approach to the Sultan having failed, as Herzl recognized, he began thinking of a sort of transit camp near Palestine where the Jews could be settled until the time when they could return to Zion itself. The Ottoman empire was shaky and its future uncertain. Britain, the greatest imperial power in the world, now moved into the foreground as the sponsor Herzl had always had in mind. He had said in 1897:

> From the first moment I entered the Movement, my eyes were directed towards England, because I saw that by reason of the general situation of things there it was the Archimedean point where the lever could be applied. The still existing happy position

of the English Jews, their high standard of culture, their proud adherence to the old race caused them to appear to me as the right men to realise the Zionistic idea.[3]

Herzl's indefatigable diplomacy turned to Cyprus or a place just on the Egyptian side of the frontier with Palestine as a place of refuge for the Jews. In a letter to Lord Rothschild he suggested that El Arish in the Sinai peninsula might appeal to the British government, it being the point where their Egyptian and Indo-Persian interests converged. It was a shrewd suggestion. El Arish is a shallow depression, or wadi, running northwards in the Sinai peninsula to the Mediterranean just inside Egypt, and a short step into Palestine. The plan was not merely for a settlement in the El Arish valley but also lands to the west towards the Suez canal.

A meeting was arranged in the autumn of 1902 between Herzl and Joseph Chamberlain, the British Colonial Secretary, through the intermediacy of Leopold Greenberg, the Zionist editor of the *Jewish Chronicle* and a political radical from Birmingham, the city which was Chamberlain's power base. Chamberlain was a flamboyant character and the very personification of England's late-Victorian imperialism. But Joe Chamberlain, 'the famous master-figure of England' as Herzl called him, did not make an impression of brilliance. 'Not a man of imagination', Herzl noted in his diary: 'A matter-of-fact screw manufacturer, who wants to expand the business. A mind without literary or artistic resources, a business man, but an absolutely clear mind.'[4] Chamberlain was enthusiastic about Herzl's plans. But he made clear that Cyprus was not a possible idea because of the inevitable opposition of the inhabitants. On the other hand, Chamberlain said, El Arish was well worth considering.

Herzl told Chamberlain that the situation of the Jews in eastern Europe was desperate. The influx of these Jews into Britain had caused Salisbury's Conservative government to appoint a Royal Commission to consider whether there ought to some control over immigration. Herzl had given evidence to the Commission in July 1902, only months before he met Chamberlain. His anxiety, he told Chamberlain, was to find somewhere the Jews could go and feel safe, and where their everlasting wanderings could cease. It was Palestine, he said, that would satisfy their deepest aspirations.

Chamberlain may have been genuinely affected by the plight of the Russian Jews, but there were also other considerations that attracted him in the proposal.

Britain could attain the first position in the sympathies of that almost mythical community of influence and power by whom British ministers and officials seem to have been bemused: world Jewry. She could secure Jewish capital and settlers for developing land which was already within the British sphere of influence in the Middle East and, when the time came for the inevitable collapse of the Ottoman Empire, a friendly Jewish settlement in Palestine could be of great service to Britain's imperial designs. Herzl was right that Chamberlain wanted to expand the business.

Chamberlain told Herzl that there might be difficulties about El Arish and that it was possible that 'we would have the same trouble with the native inhabitants'. 'No', said Herzl, 'we will not go to Egypt. We have been there.'[5] Chamberlain laughed, but he knew what Herzl was driving at: a place for the Jews to gather as a jumping-off point for the land of Israel. However, the El Arish scheme was within the jurisdiction of the Foreign Office, not Chamberlain's Colonial department. Chamberlain arranged for Herzl to see the Foreign Secretary, Lord Lansdowne. Lansdowne showed interest but he in turn passed on the plan to Lord Cromer, Britain's Consul-General in Cairo, by whom he said he would be guided. Greenberg was to go out to Cairo to explain the El Arish scheme to Cromer.

The office of Consul-General in Cairo did not sound very influential, but in fact it was. Egypt, although under nominal Turkish suzerainty, was a British colony in almost everything but name. The Agent and Consul-General, the senior British official there, exercised a great many of the functions of a governor. Herzl drew a picture of Cromer which was not flattering. He thought the consul-general the most disagreeable Englishman he had ever met: 'Rather too much morgue, a touch of tropical distemper, and a streak of absolute vice-regalism'.[6]

Despite Greenberg's efforts, the Egyptian government objected to the scheme. The water resources for the project would have to come from the Nile and could not be spared. Cromer thought that the scheme, which would be bound to involve a large-scale cosmopolitan settlement, would only add to his problems, and he eventually gave the El Arish scheme its quietus during the summer of 1903.

Meanwhile Chamberlain had left for a long trip to Africa and it seems that the Jewish problem had remained on his mind. When he came back in the spring of 1903 he suggested to Herzl that suitable land could be found for a Jewish settlement in East Africa, but he assumed that it was too far from Palestine to be of interest. This idea came to be known as the 'Uganda' scheme, although what was suggested was land in the East African Protectorate, shortly to become the colony of Kenya. However, the name 'Uganda' stuck, and among the opponents of the scheme it acquired pejorative overtones. Herzl was at first against the idea for the reason assumed by Chamberlain, that East Africa was not Zion, but he was persuaded by Greenberg that any offer from the British government was not lightly to be put aside. To turn it down, Greenberg argued, would be dangerous, whereas to entertain it might, in the end and with skilful negotiation, bring the prospect of Zion closer. Herzl was persuaded. The plight of the Russian Jews weighed on his mind and by now he knew that the El Arish plan was virtually dead. There seemed to be no alternative.

Greenberg was assisted in formulating these schemes by a London firm of solicitors, Lloyd George, Roberts & Co., in which David Lloyd George was a partner. Lloyd George was then a member of Parliament and of the Liberal Party, which at that time was in opposition. He was no doubt chosen by Greenberg because he knew his way through the corridors of Westminster; but he was not yet a committed Zionist.

Meanwhile, events inside Russia had made the position of the Russian Jews more precarious and their escape more urgent. They went in daily fear of their lives. In the spring of 1903 reports began to reach western Europe of a massacre of Jews at Kishinev. There were forty-five dead and six hundred seriously wounded. The numbers may seem small, but at the opening of the twentieth century it was a harbinger of what that dreadful century had in store.

Chaim Weizmann wrote that the Kishinev pogrom, which occurred at Easter time and coincided with the last days of Passover, sent a thrill of horror through the Jewish world. He was convinced that the massacre was deliberately organized, carefully planned and carried out under the eyes of the Russian civil and military authorities. It appeared that the Jews had allowed themselves to be slaughtered without offering any general resistance. Weizmann returned to Russia and set about organizing self-defence groups in the larger Jewish centres.[7]

It was not only the imminent danger to the Jews of the Pale that was on Weizmann's mind in the first half of 1903. He was also anxious about the divisions which were weakening Zionism. The younger Jews in Russia were being drawn into the revolutionary socialist movement which was astir and would eventually erupt in 1905, and then decisively in 1917. At the other end of the spectrum were the orthodox faction, passive, reliant on the old religious forms and out of touch with increasing numbers of young Jews. Weizmann himself was still loyal to Herzl, indeed he revered him, but he was increasingly uneasy about the direction of his leadership. He was a leading member of the so-called 'Democratic Fraction'. This group was dedicated to practical action and disenchanted with fine speeches. To Weizmann and the 'Fraction', Herzl's feverish diplomacy seemed to be leading nowhere.

In May 1903, on his return from Russia, Weizmann set out his anxieties in a long letter to Herzl.[8] He gave his leader a detailed account of the plight of Jewry inside the Russian empire, and the defection of many of the Zionist youth. The letter was courteously expressed but it made clear the writer's anxiety about the future of Zionism. Herzl, for his part, regarded the Democratic Fraction as a dangerous splinter. In his reply to Weizmann he was frank. 'I regard you, Dr Weizmann, as a person who has been temporarily misled, but nevertheless a useful force who will once more find his way back . . .'[9] The rift in the ranks was to come into the open later in the year at the sixth Zionist Congress.

Herzl had a Utopian conception of what the Jewish state would be like. He attempted an imaginative account in his novel *Altneuland* (Old-New Land), which he started to write in 1899 and published in 1902. The book owed more to western European notions of civil society than to Jewish cultural traditions. Two friends, one Jewish and the other gentile, are disillusioned and weary with life. They decide to withdraw to a remote island in the Pacific. On the way there they spend a few days in Palestine. They saw, as Herzl had seen in his visit in 1898, a decayed and desolate land. They return refreshed twenty years later. Everything has changed. The Jewish State has been realized. The ancient city of Zion has been left intact, and is now surrounded by leafy suburbs, Haifa is a world city, the desert has bloomed and the country flourishes. The economy is 'mutualistic', or cooperative, education is free and the social order is based on justice and freedom. The festivals of Judaism are observed but religion plays no part in public life. There is no racial antagonism. The Arabs, free to worship in their mosques, live side by side with the Jews from whom they have learned much. Even outside Palestine an idealized order prevails. Jews are still scattered through other countries and have found peace there. Anti-Semitism has vanished.

The importance of *Altneuland* lay in what it revealed about Herzl's inner thinking. It was a vision too shallow and too suffused with a spirit of western European enlightenment for most Zionists. A storm blew up and troubled the movement which was already riven by faction. Weizmann disliked the book. He was a pragmatist and opposed to visionary schemes with no foothold in reality. He told Vera Chatzman that the book was bound to cause fierce repercussions at the forthcoming Congress, and that the struggle between east and west within Jewry was worsening. Ahad Ha'am wrote a scathing review, saying that Herzl had drawn a picture of a Jewish homeland without a Jewish culture.[10]

The Kishinev massacre at Eastertime, 1903, had thrown a ghastly light on the Jewish question in Russia. The common report was that Vyacheslav Plehve, the Minister for the Interior, a former Chief of Police and a political figure of unenviable notoriety for his anti-Semitism, was answerable for the crime, either through complicity or worse. Herzl decided to see him if he could. He succeeded in obtaining an appointment through the intermediacy of a Polish noblewoman. Plehve, she reported to Herzl, would be happy to make the acquaintance of so interesting a personality as Dr Herzl, and would 'heartily support a movement for Jewish emigration without the right of re-entry'. In June, Plehve made it clear that he was prepared to assist the Russian Zionists to emigrate, but the Tsarist government would not tolerate propaganda in favour of a Jewish national movement within Russia.[11]

Herzl considered it his duty to negotiate with anyone in whose hands a solution might lie and he chose to ignore Plehve's record. Russia had an obvious interest in facilitating Jewish emigration. In early August 1903, therefore, he visited Russia, and had an interview with Plehve. He asked for Russian intervention with the Sultan to secure a charter for colonization in Palestine, and financial aid for emigration. Plehve agreed at once. Weizmann was angry when he learned that Herzl had seen Plehve. He thought that a meeting with the man who had the blood of Kishinev on his hands was humiliating – and pointless. Plehve did as he had promised. However, Russia's diplomatic intervention with the Sultan fell on deaf ears.

On the way back from St Petersburg Herzl visited Vilna. The streets were tumultuous with cheering Jews. 'Address after address praised me wildly beyond my deserts, but the unhappiness of these sorely oppressed people was only too genuine.'[12] He was received as a redeemer. He began to think that everything, even the return of his people to their ancient home, must for the moment be subordinated to their safety.

It was in that frame of mind that Herzl met the sixth Zionist Congress on 23 August 1903. There, for the first time, delegates were told of the 'Uganda' offer. Few of the delegates knew that Herzl had been negotiating with the British government about alternatives to Zion. Instead of the usual map of Palestine hanging behind the speakers' platform, the delegates saw a map of East Africa. The British government's offer was contained in a letter from Lord Lansdowne. Although it was subject to a number of provisos, it stated that the government would be prepared to consider favourably the establishment of a Jewish colony or settlement in East Africa, the grant of a suitable area of land, the appointment of a Jewish local governor and a degree of local autonomy under the general control of Britain.

The first reaction of the delegates was elation. They were moved and proud. Here at last was a concrete offer of a refuge and a homeland from the greatest world power of all; and recognition of the Jews as a nation. The view that it was England and not any other country to which the Zionists should look seemed to be strikingly confirmed. But excitement quickly gave way to doubt. The 'Uganda' offer opened a deep split in the movement and left bitterness in its wake. The Land of Israel was of the essence of Zionism. Take that away, as the 'Uganda' offer did, and the movement might never find its way back to Zion. A homeland anywhere else was to many Jews a fantasy or even a form of idolatry.

Weizmann was now aged twenty-nine, a junior Russian delegate to the Zionist Congress, but otherwise without office in the Zionist Organization and only slightly known to Herzl and the other leaders. After some initial hesitation he became one of the most passionate opponents of the 'Uganda' plan. He gives an account in his autobiography, *Trial and Error*, which, although written nearly a half century later, still bears the marks of anger which 'Uganda' aroused in his mind.[13]

Herzl introduced the 'Uganda' offer to Congress. His speech was, in Weizmann's words, cautious, dignified and guarded. His proposal was no more than for an investigating committee to be sent out to East Africa and report. He spoke of the flood of Jewish emigration from Russia, which since Kishinev had been rising to the rate of a hundred thousand a year, and described how that great human tide might be deflected to East Africa. He told Congress that he had not lost sight of Zion, and that East Africa was only an emergency expedient, a *Nachtasyl* (night shelter). In the heated debate which followed there was a dramatic moment when a young woman ran on to the platform and tore down the map of East Africa which was hanging behind the speaker's rostrum.

The Russian delegation met separately. The leader of the delegation was Menahem Ussishkin, but he was away – in Palestine. Ussishkin (1863–1941) had been born in what is now Belarus and had been a member of *Choveve Zion* (Lovers of Zion) from his early youth. He was a member of the Executive of the Zionist Organization and was a leading figure in the anti-Ugandist faction. The strength of his conviction was made clear in a message he sent from Jaffa about founding a Hebrew University in Jerusalem. 'I am ready to work heart and soul for the founding of the University here and I shall oppose its establishment elsewhere with all my strength.'[14] The discussion among the Russian delegates was emotional. 'They argued, fumed and wept – some sat on the floor mourning as one mourns for the dead.'[15] Weizmann and his father, who was also a delegate, were on opposite sides. His father was a practical man who thought that there was nothing to lose by accepting the 'Uganda' offer. But the son passionately opposed. He thought those who were in favour of the offer had fallen prey to a curious inferiority complex, and he made a violent speech which swayed many. His own conception of Zionism and the way in which it could be made reality on the ground in Palestine was forming. He expressed what he felt at the time of the 'Uganda' controversy in a speech he made to a students' meeting.

> What we want is not some kind of underhand colonisation, as our opponents argue. All we say is that five thousand settlers without a charter are better than a charter with no settlers. The charter can be secured when we are in Palestine. Zionism is not simply an answer to present distress; for us it is a complete world outlook which encompasses all the values of our lives . . . The Jewish people are sitting on a volcano, and this position will continue until an appalling disaster occurs . . . Then ultimately the solution to the Jewish question will be found. This unique solution is that of national Zionism: the revival of Israel in its historic land![16]

When Herzl's proposal for a commission to go out to East Africa was put to Congress, it was carried by 295 votes to 178. However, the dissident minority was large enough for it to be clear that acceptance of the British offer would probably be futile. The bulk of the 'nay-sayers' came from the Russian delega-tion, the very section of Jewry whom the proposal was designed to help most. To the western Jews it was beyond understanding. The Russians walked out of the hall, disgusted. After the vote had been taken, Herzl came to see the Russian delegation. He looked exhausted and haggard from the strain of seeing his life's work threatened by faction, and from the heart disease which would give him less than another year. He chided them for having left the hall and asked them to come back. He made a last plea for the need to find an immediate refuge for the masses of homeless. He was listened to in complete silence. It was the last time Weizmann saw him. He died the next year, aged forty-four.

After it was all over, Weizmann wrote to Ussishkin about the lessons of the Congress. He was disparaging about what he called 'African fever', and said that it was essential to come to the next Congress 'armed, and with an integrated view regarding the future of the cause – above all, the Palestine cause.' If we fail to do so, he continued, 'we shall not be able to have even the 178 nay-sayers, and we shall be powerless in the face of the solid block of *Mizrahi* [rabbinate party] and the western Zionists who, in the name of "the Jewish people" will say that Palestine cannot be had, that the people are starving, and therefore we must grab Africa!'[17]

East Africa was in any case an impossible idea. When the British settlers learned what was on foot, they reacted sharply. Lord Delamere, the undisputed leader of the white pioneers in East Africa and what would now be called a 'hard-liner', protested in a choleric cable to *The Times* on 29 August 1903 against 'the introduction of alien Jews'. He asked, 'Is British taxpayer, proprietor East Africa, content that beautiful and valuable country be handed to aliens? Have we no colonists our own race?'

The day before this outburst appeared, *The Times* printed a letter from Lucien Wolf, a prominent Anglo-Jewish opponent of Zionism. He thought the 'Uganda' scheme was open to the gravest objections, particularly the experiment in Jewish self-government. 'From the point of view of colonial administration,' he wrote with no little pomposity, 'the precedent would certainly not be a happy one ... The essentially British character of our Colonies would not be strengthened if we devoted ourselves to accentuating the alien characteristics of white colonists, who otherwise would easily assimilate themselves with their British neighbours.' He foresaw that the result of granting 'these unhappy people' municipal autonomy would be the establishment of a Polish ghetto in East Africa.[18] It was a warning of what the Zionists were to expect from Anglo-Jewry.

On the same day *The Times* published an editorial on the subject. The editor's gloomy conclusion was that 'full-blown Zionism had better stand over – perhaps for ever'. By the end of 1903, Lansdowne had written of the 'Uganda' plan, 'We shall probably be well out of it! But it was right to treat the application considerately.'[19]

For Weizmann it was a turning point. On 4 July 1904 Herzl died in Vienna a disappointed man. His plan for a homeland in accordance with public law and with the support of the Powers had foundered. As Jews from all over Europe gathered for his funeral, Weizmann realized that a fresh start would have to be made. As he wrote, 'I closed the first chapter of my Zionist life, and set out for England, to begin the second.'[20]

6

England

Why did Chaim Weizmann go to England, and why then in 1904? He does not explain in his letters, but in his autobiography he says that it was no accident. It was, he says, a case of *reculer pour mieux sauter*. 'I was in danger of being eaten up with Zionism with no benefit to my scientific career or to the movement.'[1] The income from his patent was running down. The teaching post in the University in Geneva had no future that could satisfy him. He would soon be short of money again. He chose England intuitively as the country, above all other European countries in the early twentieth century, whose name was held in honour for its tolerance and its moderation by Jews everywhere, especially by the masses in eastern Europe. And, as he always had thought from his Russian childhood, England would show tangible sympathy for the Zionist movement and the Jews would in the end find their champions in the English.

Weizmann's affection for England was a constant thread which ran through his life. He liked and admired the English. Unhappily for him he trusted them too well. In 1917, however, the triumph of the Balfour Declaration would seem to confirm his judgement and his trust, and everything he had supposed about Britain from his earliest childhood would seem to be true.

He became a British subject in 1910 and on his naturalization took the name 'Charles' instead of Chaim; but he used it only on ceremonial occasions, as when after the war in 1920 it was proposed by Herbert Samuel and others that he be knighted – a suggestion that was not proceeded with because Lloyd George thought it then inopportune. That it did not happen probably disappointed him. He hoped too that he would be rewarded for his biochemical work by a professorship at Manchester, as he had been promised, and that he would be elected a Fellow of the Royal Society. He won neither of these honours, and greatly wanted both. But no honour that his adopted country could confer was as dear to him as the cause of Zionism. Warmly as he felt about England, he was conscious to the depth of his being of his Russian Jewish origins. He wrote to a sympathetic friend in 1915:

> You were good enough to ask: 'What made you take up the Zionist problem?' My answer to this question was not adequate. I never 'took the question up'. We who come from Russia are born and bred in an aspiration towards a new and better Jewish life. It must not only be a comfortable life but a *Jewish* one, a normal Jewish life, just as the Englishman leads a normal English life.[2]

After the sixth Zionist Congress in August 1903, Weizmann was at a dead end. The bitterness of the split in Zionism is evident from his letters. The Ugandists ('the Zionist rabble', as he called them) seemed to be in the ascendant. They dreamed of a fine homeland in the uplands of East Africa, and if they could not have that, they would look elsewhere. He even thought of a breakaway group to carry on the struggle for Palestine.

Weizmann told Vera Chatzman that Herzl's death had left him with a great weight on his heart and a frightening legacy. Conditions were worsening in Russia too. 'Every time I walk through the town I return home with a broken heart', he wrote to her in April 1904 from his family home in Pinsk. 'There is not a single animated face, not a single smile; all around there are only dead shadows . . . All conversations turn around emigration . . . but where to go? Entry into America is made difficult, restrictive Bills are being passed in England.'[3]

Vera and he had decided to marry, but they had agreed that she should complete her medical studies in Geneva first, so that they would be separated while he was starting a new life in England. The enforced separation was a chafing experience for them both. He wrote to her every day and complained bitterly when she did not reply to each letter. While he was in Russia in the spring of 1904 he met her family for the first time. Her mother's immediate reactions were deflating. 'Poor Verotchka,' she lamented, 'she's so young and beautiful – and he's so old!' The couple paid no attention. Vera knew the personal dilemma that was tearing her fiancé apart. She knew what research, with its switchback moments of elation and disappointment, meant to him. At the same time he was working on a plan to open an office in Geneva for a Hebrew University, his most cherished dream of all. Which should he choose, chemistry or Zionism? 'I do not want to hide this dilemma from you', he wrote to Vera. 'I am putting it before you, naked and unadorned, as I see it myself. Our lives are inextricably tied together, and it is for you to have the last word.' She did not mince her answer. She told him it was *his* duty to weigh things up, but she could not see how chemistry and Zionism could be separated. 'Surely you do not intend to take Jewish money for the cause?'[4]

He arrived in 1904 and saw an England that he knew hardly at all. He had visited London in the previous October to find out for himself what there was in the Uganda offer. His first impression was the same as those of many visitors in winter: '. . .there is slush here, foul weather, din and uproar, and a language which is not exactly comprehensible to me'. He described Whitechapel, where so many of his fellow Russian Jews had found refuge. 'What horror! Stench, foul smells, emaciated Jewish faces. A mixture of a London avenue and Jewish poverty in the suburbs of Vilna.'[5]

These were the 50,000 in the Jewish East End, about whom the Royal Commission had heard the damning evidence referred to in Chapter 3. The Jews of Whitechapel must have struck their neighbours as queer foreign fish, speaking Yiddish and observing strange religious rites and practices. In their overcrowded masses they teemed in the narrow streets and alleys. They had an appetite for work which could barely be assuaged and were prepared to work for next to nothing. These poor immigrants would do anything to better themselves and see their children speak English and be well-educated.

Weizmann had the advantage of having met Moses Gaster, the 'Haham' (head of the Sephardic communities in England) at the third Zionist Congress in 1899 and knew him for an opponent of the 'Uganda' scheme. Through him he had an introduction to Lord Percy, Under-Secretary for Foreign Affairs in charge of the African desk. He went from Percy to Sir Clement Hill, the Superintendent of African Protectorates. He saw them both again when he came to England permanently in 1904, and was amazed that the grand figures in British public life were so accessible, so affable and frank. Both Percy and Hill received him kindly, and Hill told him that if he were Jewish, he would oppose the 'Uganda' scheme absolutely. 'For a Zionist there is nothing to look for in Africa,' he said. It was music to Weizmann's ears. 'I have, in fact, assumed the role of some kind of self-styled diplomat of the Russian Zionists to the British government', he told Vera.[6]

The Uganda scheme was in any case about to fade from the scene. A

Zionist Commission went out to East Africa at the end of 1904. Its report was unenthusiastic. When the seventh Zionist Congress met in July of the following year it resolved that, while the movement was grateful to Britain for its offer, it should be declined and all future Zionist activity outside Palestine should be rejected. By then both the British government and the majority of Zionists were relieved to be extricated from what had become an embarrassing and, for the Zionists, a painful episode.

When he moved from London to Manchester Weizmann's excitement at being able to mingle with the great and the good soon gave way to the more sobering and humble circumstances of researcher in an obscure laboratory in the chemical school of Manchester University. He had chosen Manchester for his self-imposed exile because it was an important centre of the chemical industry and because the chemical school at the university had an international reputation. He had a letter of introduction from one of the senior chemists at the University of Geneva to Professor William Perkin of Manchester, but he came with very little experience and spoke little English. His basement place of work was grimy with accumulations of fog and soot, and he had to pay a fee of £6 for its use. He could not hope for a paid post in the university until he had proved himself, which might take years.

Slowly, literally and metaphorically, Weizmann lifted himself out of the basement laboratory into the light of day. To improve his English he bought the Bible, Macaulay's essays and Gladstone's speeches. His efforts evidently succeeded because in 1905 Perkin asked him to give a lecture in English (still a terrifying prospect for Weizmann), and then a tutorial class, and proposed his name for a research scholarship. He started to make friends among the Manchester Jewish community. When he had first arrived in the city he knew just one person – Joseph Massel, a printer and Hebrew poet of very modest circumstances. During his first months in Manchester he spent his Friday nights as the guest of Massel and his wife. Massel introduced him to Charles Dreyfus, the Chairman of the local Zionist group and another opponent of the 'Uganda' project. This was an influential contact. Dreyfus was chairman of the Board of the Clayton Aniline Works and he soon asked Weizmann to undertake some research for his company. He was also a key figure in the Jewish community in Manchester. Weizmann and he worked together on Zionist affairs and in January 1905 both were elected to the executive of the English Zionist Federation. Dreyfus was a member of Manchester City Council and, most importantly as it turned out, the Chairman of the local Conservative Constituency Association. At this early stage in his English life Weizmann also met Harry Sacher, a journalist on the staff of the *Manchester Guardian*, and Simon Marks and Israel Sieff. All three played important parts in the Zionist movement and became close friends of Weizmann. Marks and Sieff were later associated in the formation of Marks & Spencer. Manchester was also the home of the *Manchester Guardian*, a great liberal newspaper which had attained international repute under its remarkable editor, C. P. Scott, who was to become Weizmann's friend and a tireless advocate of Zionism.

While Weizmann was establishing a foothold in Manchester revolution broke out in Russia in early 1905. The police fired into a crowd of workers and there were many left dead. He wrote to Vera, who was still in Geneva: 'it is really terrible. *Il sonne comme l'histoire*. Blood-stained pages of Russian history; that is, not only Russian but also world history and partly our own Jewish history too . . '. The unrest and the pogroms continued throughout the year. At the end of October there was a massacre in Odessa. Over three hundred people, many of them Jews, were killed. The police took no action against the mobs. Weizmann wrote to Gaster saying that he despised himself for not being there. 'It is painful, and a terrible irony, to be teaching chemistry to *Goyim* now, and I laugh with derision at myself.'[7]

At the same time in Britain the government passed the Aliens Act restricting immigration. It was one of the last measures brought in by Balfour before he resigned as Prime Minister in late 1905. Weizmann had been active in the campaign against the legislation. He was particularly incensed by the attitude of wealthy English Jews. 'Verusya', he fulminated in a letter to his fiancée, 'I wish you wouldn't ask me how English Jewry is reacting to all this. They are petrified. They are committing a second pogrom. They have given money *on condition* their unfortunate Russian brethren do not emigrate to England. Yes, my own, I lack words to express my indignation.'[8]

The Aliens Act made the General Election of February 1906 of keen interest to the Jewish community. Balfour was in Manchester defending his seat during the election campaign. The neighbouring constituency was being contested by Winston Churchill for the Liberals. Churchill had employed his formidable invective to good effect in obstructing the first Aliens Bill and was bidding strongly for the Jewish vote. Balfour's own campaign was lost. His seat was carried away in a great Liberal avalanche and the Conservatives were not in power again until the 1920s.

Amid the hullabaloo of the election Balfour found it possible, as he often did, to withdraw from the sound and fury. While his privacy was guarded by his sisters and his secretaries, he sat quietly one afternoon in his suite at the Queen's Hotel with Charles Dreyfus, his local Chairman. Balfour raised a question which still puzzled him and bore on the Jewish vote in Manchester. He naturally knew about Chamberlain's 'Uganda' offer and he wanted to know why, when they were so desperately in need, the Jews had turned it down. Dreyfus said that there happened to be in Manchester just then a young Russian Jew, a lecturer at the University in biochemistry, who was one of the younger leaders of the Zionist movement and who could explain the reasons better than he. Balfour asked to see him and a fifteen-minute appointment was made. So in January 1906 Balfour and Weizmann met for the first time. Their discussion lasted for more that an hour and contained within it the germ of the Balfour Declaration.

Weizmann reported his meeting with Balfour in a letter to Vera dated 9 January 1906. 'My dear little child,' he wrote, 'there is great excitement here over the elections. Balfour's chances are slender, Churchill's good. I had a meeting with Balfour today, and had a long and interesting talk with him about Zionism. He explained that he sees no political difficulties in the attainment of Palestine – only economic difficulties . . . Nothing new otherwise.'[9]

In that perfunctory manner he described the encounter which was to change the history of Zionism. Balfour's account did it more justice. The conversation had made Balfour understand that for Zionist Jews, race, religion and geography were linked in a unique way and were three aspects of a single concept. He told his niece, Blanche Dugdale: 'It was from that talk with Weizmann that I saw that the Jewish form of patriotism was unique. Their love for their country refused to be satisfied by the Uganda scheme. It was Weizmann's absolute refusal even to look at it which impressed me.'[10]

Forty years or so later Weizmann recollected the conversation in detail.[11] Balfour sat with his long legs stretched out in front of him with an imperturbable expression on his face. They plunged at once into the middle of the subject. Why,

Balfour asked, are some Zionists so bitterly opposed to Uganda? The British government really wanted to do something to help: the problem was a practical one, and the government had put forward a practical solution. Weizmann gave his answer in halting English which only began to flow as he warmed to the subject.

> In reply I plunged into a long harangue on the meaning of the Zionist movement. I dwelt on the spiritual side . . . Nothing but a deep religious conviction expressed in modern political terms could keep the movement alive . . . Any deflection from Palestine was – well, a form of idolatry. I added that if Moses had come into the sixth Zionist Congress when it was adopting the resolution in favour of the Commission for Uganda, he would surely have broken the tablets once again.

Weizmann recalled that at this point he looked at his listener and wondered whether the appearance of interest might be only courtesy. 'I felt that I was sweating blood and I tried to find some less ponderous way of expressing myself. I was ready to bow out of the room but Balfour held me back . . .'

> Then suddenly I said: 'Mr Balfour, supposing I were to offer you Paris instead of London, would you take it?'
>
> He sat up, looked at me and answered: 'But Dr Weizmann, we have London.'
>
> 'That is true,' I said. 'But we had Jerusalem when London was a marsh.'
>
> He leaned back, continued to stare at me, and said two things which I remember vividly. The first was: 'Are there many Jews who think like you?'
>
> I answered: 'I believe I speak the minds of millions of Jews whom you will never see and who cannot speak for themselves, but with whom I could pave the streets of the country I come from.'
>
> To this he said: 'If that is so, you will one day be a force.'
>
> Shortly before I withdrew, Balfour said: 'It is curious. The Jews I meet are quite different.'
>
> I answered: 'Mr Balfour, you meet the wrong kind of Jews.'

Weizmann had 'dwelt on the spiritual side'. He appeared to sense that it was this that would grasp Balfour's mind. Once grasped, it maintained its hold. Balfour wrote about the spiritual side of Zionism much later, saying that he was convinced that the position of the Jews was unique.

For them race, religion and country are inter-related, as they are inter-related in the case of no other race, no other religion and no other country on earth. In no other case are the believers in one of the greatest religions of the world to be found (speaking broadly) only among the members of a single small people; in the case of no other religion is its past development so intimately bound up with the long political history of a petty territory wedged in between states more powerful than it could ever be; in the case of no other religion are its aspirations and hopes expressed in language and imagery so utterly dependent for their meaning on the conviction that only from this one land, only through this one history, only by this one people, is full religious knowledge to spread through the world.[12]

Now, immediately after his conversation with Weizmann, Zionism may have appeared to Balfour to be the answer to the problem of the future of the Jews in a gentile world. What is certain is that he himself became a Zionist from that time. But he continued to be perplexed by the attitude of some of the leading English Jews. Weizmann had explained the difference between the mentality of the Jewish masses in eastern Europe and that of the emancipated Jews of the West. The eastern Jew had preserved intact the Jewish tradition and the Hebrew tongue as a living language. Zion was a hope and an article of faith. That meaning had been lost for many western Jews. 'Why should they oppose it?' Balfour demanded. 'Why can I afford to be a Zionist and not they?'[13]

7

Palestine before the War

After their first meeting in January 1906 Balfour and Weizmann did not see each other again for eight years. The first meeting had made Balfour interested intellectually in Zionism and to declare himself a Zionist. But he was evidently not sufficiently engaged to make him want to pursue the subject. He had the habit of mind of the collector. He could withdraw from active interest in Zionism or any other preoccupation. What Isaiah Berlin called 'the long and fascinated flirtation' between Balfour and Weizmann, from which so much of the life of the Zionist movement sprang, paused from time to time. In any case the Jews and Palestine was not a topic in the forefront of the British government's mind in the years leading up to the First World War. The next meeting of the two was in the wholly different circumstances of wartime.

By 1905 the world that Balfour had known and in which he had lived his political life was breaking up. The old certainties were being questioned. The Conservative Party he had led, and that had alternated in power with the Liberals in a balance so regular that it seemed to move according to some natural law, was dismissed and languished in opposition or coalition under a Liberal leader for seventeen years. By then a social revolution had taken place. The changes were both precipitated and made more violent by the war. Balfour's class that had formed the natural repository of government was losing its hold on power. The enlarged electorate had brought the Labour Party into being. It would outflank the Liberals and make them close to being an anachronism. The House of Lords, with its in-built Conservative bias, had been emasculated and turned into little more than a chaperone of the Commons, a pretence for an ostensibly bicameral system. Balfour, fifty-seven when he resigned, would never become Prime Minister again. He had become an elder statesman, a figure whose wisdom and experience were unquestioned, but whose ability to move events was more doubtful.

The pre-war years were a sterile time for Zionism. The Turkish revolution of 1908 had made impossible Herzl's idea of a Jewish homeland in Palestine legitimized by a charter granted by the Sultan. The 'Young Turks' who were the new power at Constantinople proved to be even less amenable to that idea than the Sultan. Interest in Zionism waned in England where it was felt that the movement, with its international headquarters in Berlin, was drifting into the German orbit.

Weizmann was frustrated by the inability of his fellow Zionists, particularly in England, to throw off the distracting effects of the Uganda dispute. He travelled about the country talking to Zionist groups trying to promote unity in the movement. The extreme conservative rabbinate and their congregations held to their view that the movement to bring the Jews back to the Promised Land was a blasphemous attempt to pre-empt the biblical millennium. The Ugandists were still looking for a land anywhere that was a safe haven. The western assimilated Jews saw Zionism as a threat to their hard-won emancipation. Many of Weizmann's Russian Jewish contemporaries were involved in the international socialist movement that was waging a war to the knife with the Tsar. All these forces were ranged against what Weizmann believed with absolute conviction was the true Zionism, the campaign for a national home in the Land of Israel.

The Zionists, whose tendency one could be forgiven for thinking was fissiparous, were now divided between the so-called 'Politicals' and 'Practicals'. On one side the Politicals were Herzl's followers whose creed was that the Jews should not move until they had found a home which was theirs by right – sanctioned by the sovereign power and 'secured by public law'. On the other hand were the Practicals for whom a political programme was not the important thing. What was vital was building in Palestine both a physical presence by acquiring land, and a moral presence by founding the institutions for a specifically Jewish culture. Weizmann set himself to find a combination or compromise of the two. The search for international approval, he argued, would be more likely to be fruitful if there were already an impressive Jewish presence on the ground in Palestine.

At the eighth Zionist Congress in 1907 wholesale changes were made to the Executive and it was decided to appoint representatives in Palestine and Turkey. Arthur Ruppin, a young German economist and statistician of formal manner whom Weizmann described as 'almost Prussian', was sent out to Palestine in the spring of 1907 to organize a colonization department. In the following year Victor Jacobson, an active Russian Zionist who had been in Berlin at the same time as Weizmann, was appointed the organization's representative in Constantinople. Ruppin settled in Palestine in 1908. His work there earned him the title of 'Father' of Zionist colonization. He more than any other person was responsible for the building and consolidation of the Jewish presence in Palestine in the years immediately before the war.

Weizmann made his own first visit to Palestine in 1907. At the Congress that year he was challenged by an old Viennese disciple of Herzl to go out and investigate the possibility of manufacturing essential oils. He accepted the challenge although in the end the project came to nothing. Instead of returning to Manchester after the Congress, where he had left his wife and their only weeks-old first child, he travelled on by a roundabout route to the eastern Mediterranean to see for himself the land which he had dreamed of constantly since childhood.

'A dolorous country it was on the whole,' was his first impression, 'one of the most neglected corners of the miserably neglected Turkish empire.' The Jews lived mostly in the cities, Jerusalem, Hebron, Tiberias, Safad, Jaffa and Haifa, forming communities devoted to piety. 'The dead hand of the *challukkah* lay on more than half the Jewish population', wrote Weizmann. He explained what the term meant. 'For many generations pious European Jews had made it a practice to migrate to Palestine in their old age, so that they might die on holy soil.'[1] They were supported by charity and in most cases their sole activity was to pray and to study sacred texts. Occasionally they were in business in a small way.

Weizmann's most unhappy experience in his three-week tour was his sight of Jerusalem. He saw there 'a miserable ghetto, derelict and without dignity'. All the grand places belonged to others. There were innumerable churches of every sect and nationality. All the world had a foothold in the city except the Jews. Herzl had a similar impression of squalor when he was in Jerusalem nine years earlier. He visited the Wailing Wall, the holiest place for Jews in the world. 'Deep emotion', he wrote in his diary, 'is rendered impossible by the hideous, miserable, scrambling beggary pervading the place.' He added characteristically: 'If Jerusalem were ever ours, and I were still able to do anything about it, I would begin by cleaning it up

... I would build an airy, comfortable, properly sewered, brand new city around the Holy Places.'[2]

There were some twenty-five Jewish agricultural settlements in Galilee in the north, and along the coast, mostly employing Arab labour. Here Weizmann found the pioneering spirit he was looking for. Arthur Ruppin agreed that the future of Zionism lay with the settlers and he thought that the country could absorb large numbers for agricultural development. The two met while Weizmann was staying in Jaffa and went for a walk in the sand dunes outside the town. When they had got well out into the sand, Ruppin stopped and announced with Germanic formality: 'Here we shall create a Jewish city!'[3] It was the first vision of Tel Aviv, the city which would outstrip Jaffa and become the secular capital of Israel. Weizmann wrote to his wife:

> I very much regret not having gone to the colonies directly, instead of spending one and a half days in Jaffa where people concern themselves only with squabbles, gossip and home-made politics ... In the colonies one feels altogether different. It's worth a lifetime to glimpse the work of Jewish hands, to see how, after 20 years of toil, former sand and swamps support flourishing orchards ... the potentiality of Palestine is immense ... If our Jewish capitalists, say even the Zionist capitalists, were to invest their capital in Palestine, if only in part, there is no doubt that the lifeline of Palestine – all the coastal strip – would be in Jewish hands within 25 years. No force in the world would then be able to destroy what was built.[4]

When he returned he described his experiences to a Zionist gathering in Manchester. He told them that there was one matter which seriously affected the welfare of the agricultural colonies, and that was the Arab labour question. In most of the colonies Arabs formed between sixty and eighty per cent of the labour force. This meant that the Arabs were being civilized at the expense of their Jewish neighbours, and it placed the prosperity of the Jewish colonies too much in the hands of the Arabs. The Arab, he said, retained his 'primitive attachment' to the land, and by being constantly employed on it there was a danger that he might feel himself indispensable and with a moral right to it. 'The Jewish colonies could not be regarded as really Jewish so long as the Arabs formed so powerful a labour force in them.' To avoid this danger he suggested that Jewish workers be introduced in larger numbers, whose superior intelligence and superior civilization would render their labour more valuable to their employer.[5] Weizmann's argument was that a skilled Jewish working class was vital for the purposes of Zionism; but it had as a consequence a virtual boycott of Arab labour.

He told his Manchester audience that the colonies he visited were scattered and separated. The plots of land which would connect them, he said, were of strategic importance and should be bought by the Jewish National Fund. Then there could be 'one united centre belonging entirely to Jews'. Later, at the Zionist Congress in 1913, Ruppin went further. He said that the objective in view was the creation of a 'Jewish milieu' and a closed Jewish economy, in which all producers, consumers and middlemen were Jewish.[6] What the leaders of 'practical' Zionism had in mind was the physical and economic framework of an autonomous Jewish state.

Did these Zionists of the time give thought to whether their plans could be accommodated peaceably in an Arab country? There is little evidence that they did. Their priorities were the safety of life and limb of Russian Jews in a refuge from pogrom and persecution, and the realization of a dream which had been nursed for nearly two millennia; the one borne of desperation, and the other a spiritual command.

There were, however, some educated Palestinian Arabs who were alarmed by the growth and implications of Zionism. One who recognized the threat early was Yusuf Ziya al-Khalidi, a member of an old Palestinian family. He had been educated at the Malta Protestant College and the Imperial Medical School in Constantinople. He spoke French and English as well as Kurdish and Turkish, and had learned some Hebrew. He had served as an Ottoman diplomat and was for ten years mayor of Jerusalem. An outspoken liberal who was not afraid to take an independent line, he earned the Sultan's displeasure. He had not only watched the growth of Zionism from its earliest days. He corresponded with several influential Jews on a regular basis. He was a standing refutation of the notion that the Palestinians were not worth much attention. In March 1899 he wrote a remarkable letter to Zadok Kahn, the Chief Rabbi of France and a friend of Herzl, expressing his concern about Zionism. The letter was written in French from Constantinople where Khalidi was serving in the Imperial parliament as deputy for Jerusalem. The Chief Rabbi sent it on, as was intended, to Theodor Herzl.

The idea [of Zionism] in itself is only natural, good and just. Who could deny the right of the Jews to Palestine? Dear God, historically it is certainly your country. And what a marvellous spectacle if the Jews were reconstituted once more as an independent, respected and happy nation that could give poor humanity the same moral gifts as in days gone by. But unfortunately the destiny of nations is governed not only by abstract concepts, however pure ... One must take account of reality and established facts, the force, yes, the brutal force of circumstance. The reality is that Palestine is now an integral part of the Ottoman Empire, and what is more serious, it is inhabited by others ... What material forces do the Jews have to enable their ten millions to impose their will upon 390 million Christians and 300 million Moslems? ... Even those nations most favourably disposed towards the Jews, the English and the Americans, would never consent to go to war against the other inhabitants to help the Jews settle in Palestine ... Dear God, the earth is big enough, there are still uninhabited countries where one could settle millions of poor Jews who may perhaps become happy there and one day constitute a nation. That would perhaps be the best, the most rational solution to the Jewish question. But in God's name let Palestine be left in peace.[7]

Herzl replied directly to Khalidi. He wrote in conciliatory terms but he brushed aside all difficulties. He said that the Jews had been good friends of Turkey since Sultan Selim had opened his empire to the expelled Jews of Spain. They could provide new resources for the empire of intelligence, enterprise and financial capacity. They had no belligerent power behind them, and no hostile intent or character. By admitting the Jews the Sultan would gain faithful subjects who would make Palestine flourish. The Holy Places would remain sacred for all the world, Moslems, Christians and Jews.

He added a postscript in reply to Khalidi's suggestion that the Jews would do better to look elsewhere for a home. If the Sultan did not accept the Jews' offer, Herzl wrote, they would indeed find another home. But Turkey would thereby lose its last chance of putting its finances in order and of recovering the empire's vigour. 'C'est un ami sincère qui vous dit aujourd'hui ces choses-là. Souvenez-vous-en!'[8]

For centuries Jewish immigration into Palestine had been no more than a trickle and the Arab population paid little attention. The start of the pogroms in the 1880s changed the situation. Although most of the Jewish refugees fleeing from Russia sought asylum in the United States and Britain, the trickle into Palestine increased to a small stream. To clothe these movements in figures: it has been estimated that in the twenty-five years between 1882, when the first restrictions were imposed by Constantinople on Jews entering Palestine, until the eve of the Turkish revolution in 1908, the number of Jews in Palestine rose from about 25,000 (some five per cent of the population) to about three times that number and approaching ten per cent of the population.[9]

While Herzl led the Zionist movement there was no serious question of a mass movement of Jews to Palestine without the sanction of Constantinople. He was firmly against any creeping in through the back door. 'An infiltration is bound to end badly', he wrote in *The Jewish State* in 1896. 'It continues till the inevitable moment when the native population feels itself threatened, and forces the Government to stop a further influx of Jews. Immigration is consequently futile unless we have the sovereign right to continue such immigration.'[10]

Herzl's views about immigration were not seriously challenged until the Uganda crisis. But after the decisive sixth Zionist Congress in 1903 the 'nay-sayers', or anti-Ugandans, asserted that, in order to achieve a homeland for the Jewish people in Palestine, it was vital for 'practical work' to be done there, and the sooner the better. That implied settling Jews without the 'charter' that Herzl thought essential, and on any land that could be purchased. Land available for sale was often in the ownership of an absentee landlord. The result was the eviction of the Arab peasant farmers who had been working the land.

The Zionists paid little attention to the nascent Arab nationalist movement. The Arabs of the Ottoman empire, who constituted about half the total population of twenty-two millions, were as disappointed as the Jews by the effect of the Turkish revolution of 1908. Far from being treated as the equals of the Turks by virtue of their common Islamic faith, it soon became clear that they were to be kept in their place. The resentment this engendered gave a sharp fillip to Arab nationalism. Palestine may have been regarded as a backwater in the Arab world, and the Palestinians may not have been prominent in the nationalist movement, but the Zionists failed to read the danger signals.

Once more, Ahad Ha'am was one of a few voices raised in warning. In 1891 he had visited Palestine. On his return he wrote an article in a Hebrew journal circulating in Russia and issued a warning.

> We are in the habit of thinking that the Arabs are wild men of the desert and do not see or understand what goes on around them. But that is a great mistake. The Arabs, especially the town-dwellers, see and understand what we are doing and what we want

in Palestine, but they do not react and pretend not to notice, because at present they do not see in what we are doing any threat to their own future ... but if ever we develop in Palestine to such a degree as to encroach on the living space of the native population to any appreciable extent, they will not easily give up their place.

The warning had little if any effect. He visited Palestine again in 1912 and found what he had feared – actual evidence of Arab unrest. Many natives, he reported, whose national consciousness had begun to develop since the Turkish revolution, looked askance, 'quite naturally', at the selling of land to strangers and were doing their best to put a stop to 'this evil'.[11] His repeated warning was timely. The threat posed by Zionism was twice debated in the Turkish parliament in 1911. Arab journals reminded their readers that in the Book of Deuteronomy God had commanded the Jews to destroy the inhabitants of the Promised Land. The first acts of violence between Jew and Arab occurred in the years leading up to the First World War at the Jewish colonies where Arab farmers had been evicted from the land. The attacks on Jewish settlements may not have been organized but they laid the foundation for the organized attacks of the 1920s. Jewish settlers formed vigilante groups to defend their new homes. These transformed themselves naturally into the Jewish defence groups in the inter-war years. It was a harbinger of the bloodshed that was to come.[12]

The Balkan wars of 1912 and 1913 left the Turkish empire weakened and shorn of almost all its possessions in Europe. The wars were followed by a brief, flickering attempt by the Turks to reach an accommodation with the Zionists. Once more it was hoped that Jewish money could shore up the chronically feeble finances of the empire. Restrictions on immigration into Palestine were cautiously relaxed and there were plans for Victor Jacobson, the Zionist representative in Constantinople, and Nahum Sokolov, a Russian member of the Zionist executive, to meet prominent Arabs in Egypt and Syria.

The Arabs and the Jews, it was stated in a paper prepared for the projected meetings, are from one stock and have complementary attributes. 'The Jews have knowledge, funds and influence; while the Arabs have a vast land ... Therefore a reconciliation between both peoples will be to the good of both and to the good of all the Orient. The Arabs will receive the Jews in Arab lands as their brethren on condition that the Jews become Ottoman subjects and that Palestine will not be exclusively theirs.'[13]

Unhappily it was a false dawn. The meetings were never held and the fleeting vision of peace vanished. With the tide of Arab nationalism rising, Constantinople became alarmed by the prospect of the Arabs and Jews making common cause in Palestine. In the summer of 1914 restrictions on Jews entering Palestine were re-imposed. On 2 August Germany and the Ottoman empire signed a secret treaty and every Ottoman subject of military age was called up. A distinction had formed in the Arab mind between Jews and the Zionists, who it was claimed, were planning a state extending from the Mediterranean to the Euphrates. Arab nationalism was seized by an anti-Zionist spirit and an angry new voice was heard. One Arab radical wrote in his diary in February 1914, 'What I despise is this principle which the [Zionist] movement has set up, which is that it should subjugate another to make itself strong, and that it should kill an entire nation so that it might live, because this is as if it is trying to steal its independence...'[14] There were calls to destroy Jewish farms and to force the settlers to emigrate to save their lives. The dispiriting round of violence and revenge was starting to disfigure Palestine before war came to disturb everything in the summer of 1914.

As Vera had advised him was inevitable while they were both still in Switzerland, Chaim Weizmann ran together the two consuming passions of his life, chemistry and Zionism. He specialized in the study of fermentation and its applications to the manufacture of synthetic rubber and dyestuffs. His reputation as a biochemist grew. But when William Perkin left Manchester in 1912 he was not appointed to the vacant Chair on which he had pinned his hopes. He saw himself as the victim of academic politics, in which Perkin himself had played a part, and was very bitter about it. If there had been a university in Palestine he would have gone there and then, and he told Vera that her readiness to go with him made him very happy. 'We shall go there as *free* people, and not driven by devils.' He was pressed by his Zionist colleagues to go to Berlin to head one of the departments of the Zionist Organization, and was tempted by this too, but Vera put her foot down. She had her own career to think of and anyway disliked Germany. They stayed in England and Manchester – with decisive consequences for Zionism.

At the beginning of 1914, Weizmann at last met Baron Edmond de Rothschild.

He wrote to Vera in a state of high excitement from Paris. 'So it has happened! I saw the Baron and spoke to him for three quarters of an hour. He is *for the University* and for reasons similar to yours and mine . . . *J'y contribuerai*, he told me. He is a good Jew.'[15] The Baron had for long interested himself in Palestine; but he had stood outside the Zionist Organization. To Weizmann and the other Zionists he was a great benefactor, but his generosity seemed tainted by paternalism. He was apparently interested only in philanthropic projects for which he had given vast sums. But he was not one to condescend to explain himself, and the Zionists were mistaken. Weizmann thought him 'a curious and complex personality, one of the most interesting I have ever encountered'. He gave a thumbnail sketch in his autobiography.

> When I first met Baron Edmond he was a man in the sixties, very much alert, still something of a dandy, but full of experience and *sagesse*. Everything about him was in exquisite taste, his clothes, his home – or rather his homes – his furniture and his paintings, and there still clung to him the aura of the *bon vivant* which he had once been. In manner he could be both gracious and brutal; and this was the reflex of his split personality; for on the one hand he was conscious of his power, and arrogant in the possession of it; on the other he was rather frightened by it, and this gave him a touch of furtiveness . . . His interest in Zionism was, *au fond*, as deeply political as ours . . . But he was a nationalist with a distrust of the national movement, and of the people. He did not understand that it was not enough to give money, and not enough to settle the Jews in Palestine.[16]

The Baron did, however, understand the university. He saw it, again in Weizmann's words, 'as a great centre of light and learning, from which knowledge would radiate out to the uttermost ends of the earth, reflecting credit on Jerusalem and on the Jewish community'.[17] He also deputed his son, James de Rothschild, who was living in London, to serve on the University Committee. This delighted Weizmann. The idea of a Hebrew university was almost as old as political Zionism and one which Weizmann held most dear. While he was in Jerusalem in 1907 he had noticed that Mount Scopus was the only hill that did not have its monastery or church on the summit. It was Scopus, he thought then, where the university should stand. Ruppin was able to secure the land in the middle of the war.

At the outbreak of war Weizmann was not yet forty and had become a recognized figure in world Zionism. But he was not a member of the Executive of the international organization or even the acknowledged leader of the movement in

Britain. Both in Britain and internationally Zionism was ineffective and divided, and it awaited clear direction. Much had been achieved in the immediate pre-war years, although the factions which had plagued Zionism since Herzl's death were still having a debilitating effect. The greatest weakness was Zionism's diplomatic position. Weizmann recalled the situation on the outbreak of war seven years later in his presidential address to the Twelfth Congress of 1921. After many years of striving, he said, the conviction was forced upon us that we stood before a blank wall which it was impossible to surmount.

The close relations which the Zionists had had with Britain during the Balfour government between 1902 and 1905 had given way to indifference and a degree of frigidity after Balfour's fall. The French considered that the Zionist Organization was working for Germany, while the Germans accused the movement of aiding Germany's enemies. Turkey had thrown its hand in with Germany. There seemed merit, even necessity, in Zionist neutrality when war was declared. Hostilities between the great powers meant, it seemed, that the Zionists could not get a hearing in either camp. But just at the point when the outlook seemed darkest the direction of events passed to other hands.

Chaim Weizmann
The Weizmann Archives, Rehovot, Israel

Theodor Herzl on the balcony at the Hôtel des Trois Rois, Basle, overlooking the
Rhine (1901)
Central Zionist Archives, Jerusalem

Chaim Weizmann and Arthur Balfour in Palestine (1925)
The Weizmann Archives, Rehovot, Israel

Sir Mark Sykes (1919)
By Leopold Pilichowski, private collection, Courtauld Institute

CP Scott
With kind permission of Guardian News & Media Ltd, Copyright 2005

8

Messianic Times

'Messianic times have really come', wrote Weizmann to his wife from London in December 1914.[1] Five months earlier, as war broke out in Europe, the times were anything but messianic. The international Zionist movement was at a low ebb and the war threatened it with disintegration. Its headquarters were in Berlin and its members found themselves in the armies on both sides. The democracies of France and England might seem to be the natural allies of Zionism, but Russia with its hated Tsarist regime was also a member of the Triple Entente. There was a movement to change the headquarters from Berlin to Copenhagen, but Weizmann favoured the United States. On 18 October 1914 he wrote to Shmarya Levin in New York about the problems facing the movement. Levin had been born in Russia and Weizmann had known him since his student days in Berlin, but he was now settled in the United States where he was working to establish a Zionist organization there. He had written to tell Weizmann of the American plans to establish a provisional executive committee. Weizmann replied, 'I have no doubt that that this is the only way to keep the organization from disintegrating, and you and our American colleagues will have the immortal merit of having supported the cause at a difficult time for the whole world and for all Jewry.' He went on:

> Unfortunately, the world now belongs to the guns. But as soon as the situation clarifies, we could with a clear conscience point out to both France and England the abnormal and cruel position of the Jews who have soldiers in all armies, who fight everywhere and are recognised nowhere ... We could show the interest of all those nations now fighting for small nations in securing for the Jewish nation also the right to exist ... The force of our moral claim must be self-evident and the political conditions for the realisation of our ideal will be favourable. It is necessary to prepare for such a time, and preparations can be successfully begun only when the roar of the guns has somewhat quietened down ... It is necessary to unite the large, conscious Jewries in England, America, Italy and France, and also the democratic movements in America and Russia ...'[2]

Great Britain declared war against Turkey on 5 November. The Ottomans, whom Herzl had courted so tirelessly and whose acquiescence in a Jewish national home in Palestine was considered so vital, had become an enemy of Britain. The traditional British eastern policy of propping up the Turkish empire was abandoned, and her aim was now its destruction. At the annual Guildhall speech on foreign affairs a few days after the declaration of war against Turkey, Herbert Asquith, the Prime Minster, said that Turkey had committed suicide, and would assuredly lose her empire in Asia as she had already lost her European possessions.

One of the first to see the implications of this for the ultimate destiny of Palestine was Herbert Samuel, the President of the Local Government Board and the first member of the Jewish community to sit in a British cabinet. (Disraeli was never a member of the Jewish community and was baptized when he was a boy.) Samuel's family were long-established and assimilated members of the Jewish community and had little sympathy with Zionism. He was brought up in strict conformity with Jewish beliefs and observance, but from an early age he ceased to believe in the orthodox theology of Judaism, although always remaining proud of his Jewish heritage. His leading characteristics were reliability and a level head. He could be depended upon to view with scepticism any adventurous or romantic scheme, and to keep his feet firmly on the ground. It was said of him that he never 'cherished a sentiment or coquetted with an illusion'.[3] Those who thought that reckoned without the extraordinary power of Zionism to kindle flames in the most unpromising material. Everything about Samuel led his contemporaries to think that he must be opposed to Zionism, whereas in fact he had for some time been sympathetic.

Sir Edward Grey was the first member of the cabinet to whom Samuel disclosed his hitherto unknown views about Zionism. The two had a long conversation in November 1914. Samuel's selection of Grey, the long-serving Foreign Secretary, was significant. Grey knew more than anyone else about the tortuous path of pre-war European diplomacy, and the potential significance of Palestine for Britain.

Samuel told Grey that he had never been a Zionist because the possibility of the Return of the Jews had always seemed so remote. But now that one of Britain's war aims was the dismemberment of the Turkish empire he felt differently and thought the establishment of a Jewish state in Palestine was a real possibility. 'The Jewish brain is rather a remarkable thing', he observed, 'and under national auspices, the state might become a fountain of enlightenment and a source of a great literature and art and development science.'[4] He thought too that Britain should be closely involved because the proximity of Palestine to Egypt would make it of strategic importance to the British empire. Grey, a usually cautious man, agreed and went so far as to say that the Zionist idea had 'always had a strong sentimental attraction for him'.[5] A brief talk that Samuel had with David Lloyd George at about the same time revealed that he too was well disposed to Zionism. Lord Haldane, the Lord Chancellor, was also sympathetic.

Emboldened by this support from his cabinet colleagues, Samuel circulated a memorandum for cabinet in January 1915 advocating British annexation of Palestine after the Turks had been defeated, and linking it with support for Zionist aspirations. Herbert Asquith, the Prime Minister, was astonished. He thought the idea of making Palestine a Jewish national home the stuff of fantasy, and at once wrote to Venetia Stanley about it. Venetia Stanley was a young girl less than half Asquith's age. He had known her as a child and she was only twenty when in 1907 she was enrolled in what his wife, Margot, called his 'little harem'. The letters from the statesman to the young girl (none from her to him survive) form one of the most remarkable series in British political history. Asquith had a penchant for the society of clever, attractive women, deriving particular pleasure from writing to them and retailing to them everything that was happening at Westminster, regardless of his obligations of confidence. Now he made light of Samuel's memorandum.

> He thinks we might plant in this not very promising territory about three or four million Jews and that this would have a good effect on those (including I suppose himself) left behind . . . It reads almost like a new edition of *Tancred* brought up to date. I confess I am not attracted by the proposed addition to our responsibilities. But it is a curious illustration of Dizzy's favourite maxim that 'race is everything' to find this almost lyrical outburst proceeding from the well-ordered and methodical brain of H S.[6]

Whether or not Samuel was aware that his memorandum had done no more than amuse the Prime Minister, he was not discouraged. He took steps to find out what the true situation in Palestine was and revised his memorandum. In March

1915 he circulated the new version.[7] Although it is not known whether it was ever considered by cabinet, it is a document of great interest and perceptiveness; and it helps to show why in the end the British government embraced the aims of Zionism nearly three years later.

The memorandum begins with the question of what should be the future of Palestine, assuming the breakup of the Turkish empire as a result of the war. Samuel canvassed five possibilities: annexation by France, leaving it to Turkey, some form of international regime, an autonomous Jewish state and a British protectorate. The first three options were dismissed. As to the fourth, he considered the time was not yet ripe for an autonomous Jewish state. Jews represented only a small minority of the population. 'The dream of a Jewish State, prosperous, progressive, and the home of a brilliant civilisation, might vanish in a series of squalid conflicts with the Arab population ... To attempt to realise the aspiration of a Jewish State one century too soon might throw back its actual realisation for many centuries more. These considerations are fully recognised by the leaders of the Zionist movement.'

Samuel's conclusion was that a British protectorate was the right solution. It would be a safeguard for Egypt, he argued. To conciliate the susceptibilities of the Greek and Roman churches and Islam, the protection of the Holy Places could be the responsibility of an international commission. Jewish immigration would be carefully regulated, but in time the Jewish people would grow into a majority and justify a measure of self-government. However, it was unrealistic to think that a country the size of Wales, much of it barren mountain and part of it waterless, could hold the nine million Jews in the world. The Jewish state Samuel envisaged would be a centre of spiritual and intellectual greatness capable of raising the character of the individual Jew, wherever he might be. He added: 'The sordid associations which are attached to the Jewish name would be, to some degree at least, sloughed off, and the value of the Jews as an element in the civilisation of the European peoples would be enhanced.'

Asquith was unmoved by Samuel's eloquence. 'I think I told you', he wrote to Venetia Stanley, 'that Herbert Samuel had written an almost dithyrambic memorandum urging that in the carving up of the Turks' Asiatic dominions we should take Palestine, into which the scattered Jews could in time swarm back from all the quarters of the globe, and in due course obtain Home Rule (what an attractive community!) Curiously enough, the only other partisan is Lloyd George, who I need not say does not care a damn for the Jews or their past or future, but thinks it will be an outrage to let the Christian Holy Places – Bethlehem, Mount of Olives, Jerusalem etc. – pass into the possession or under the protectorate of "Agnostic, Atheistic France".[8]

Asquith was quite unable to take Zionism seriously and remained sceptical well into the Mandate years between the wars. He also had a tendency to throw away something that was serious for the sake of a witty phrase, and he sometimes misjudged his colleagues. In this instance he did both. He was particularly simplistic about Lloyd George. The Welshman's interest in Zionism was genuine. The romance of the Jews being enabled at last to go back to their biblical home appealed to him. But it was not piety that drew him. It has been well said by Lloyd George's biographer that 'he was attracted by the Gospels, as by other bible stories, but to him the founder of Christianity was a prophet of social reform rather than a personal redeemer'.[9] As a Welshman he was genuinely interested in a small nation's right to live its own undisturbed life, but it was a pragmatic interest that was always mixed with arguments of expediency. He may have cared about small nations but he cared more about the future security and development of the British empire.

Although the time was not yet ripe for Samuel's unexpected foray into Zionism, another avenue now opened up that was at least as promising. On 16 September 1914, Weizmann wrote to Leopold Greenberg, the editor of *The Jewish Chronicle*, and told him that he had had a long talk that day with C. P. Scott, the editor of the *Manchester Guardian*. Scott, he said, was prepared to 'help us in any endeavour in favour of the Jews'. He would be willing to see Sir Edward Grey when 'we had a practical proposal to submit', and, he added, 'Scott carries great weight and he may be useful.'[10] It was an understatement. Scott was the confidant of David Lloyd George, the engine of the government and its key member, and knew most of the senior figures on both sides of politics. Any of them was apparently willing to see him at any time. He travelled constantly between Manchester and London using the train by day and night. His diary, which he kept on odd scraps of paper and which was mostly written on the train, gives a unique picture of wartime politics.

Weizmann had met Scott by chance at a party. He found the great editor so unaffected, open and charming that he wrote to him immediately after their meeting. He said that it was the first time in his life that he had spoken out to a non-Jew on all his intimate thoughts about the realization of his dream. 'If I had spoken to a man who I value less,' he said, 'I would have been very diplomatic.' Scott's sympathy with Jewish ideals was well known and was reflected in the columns of his newspaper, and he grasped the essence of Weizmann's Zionism in one casual meeting. He found Weizmann 'extraordinarily interesting – a rare combination of the idealism and the severely practical which are the two essentials of statesmanship. What struck me in his view was first, the perfectly clear conception of Jewish nationalism – an intense and burning sense of the Jew as Jew . . . and secondly, arising out of that, and necessary for its satisfaction and its development, his demand for a country which for him . . . could only be the ancient home of his race.'[11]

On the first occasion when they met Scott said, as he was to say many times in the course of their friendship, that he would like to do something for Weizmann. His suggestion was that he put him in touch with Lloyd George, then the Chancellor of the Exchequer, and other members of the cabinet. He also pointed out that there was a Jew in the government, Herbert Samuel, and as it happened Weizmann saw Samuel first.

To Weizmann's surprise (for he had assumed that Samuel would have the conventional anti-Zionist attitudes of establishment Anglo-Jewry) Samuel said that Weizmann's demands were too modest. He, Samuel, 'would expect Jewry to move immediately the military situation was cleared up . . . the Jews would have to build railways, harbours, a university, a network of schools . . . He also thinks that perhaps the Temple may be rebuilt, as a symbol of Jewish unity . . .'. Weizmann remarked that he was pleasantly surprised to hear such words from Samuel, and that if he were a religious Jew, he would have thought the Messianic times were near. Samuel added that these ideas were in the mind of his cabinet colleagues and he advised Weizmann to work quietly and 'prepare for the hour to come'.[12]

The interview with Lloyd George took place over breakfast on 3 December 1914 with Scott, Samuel and Josiah Wedgwood, the radical Liberal politician, also present.[13] Weizmann was nervous among these great figures. He was shocked that they could talk about the war in such a flippant way and did not understand that it was the English style to conceal seriousness. It gradually became apparent to him that everyone there was sympathetic to Zionism. Lloyd George promised to give Palestine serious thought, but he warned Weizmann that there would be tenacious opposition from certain Jewish quarters and prophesied that Edwin Montagu, lately appointed as Chancellor of the Duchy of Lancaster, would be one of the most bitter opponents.

How true this was became clear in March 1915 when Montagu produced a violent counterblast to Samuel's memorandum. Montagu considered that the idea of founding a Jewish state under British protection would be a disastrous policy. He denied that there was such a thing as a Jewish race as a homogeneous whole, still less a Jewish nation. He could not see any Jews he knew tending olive trees or herding sheep in Palestine, and, he asked, what of the Jews left behind? Was not sympathy for Zionism in the Protestant world very often a thinly cloaked desire to get rid of the Jewish ingredient in the population? He regarded Samuel's proposal, 'trimmed with rather thin arguments of strategy and foreign policy, as a rather presumptuous and almost blasphemous attempt to forestall Divine agency in the collection of the Jews which would be punished, if not by a new captivity in Babylon, by a new and unrivalled persecution of the Jews left behind'.[14]

The key was in the last few words. Although Montagu was talented, was a close associate of Asquith and had climbed high, he was sensitive and prickly, and he saw anti-Semitism round every corner. His answer to the scourge of his people was that the Jews should stop asking favours and cease to complain of their disadvantages. If only they would take their place as nonconformists like any other, they might find their way to esteem.

Asquith was entertained by the squabble between the two Jews in his cabinet, and he kept Venetia Stanley informed. 'By the way, the Assyrian [Asquith's rather unkind name for Montagu] has just produced a very racy memorandum on the subject of the restoration of the Chosen Race to the Promised Land. It contains some rather vicious digs at Cousin Herbert . . .'[15] Although his jokes were sometimes disagreeable, Asquith had no real prejudice against the Jews. He enjoyed making fun of those he knew, particularly in correspondence with his beloved Venetia Stanley. He was shaken and mortified when she told him in May 1915 that she was engaged to be married to Edwin Montagu.

Montagu was not alone in his view about Zionism, but few others held it with such vehemence. Although both the Chief Rabbi, Dr Hertz, and the spiritual leader of the Sephardic community in Britain, Dr Moses Gaster, were Zionists, almost the entire lay Anglo-Jewish establishment disliked and opposed the movement. With great difficulty they had achieved wealth, respect, position and what they conceived as security in Britain. They had contributed to all aspects of British life. Their loyalty to the country was undoubted. The suggestion that Jewry was a nation, dispersed and fragmented but still a nation, seemed to them an unreal conception. There is no word adequate to describe all persons of Jewish ancestry. 'Nation' is as unsatisfactory as 'race'. But to speak of 'Jewish nationality' was worse than a fiction to the ears of an assimilated British Jew. It was a term fraught with danger. For if he owed loyalty to Jewry, how could he give unqualified allegiance to Britain? In a word, the Zionists were rocking a boat which had achieved only a precarious equilibrium.

The focus of opposition to Zionism in the Jewish community in England was the 'Conjoint Foreign Committee'. This committee had been formed in 1878 jointly by the Board of Deputies of British Jews and the Anglo-Jewish Association, the two main lay bodies of Anglo-Jewry, to act as the voice of British Jewry in matters affecting Jewish communities abroad. Since its formation the committee had bent its efforts to secure a more tolerable existence for the millions of Jews who were suffering persecution in foreign countries. Its members were drawn exclusively from the assimilated Jewish bourgeoisie who had put down firm roots in England, and none was a Zionist. In fact all were opposed to it.

The President of the Anglo-Jewish Association was Claude Montefiore, a scholar and philanthropist, and a leading figure in the liberal reform movement within the Jewish community. His opposition to Zionism was principled. He believed that it was a defeatist creed, and that it was born of despair that anti-Semitism could ever be defeated by reason and tolerance. He also considered that Zionism was an essentially secular creed and that it stressed Jewish nationalism rather than religion.

The Secretary of the Conjoint Committee was Lucien Wolf, a man of quite different character. Wolf was also a scholar and a gifted man, but he was both touchy and pompous. He enjoyed good relations with the Foreign Office, and considered that he knew how to handle its senior officials. He took the view that he had the exclusive right to act as spokesman for the Jewish community in its dealings with the government, and he resented the intrusions of a parvenu Russian chemist from Manchester, who had no official standing in Jewry, into the upper echelons of Whitehall. Wolf considered that Zionism was an east European movement with its principal following in the East End of London. This was simple snobbery, and, as Weizmann reported to Ahad Ha'am, he had told Balfour it was an error into which many west European statesmen had fallen to think that east European Jews were a 'pack of *schnorrers*' (importunate beggars).[16]

It was hardly surprising that the Zionists and Wolf were unwilling collaborators or that when they were brought together during the first half of 1915 temperatures rose. They were to clash again. Weizmann concluded that sympathetic gentiles understood Zionism better than assimilated Jews. 'It is not easy to argue with a complex', he wrote.[17]

At the end of 1914 and at the prompting of C. P. Scott, Lloyd George saw Weizmann. He advised him to see Arthur Balfour, a suggestion that Weizmann promptly followed up by invoking the good offices of Samuel Alexander, the Professor of Philosophy at Manchester, who happened to know Balfour well. Balfour had played no active political role since retiring from the leadership of the Conservative party in 1911. His somewhat remote style of leadership had broken under the strain of trying to hold the Conservative party together through the crisis that year in which the Liberals destroyed the power of the House of Lords. Some of his colleagues thought that he would gradually withdraw from the centre of things, but he remained in touch and became a regular member of the Committee of Imperial Defence in 1912. He was out of government until May 1915 when he joined the wartime coalition under Asquith as First Lord of the Admiralty.

On 12 December 1914 Balfour and Weizmann had a long talk. Weizmann wrote two accounts while the meeting was still fresh in his memory. The first was to Ahad Ha'am and the second is contained in a longer report addressed to the executive of the International Zionist Organization, but intended for Nahum Sokolow and Yehiel Tschlenow, both Russian members of the Zionist executive who had lately come to England.[18]

Balfour had forgotten nothing over the eight years which had passed since they last met. When Weizmann said that it was a pity that the Zionists' work had been interrupted by the war, Balfour replied, 'You may get your things done much quicker after the war.' He then said flatly that the Jewish question in England would remain insoluble until either the Jews became entirely assimilated by intermarriage, or there was a normal Jewish community in Palestine.

The conversation then turned from the practical to abstract ideas. Balfour said that he had had a conversation with Richard Wagner's widow, Cosima, in Bayreuth two years earlier, and that he shared many of her anti-Semitic ideas. Far from being shocked by this, Weizmann interrupted and offered to tell Balfour what she had said. Frau Wagner would have said that the German Jews had taken part in building Germany, indeed they had captured the German stage, press, commerce, the universities and so on; and she no doubt resented having to receive all this moral and material culture at the hands of Jews. Weizmann went on that he agreed with Frau Wagner as to the facts, but he was in entire disagreement as to the conclusions to be drawn. The very crux of the Jewish tragedy was that those Jews who were giving their energies and their brains to the Germans were doing it in their capacity as Germans. They were enriching Germany and not Jewry. They had to hide their Jewishness in order to do their work in Germany. The tragedy is, he said, that we do not recognize them as Jews, and Frau Wagner does not recognize them as Germans.

Balfour was very *frappé* by this view, Weizmann reported. It was a strange irony that this passionate Jewish nationalist and his British sympathizer should find themselves in agreement with an apostle of anti-Semitism. Weizmann emphasized, as he did many times later, that Palestine could offer no solution to the Jewish question in Russia with its millions of Jews. The country was small and could not support more than about two and a half million people, of which the Jews were only a small fraction. The significance of Palestine was different. There and nowhere else a Jewish nation could be built from within, with its own forces and its own traditions which would establish the status of the Jews and would create 'a type of 100 per cent Jew'. He illustrated this by citing the Zionists' colonizing activities in Palestine and the educational work that was being done, and he gave an account of the struggle to make Hebrew the first language.

Balfour asked whether Weizmann wanted anything practical. Weizmann replied no, he only wished to explain the tragedy of the Jews. He would like to see Balfour again, with his permission, when the roar of the guns had stopped.

Balfour saw Weizmann out into the street and held his hand in silence for a moment. 'Mind you come again to see me', he said, 'it is not a dream, it is a great cause and I understand it.'

Blanche Dugdale gives a similar account of the meeting in her biography of Balfour. Her narrative can only have come from Balfour himself, and she herself was a committed Zionist. Thus, although Weizmann occasionally gilded the lily in his letters for dramatic effect, his accounts of the conversation must be taken as corroborated by Balfour, and accordingly accurate.[19]

The meeting with Weizmann throws into relief the differences between Balfour's view of Zionism and those of the other sympathizers at Westminster. Samuel had laid out the various possibilities for administering Palestine when the time should come for dividing the Turkish spoils among the victors. He had come down in favour of a British protectorate for reasons that were strategic. The idea of regenerating Jewry and forming a self-governing community in the country, although much in his mind, was still secondary and would follow only in the fullness of time. Lloyd George was described by Lord Reading (Rufus Isaacs) as affected by a poetic vision of Zionism. But Lloyd George was a hard-headed poet at best. He was a brilliant opportunist. His imagination may have been kindled by a sort of mysticism about the Return, but to burn steadily it needed also to have fuel supplied by the imperial advantages of securing Palestine for Britain.

Weizmann had a meeting with Baron Edmond de Rothschild in Paris only days after the conversation with Balfour. Weizmann's impression of the Baron which he had formed at their first meeting in January 1914, nearly a year earlier, was confirmed. He found that the philanthropist's attitude to Zionism was a good deal cooler and more cautious than that of Balfour. The Baron thought that 'the whole thing has come to us five or ten years too soon'. The war had caught the Zionists in the middle of their activities. There was a danger from the Catholics who, he considered, would do everything in their power to prevent the establishment of the Jews in Palestine. There was a second danger coming from the English Jews 'of the type of Claude Montefiore and his followers'. The Baron's advice, however, was to ignore this group as in his opinion 'they were of no value, being themselves shaken in their position'. The Zionists should work quietly through a very small committee and 'only enter the public arena when our plans were fully matured'. It would be important also to clear up the diplomatic position between France and England. By this he meant that as both countries had designs on Palestine, the problem had better be clarified and, if at all possible, resolved.[20] This was admirable advice in every particular. So far as it lay in their power, the Zionists adopted it.

9

Placating the French, inciting the Arabs

In November, 1914 Maurice Paléologue, the French Ambassador to Russia, was received by Tsar Nicholas II. According to Paléologue's diary the Tsar was in an informal mood. He leaned back in his chair smoking and mused about the fate of the Turkish empire after the war was over. His view was that the Turks must be expelled from Europe, and that Constantinople should be neutral under an international regime. Paléologue politely interrupted the Tsar to remind him that France had a 'precious heritage' of historical memories and moral and material interests in Syria and Palestine. 'May I assume', he asked, 'that Your Majesty would acquiesce in any measures the Government of the Republic might think fit to take to safeguard that inheritance?' 'Certainly', the Tsar responded warmly, and turned the conversation back to the Balkan possessions of the Ottoman empire.[1] But when the time came to make good the French claims, the Tsar had abdicated and a year later in 1918 had been murdered with all his family by the Bolsheviks in an obscure cellar in Ekaterinburg.

'The moral and material interests' that the French claimed extended along the entire eastern coast of the Mediterranean from Syria down to the Egyptian frontier. They were in the habit of referring to the whole area as 'la Syrie intégrale'. The British government knew they would have to take careful account of these claims which, put in historical context, went back to the Crusades. Ever since that time, France had considered itself the true guardian of the Holy Places of Christendom. They claimed a particular connection with the coastal region of Syria-Lebanon, where Christians lived under their protection and where they had developed extensive commercial interests, including the railway running from Aleppo to Damascus, with an extension southwards into the heart of Arabia to Medina in the Hejaz. It rankled that the British had managed to squeeze the French out of Egypt – by force in Napoleon's time, and then by something approaching a confidence trick in the 1880s.

British duplicity in the Near East continued to inflame French sensibilities. Even as late as the Second World War, General de Gaulle complained of 'the English game settled in London by firmly established services, carried out on the spot by a team without scruples but not without resources, accepted by the Foreign Office, which sometimes sighed over it but never disavowed it . . . aimed at establishing British "leadership" in the whole Middle East'. British policy, he concluded, would therefore endeavour to replace France at Damascus and Beirut.[2] Such feelings went deep and had some justification.

Tsar Nicholas had assured the French Ambassador that after the war Constantinople would be under international control. It came as a rude shock therefore when in March 1915, barely four months after Paléologue's audience with Nicholas, the British and French governments were told that anything short of Constantinople and the Bosphorus being incorporated into the Russian empire would be regarded by Russia as insufficient. This was an event which greatly concentrated the minds of London and Paris. Russia had made the first move for the spoils of the Turkish empire: Britain and France must stake their own claims. In April 1915 Asquith set up an inter-departmental committee under Sir Maurice de Bunsen, an experienced diplomat, to advise the government what should be the British 'desiderata in Turkey in Asia', or more plainly, what did Britain want in the scramble for the Ottoman empire after the Turks had been defeated?

The members of the committee were senior officials of various interested departments with the exception of Sir Mark Sykes, who was made a member on Kitchener's suggestion. Early in 1915 Sykes had been introduced to Oswald Fitzgerald, Kitchener's personal secretary and confidant, and was so brought within the War Minister's orbit. He was just thirty-six and without departmental experience, but he was destined to play a short but crucial part in carrying the policy of the Balfour Declaration to fruition. He had an unusual background. His parents were members of the Yorkshire gentry. There were thirty years between them and a similar gap in compatibility, and they soon decided to live apart. At the age of three Sykes was received into the Catholic Church with his mother, but not his father, who nonetheless gave the conversion his blessing. His schooling was a thing of fits and starts, by private tutors and by Jesuits. He went down from Cambridge after two years without a degree. From an early age he accompanied his father on long journeys abroad, and he spent two of his Cambridge terms wandering in the Near East. He had written books about his experiences and illustrated them with witty cartoons.

Although he was Kitchener's representative on the committee, he saw little of that formidable personage. Instead he made a daily report to Fitzgerald, and received through him Kitchener's instructions for the next day. 'I acted, Fitzgerald spoke, he [Kitchener] inspired' was Sykes' description of the triangular relationship. Sykes made one important new contact on the committee. This was its secretary, Maurice Hankey, who in 1916 was to become the cabinet secretary and the most influential single British official during the war.

Sykes had a very quick and fertile mind and rapidly became the driving force in the committee. Within a month of its being set up, he had formulated proposals for the policy to be pursued in Turkey's Asian empire. His paper canvassed the alternatives of partitioning the empire among the allies, or leaving the empire intact and dividing it into spheres of influence. In either case the British zone would comprise Mesopotamia and Palestine, including the port of Haifa, and the French were allocated the northern part of Syria and the northern part of what is now Iraq. The old Ottoman divisions of the empire were ignored and Sykes proposed to start from scratch and redraw the map of the Middle East.

The committee reported at the end of June 1915. It adopted Sykes' plan for a division into spheres of interest, but in one important respect it departed from his proposals. It firmly declined to make any recommendation at all about Palestine. De Bunsen recognized an explosive topic when he saw one. The report read:

> Still less do the Committee desire to offer suggestions about the future destiny of Palestine . . . They have felt free to deliberate on the assumption that the French claim will be rejected, since they are convinced that the forces opposed are too great for France ever to make the claim good, but for the same reason they consider that it will be idle for His Majesty's government to claim the retention of Palestine in their sphere. Palestine must be recognised as a country whose destiny must be the subject of special negotiations in which both belligerents and neutrals are alike interested.[3]

Kitchener was not surprised by the show of Russian aggression over Constantinople. At the outbreak of war he had been appointed War Minister. There was no other man alive who could then have commanded so much public confidence as head of the War Office. He had been brought home from Egypt, where he had been Agent and Consul-General since 1911. During his period in Cairo he restored much of the prestige which had attached to the Agency in Cromer's time. In his long and successful military career Kitchener had gathered round him a group of young soldier-disciples. They believed with him that Russia was the main threat to British imperial designs in the East; and that a bulwark against Russian expansion southwards should be created in the form of a large Arab client state of Britain extending from the Persian Gulf to the Mediterranean. This strategic consideration was an element in the formation of a pro-Arab tendency in the Foreign Office which would prove to be lasting.

The fascination which the Arab world held for the British can be traced back as far as the middle of the nineteenth century when the extraordinary exploits of Richard Burton held the country spellbound. In 1853, disguised as a Dervish and adopting the name of 'Al Haj' (the pilgrim), Burton made his way overland across the Arabian peninsula. His account of that epic journey became and remained the most popular of all his writings. Englishmen were captivated by the picture of a civilization that was intricately refined yet pure as the desert the Arabs inhabited. The attraction was strengthened and intensified as the legend of T. E. Lawrence and the Arab nationalist rising unfolded. The more impressionable young men in the Cairo Agency imbibed the rarified air of this romance.

How did Palestine fit into the Cairo Agency's plans? This is what Ronald Storrs, the Oriental Secretary, had to say in a letter of 28 December, 1914 to Kitchener's secretary, Oswald Fitzgerald.

> With regard to Palestine, I suppose that while we naturally do not want to burden ourselves with fresh responsibilities such as would be imposed upon us by annexation, we are, I take it, averse to the prospect of a Russian advance southwards . . . or of a too great extension of the inevitable French protectorate over the Lebanon . . . a buffer state is most desirable, but can we set one up? There are no visible indigenous elements out of which a Moslem Kingdom of Palestine can be constructed. The Jewish state is in theory an attractive idea; but the Jews . . . are very much in a minority in Palestine generally, and form indeed a bare sixth of the whole population . . . Would not the inclusion of a part of Palestine in the Egyptian Protectorate with the establishment at Jerusalem of a mixed Municipality chosen from a large number of elements and granted wide powers be a possible solution?[4]

Nothing more was heard from the Cairo Agency of any such plans for Palestine; but speculations of this sort were overtaken by direct negotiations between Cairo and the Arabs. These started in an improbable way. The first contact was made by Abdullah, one of the sons of Hussein, King of the Hejaz and Sherif of Mecca. The title of 'Sherif' means 'successor' and denotes a direct descendant of the Prophet Mohammed. Abdullah stopped in Cairo in February 1914 on his way to Constantinople. He saw Kitchener and told him that there was trouble between the Sherif and his overlord, the Sultan, in the Hejaz, the broad strip of land lying along the eastern side of the Red Sea and containing the holy cities of Mecca and Medina. Kitchener was given to understand that the difficulties were serious and could result in the Sherif being deposed. Abdullah enquired if the British government would use its good relations with Constantinople to prevent an open split.

Kitchener read this as an attempt by a rebellious subject to recruit the British as his auxiliary against a then nominally friendly power, and he declined to help. In the event, the Sherif composed his differences with the Sultan, but Abdullah paid another visit to Cairo in April. This time it was Storrs who saw him, at the Khedive's Palace. Storrs described his enchanted impression of Abdullah.

> He intoned for me brilliant episodes of the Seven Suspended Odes of Pre-Islamic poetry, the Glories and the Lament of Antar Ibn Shaddad, during which we must have accounted for whole quarts of rich Khedivial coffee. Travelling by a series of delicately inclined planes, from a warrior past I found myself in the defenceless Arab present, being asked categorically whether Great Britain would present the Grand Sharif with a dozen, or even half a dozen machine guns.[5]

Storrs was not merely enchanted by Abdullah. It seems that he conveyed that, although the British government had declined to supply arms to the Arabs, the refusal might not be as final as it appeared.[6] Storrs, as the Oriental Secretary, was the expert on Arab affairs at the Cairo Agency. Although he was an able man, it was a misfortune that he should have been entrusted with a vital role in the negotiations with the Sherif and his sons. As he claimed himself in the article he wrote on T. E. Lawrence in the *Dictionary of National Biography*, it was he, Storrs, who 'had initiated the negotiations which culminated in the Arab Revolt'. He drafted and translated the letters to and from Mecca, and had control over the choice of messenger to convey them.

Flippant and overconfident by turns, Storrs was easily influenced by both the charm of the Arab notables and the regard he had for the elegance of his own erudition. By hints and embellishments, sometimes reckless, of his instructions from the Foreign Office in London, he carried the negotiations to a dangerous pass. To London he urged bidding up the Arab chieftains lest they throw in their lot with the Turk. To the Sherif he conveyed that the time was near for a general Arab rising in support of Britain's struggle against the Ottoman empire, which would lead to their own long-awaited freedom. He laid stress on the restoration, with British help, of the Caliphate from the usurper Turk to the Sherif, its rightful holder. 'Caliph' means lieutenant or vicar and connotes the person who is entitled to succeed to the spiritual and temporal monarchy which the Prophet had created.

Storrs was not alone among the senior British officials in the Middle East in thinking that an Arab rising against the Turks should be actively encouraged in the service of Britain's interests. General Sir Reginald Wingate, Kitchener's successor as commander-in-chief, or 'Sirdar' of the Egyptian army and Governor-General of the Sudan, was of like mind. So was Wingate's agent in Cairo, Captain Gilbert Clayton, who also had served with Kitchener in the Sudan campaign, and who in October 1914 became the head of the Egyptian military intelligence services. So too was General Sir John Maxwell, the GOC in Egypt and another who owed his post to Kitchener. These men formed an influential group in the formulation of Middle Eastern military policy.

The group's influence over the course of the negotiations with the Sherif was enhanced by a number of factors. They were all Kitchener's men. Storrs in particular had a close personal rapport with him which he is at pains to elaborate in his memoirs, *Orientations*. Although Kitchener consulted Grey, the Foreign Secretary, about the instructions he sent to Cairo, Grey's own views were not always consistent. Under stress his hand was no longer steady on the tiller and, as Lord Esher put it, he was 'never intended for the service of Mars'.[7] The Indian government also had an interest in British-Arab affairs, aggravating further the difficulty of formulating and carrying out a coherent British policy. The India Office was distrustful of Cairo's adventures in Arabia and protested vigorously. Its own interests included Mesopotamia and its constant anxiety was a nationalist rising in India. With a substantial Moslem population, the Indian government was alarmed about what Cairo was stirring up in Arabia. Their objections were resented in Cairo and were overborne by the Foreign Office.

In January 1915 Sir Henry McMahon was transferred to Cairo and appointed High Commissioner, into which the office of Consul-General and Agent had been transmuted when the British protectorate in Egypt was declared in 1914. He was Kitchener's choice and it was not intended that he should stay long in the job. It was thought that the war would be over quickly and that Kitchener could equally quickly resume his duties in Cairo. As High Commissioner, McMahon was charged with the negotiations with the Sherif Hussein to stimulate an Arab revolt and so disrupt the Turkish war effort. He was sadly ill-equipped for the task. He came from the Indian civil service, had no experience of Egypt and could speak no Arabic. The negotiations called for acuity and unusual diplomatic gifts. McMahon was an honourable man, but he was slow and willing to go to almost any lengths to avoid making a decision. He did not share his colleagues' enthusiasm for the Arab movement, and thought it an unhappy trick of fate that, because of the military exigencies in the Middle East, he should have been saddled with the Sherifian negotiations. He wrote to Wingate afterwards and showed his true feelings.

> It was the most unfortunate date in my life when I was left in charge of the Arab move-
> ment and I think a few words are necessary to explain that it is nothing to do with me: it is
> a merely military business. It began at the urgent request of Sir Ian Hamilton at Gallipoli.
> I was begged by the Foreign Office to take immediate action and draw the Arabs out of
> the war. At that moment a large portion of the [Turkish] forces at Gallipoli and nearly
> the whole force in Mesopotamia were Arabs . . . I was told to do it at once and in that
> way I started the Arab movement.[8]

The negotiations between the Arabs and the British were conducted by correspondence in a series of letters passing between McMahon and the Sherif Hussein between July 1915 and March 1916. They were kept secret until as late as 1939 when they were published as a White Paper at the request of the Arab delegation to the Palestine conferences of 1938–9.[9] Ever since they were written they have been pored over and argued over with as much ingenuity and intensity as Chancery lawyers bring to bear on the ambiguities of a disputed will. The Arabs believed that by the letters McMahon had promised Palestine to them. The British and the Zionists argued the contrary.

The opening letter from the Sherif dated 14 July 1915 was received in Cairo with astonishment and, in Storrs' case, derision. The Sherif demanded, as the price for a military uprising against the Turks, that all of Arab Asia from the Persian Gulf to the Red Sea, and from the Egyptian frontier northwards along the Mediterranean as far as Mersin on the south-east coast of Anatolian Turkey, should become an independent kingdom under his rule. The reply from McMahon stated that it seemed premature in the heat of war and while the Turk remained undefeated to discuss limits and boundaries; but it promised a welcome to the resumption of the Caliphate by 'an Arab of true race'. The Sherif returned to the charge on 9 September. He had received McMahon's letter, he said, 'with great cheerfulness and delight', but he had nonetheless the impression of ambiguity and of 'a tone of coldness and hesitation' about limits and boundaries. This subject had of necessity to be settled immediately.

By early October 1915 the High Commission was in a state of high excitement. It was convinced that the Arab question had reached a critical stage. The reason for the excitement was the arrival in Cairo of a young Arab Lieutenant in the Turkish army who had deserted at Gallipoli. His name was Mohammed Sharif al-Faruqi. Clayton interrogated him. Faruqi told Clayton that the Arabs were united and were waiting patiently for Britain to deliver them from Turkish oppression, and that there was now a large, solid Arab party behind the Sherif; but, he said, the Arabs' patience was not inexhaustible, and if the Sherif's proposals were not accepted, they would be thrown into the arms of the enemy. Faruqi was a deserter and an adventurer. He did not even know the Sherif. Clayton had no means of corroborating his account. Anything he said should have been treated with extreme caution. In fact, much of the story was untrue. The Sherif did not have a following that was large and solid. The Arabs were not united, and it was mere speculation that they would ever throw in their lot with the Turks. Nevertheless McMahon accepted it whole. He composed a somewhat alarmist cable for Maxwell to send to Kitchener faithfully reflecting Faruqi's story.[10] After seeking further details of the Arab demands, Grey, prompted by Kitchener, authorized McMahon to convey the British proposals to the Sherif.

These were contained in McMahon's letter to the Sherif of 24 October 1915. This stated that the districts of Mersin and Alexandretta (a Mediterranean port in northern Syria) should be excluded from Hussain's demands. Also to be excluded was that part of Syria lying to the west of the districts of Aleppo, Hama, Homs and Damascus. These four towns lay on a north–south axis along the line of the railway built by the French and having an extension southwards into the Hejaz. The object of the exclusions was to allow for French claims, but the origin of the Aleppo, Hama, Homs, Damascus line is unclear and has been the subject of exhaustive and ultimately futile debate.[11]

As to the rest of the Sherif's territorial demands, McMahon stated, wherever Britain was free to act without detriment to France, Britain would support the independence of the Arabs, and would have the sole right to offer advice and help in forming governments in all the remaining areas. McMahon and his superiors in London considered that this left Britain free to make the best bargain they could with France, while giving Britain primacy in its future dealings with the Arabs.

The language of this crucial letter is so opaque, and doubtless even more so to the Sherif when translated by Storrs into Arabic, that almost anything can be read into it. Yet it has been the nub of the claim that the British government promised Palestine to the Arabs. What does the reference to the four Syrian towns mean? How far north and south should the line joining them be extended? Was everything not expressly excluded meant to be included? Palestine was nowhere mentioned by name in the McMahon–Sherif correspondence. Sir Arthur Hirtzel, political secretary at the India Office and a very clear-sighted official, pointed this out in a paper of 9 November 1915. He appears to have read the correspondence as giving Palestine to the Arabs – or at least leaving it dangerously vague. 'The problem of Palestine has not been expressly mentioned in these negotiations', he wrote. 'Jerusalem ranks third among the Moslem holy places, and the Arabs will lay great stress on it. But are we going to hand over our own holy places to them without conditions?'[12]

McMahon himself believed that the letters had no binding force and would neither 'establish our rights . . . or bind our hands'.[13] Grey agreed. But Hirtzel and his political chief, Austen Chamberlain, the India Secretary, thought it irresponsible of the Foreign Office and the Cairo Agency to engage in a carefully worded correspondence of this sort and assume that they could rely on its having no binding force. Hirtzel wrote:

> Sir E. Grey does not think that McMahon's assurances matter much because the scheme
> will never materialise. But it would surely be attributing too much stupidity to the Young

Arab party to assume they will not manoeuvre us into a position in which – whether or not they get what they want – we shall not get what we want without eating some very indigestible words.[14]

Put another way, the letters were mere words writ in water, and could do no harm. Grey and McMahon were more wrong than they could have imagined.

In May 1915 a coalition government was formed in Britain and Balfour became the First Lord of the Admiralty and a member of the war committee. In December Sykes gave evidence to the committee on the de Bunsen recommendations. He had just come back from almost six months in the east, staying a week in Cairo where he had become infected by the enthusiasm for an Arab rising which was gripping the Agency. It was natural therefore that he would advocate a forward policy in his evidence to the war committee. But the time was not auspicious. Reverses in the Balkans and Mesopotamia and the traumatic failure of the Dardanelles expedition had weakened the hand of the 'Easterners' in the British cabinet: Lloyd George, Balfour and Kitchener. Those who thought that the real war must be fought and won on the western front, and that the campaigns in the East were side shows, like the new Chief of the General Staff, Sir William Robertson, were in the ascendant.

Sykes' advice to the war committee was that Britain should settle with France as soon as possible how the spoils in the Middle East should be divided between them, and then launch a powerful army northwards from Egypt. Balfour asked what should be the arrangement with France. Sykes replied, 'I should like to retain for ourselves such country south of Haifa as was not in the Jerusalem enclave . . . I think it is most important that we should have a belt of English-controlled country between the Sherif of Mecca and the French.' He meant Palestine.[15]

In the meantime the Anglo-French discussions had begun. The French nego-tiator was François Georges-Picot, who for many years had been French consul at Beirut. Picot was tough in argument and a strong believer in his country's mis-sion in the Middle East. He arrived in London in early November 1915 to begin talks with Sir Arthur Nicolson, the permanent under-secretary at the Foreign Office. Picot at once claimed for France the whole of the eastern littoral of the Mediterranean down to the borders of Egypt. In face of that sweeping demand the talks became deadlocked. Sykes was co-opted as Nicolson's adviser and took over the negotiations in December. In the same way as he had done when the de Bunsen committee was sitting, he reported each day's progress to Fitzgerald and, through him, to Kitchener.

As he had made clear to the war committee, Sykes' own view was that it was important that Palestine should be within the British sphere of interest. But the government did not feel it could go so far. The Anglo-French alliance was of paramount importance and the British were well aware that the French were carrying the larger share of the burden of the western front. The negotiations were nevertheless hard fought. Picot disputed every inch of ground and Sykes emerged with a compromise solution in January 1916. There were weaknesses in the French position too which Sykes had exploited. They did not wish to quarrel with their partner on the western front any more than Britain did, and they were not taking any significant part in the eastern war against Turkey. Nor were they likely to do so. Both sides recognized tacitly that if Britain invaded the Turkish empire from Egypt, it would be in Palestine by right of conquest.

The Sykes–Picot agreement, as it became known, was signed by its two authors in January 1916 but not ratified by Britain, France and Russia until four months later in May. It remained secret until 1917. Under the agreement, France gained the coastal strip of northern Syria together with a swath of eastern Anatolia and the northern part of modern Iraq. Britain gained southern Iraq including Baghdad and Basra. The coastal strip of Syria allocated to France left the line Aleppo–Damascus in Arab hands in accordance with the McMahon–Sherif correspondence. There was to be an independent Arab state or states in the vast hinterland stretching from the Hejaz in the south to Aleppo in the north, and a belt of central modern Iraq. The Arab hinterland was divided into two zones, A in the north and B in the south, which were the respective spheres of interest of France and Britain. France and Britain were each entitled in its own sphere to 'priority of right of enterprise', the sole right of appointing advisers at the request of the Arab states, and the right 'to establish such direct or indirect administration or control as they desire and as they may think fit to arrange with the Arab states'.

Palestine was to be separated from Syria by a line drawn from Acre to the Sea of Galilee and was to be internationally administered as agreed among the allies and with the Sherif Hussein. Haifa was to be British together with the right to construct a railway from Haifa to Baghdad.

The agreement had many critics. Lloyd George called it a foolish document and quoted Lord Curzon's remark that the 'gross ignorance' with which the boundaries were drawn could only be explained by its being 'a sort of fancy sketch to suit a situation that had not then arisen, and which it was thought extremely unlikely would ever arise'.[16] It was, however, not altogether foolish or fanciful. As between France and Britain, it was a reasonable compromise of negotiating positions which had begun far apart. French resentment against Britain after the war was caused not so much by the Sykes–Picot agreement, but by its alteration unilaterally by Britain after Allenby's conquest of Palestine.

The Sykes–Picot agreement assumed that the map of the Middle East could be redrawn after Turkey was defeated by simple strokes of the pen according to the maxim 'to the victor belong the spoils': that is, by conquest and by satisfying the imperial ambitions of the victors. This assumption was to be rudely disturbed.

The agreements with France and with the Arabs to which Britain had come in 1916 both assumed that the Arab rising would knock Turkey out of the war. That too was a false assumption. The rising in the Hejaz, when it finally came in June 1916, was a failure. The Arabs of Palestine and Syria did not help the Sherif when the flag of rebellion was raised. Arab forces, in conjunction with Lawrence's romantic exploits, had an effect on the war only when, in the following year, the British invaded Palestine. Right up to the end of the war large numbers of Arab troops in the Turkish army continued fighting against the liberation of their own people.

Storrs and others thought the Arab revolt would have another effect. It should, he wrote to a friend, 'prove in the end mortal to the Jews now reigning on the Bosphorus'.[17] This curious remark was a reference to a long-held delusion that since the Turkish revolution of 1908 an evil pro-German alliance had subsisted between the Young Turks' regime and the Jews of Constantinople and Salonika. G. H. Fitzmaurice, the dragoman (interpreter and guide) at the British Embassy, thought that the ruling Young Turks were in thrall to the Jews and the Freemasons. Jewish freemasonry, he considered, had inspired the ruling Turkish faction in the godless, levelling ways of the French Revolution, and was advancing the interests of Zionism at the same time. Fitzmaurice put about his fevered ideas as widely as he could. He was a close friend of Storrs and the Cairo Agency was infected by the fantasy of Jewish control of Turkey. It was a strand in the belief, widely held among the British governing classes, that the influence of the Jews was ubiquitous and well-nigh omnipotent.[18]

The Zionists were in ignorance of the Sykes–Picot agreement and the McMahon–Sherif correspondence until much later. But their aspirations in Palestine were well-known to the British government while these agreements were in the making, and strongly supported by several members – Balfour, Samuel and Grey at least. Yet the Zionists' hopes and claims do not seem to have merited a mention. Weizmann had a meeting with Balfour on 16 March 1915, but no record of it has survived beyond Weizmann's reference to it in a letter informing Samuel that Balfour 'would help us if the situation with regard to France would be clear.'[19] It is surprising, to say the least, that Balfour, from whom Weizmann had the clear impression only three months earlier of a strong commitment to Zionism, did not raise the cause of the Zionists while the war committee of the cabinet was considering the future of Palestine.

It was left to Captain W. R. Hall, the well-informed director of naval intelligence, to draw attention to the likely attitude of the Jews. In a letter dated 12 January 1916 to the Foreign Office for consideration by the war committee, Hall wrote very critically of the Sykes–Picot agreement, which was then awaiting ratification by the allied governments. After observing that it was an unusual arrangement to divide the bear's skin while the bear was still alive, he had this to say about Palestine and the Jews.

> Opposition may be expected from the Jewish interest throughout the world to any scheme recognising Arab independence and foreshadowing Arab predominance in the southern near east. This objection, however, will hold against all schemes which are based on a desire to conciliate or enlist pan-Arabism, and not specially against the one under discussion. Jewish opposition may be partly placated by the status proposed for the Brown area [Palestine]; but it may not be wholly or, indeed, very largely, placated.[20]

Hall had showed his letter to the First Sea Lord (the senior naval officer at the Admiralty) who had approved it. Did Balfour, who was then his political chief, also see it? Whatever the answer, Hall's warning that the Arabs and the Jews might be on a collision course in Palestine was not heeded.

10

First Steps to the Balfour Declaration

In March 1915 Chaim Weizmann heard from Herbert Samuel that the British cabinet was not only sympathetic to the Palestinian aspirations of the Jews, but wanted to see them realized. But Britain did not wish to be involved in any responsibilities. It wanted the Jews to organize their own political unit and it did not want Palestine to belong to any other great power. 'I have already had the pleasure of pointing out to you that these two views are in contradiction', Weizmann commented mildly to C. P. Scott. 'If Great Britain does not wish anybody else to have Palestine, this means that it will have to watch it, and stop any penetration of another power.' However, Weizmann thought there was a middle course that the government could adopt. The Jews would take over the country so that the whole burden of organization fell on them, but for the next ten or fifteen years they would work under a temporary British protectorate.[1]

As early as the first quarter of 1915, then, Weizmann's mind was formulating a practical way in which the Zionist dream could be realized under the sponsorship of Britain. But, on its side, the British government was as muddled about its aims in Palestine as Weizmann thought. Asquith was Prime Minister and would be in Downing Street for nearly another two years. His habit of mind was to wait on events rather than to try to take charge of them. He governed through a cabinet of twenty-two. All decisions on the direction of the war had to go from the small war committee through this unwieldy body. The war could not be run that way. The policy on Palestine, as on all politico-military issues, would not be clearly focused until Lloyd George replaced Asquith in December 1916.

One of the growing band of Asquith's critics was Sir Mark Sykes, the Conservative member for Central Hull, and the co-author of the Sykes–Picot agreement. In March 1915 he was already regarded as an expert on the Middle East, but neither Weizmann nor Samuel had ever met him. Sykes had been an unthinking anti-Semite until a Zionist opened his eyes. His attitude to Jews was founded on prejudice and the resulting picture was a caricature. He considered Jews as rootless, moneyed parasites who were in some way involved in an international power and money conspiracy. He made no distinction between the Jews of the east and the assimilated Jews of west European countries; or between Zionists and other Jews. His views about the Arabs were similarly prejudiced. How did it come about that the compass needle veered through a hundred and eighty degrees so that he became an ardent Zionist and Arab nationalist?

The first reason is that his mind was not only quick but quick to change. It did not at all embarrass him to be advancing an opinion which was diametrically opposed to one he had held previously. Between January 1916, when the Sykes–Picot agreement was provisionally signed, and May, when it was ratified by the allied powers, his mind began to move rapidly towards Zionism. Just before he went to Petrograd with Picot to seek Russia's approval to the agreement, he met Herbert Samuel and read his cabinet memorandum on Palestine, with its recommendation of a Zionist settlement under a British protectorate. It strongly affected his mind.

While Sykes was in Petrograd he had confirmation of what Weizmann had heard a year earlier, that the British government was indeed sympathetic to the Zionist ideal. Sykes learned that the Foreign Office was proposing that a declaration be made by the governments of the Triple Entente, Britain, France and Russia, supporting the settlement of Jews in Palestine. The idea had originated in the unlikely person of Lucien Wolf, the secretary of the Conjoint Committee and a fierce opponent of Zionism. As he was at pains to make clear to the Foreign Office, Wolf deplored the Jewish national movement, but he wanted the British government to do something to alleviate the plight of the Russian Jews. He was aware that great importance was attached to the so-called 'international power of the Jews', and the government's consequent wish to win over world Jewish sentiment to the allied cause. Although it was contrary to everything he believed, he felt constrained to make a positive gesture about Palestine.

In March 1916 Wolf suggested to the Foreign Office the idea of a 'formula' which, he said, would appeal to a powerful section of Jews worldwide if it were published in the form of a declaration by the government. The 'formula' was that in the event of victory the allied governments would 'take account of the historic interest which Palestine possessed for the Jewish people'. Jews settling in Palestine would be 'secured in the enjoyment of civil and religious liberty, and equal political rights with the rest of the population'; and there would be reasonable facilities for Jewish immigration and colonization.[2]

Sir Edward Grey, the Foreign Secretary, was impressed, as were his officials in the Foreign Office, by the prospect of enlisting the wholesale support of world Jewry. This was particularly so in the case of American Jews. Millions of Russian Jews had fled the terror in Russia to the United States. They were violently anti-Russian and were therefore inclined to favour Germany in the war in which the United States was still neutral.

Grey was prepared to go further than Wolf's 'formula' and propose to France and Russia an autonomous Jewish settlement in Palestine. He sent telegrams to the British ambassadors in Petrograd and Paris with instructions to sound out the Russian and French governments on a public declaration supporting Zionism which, he said, had within it 'the most far-reaching political possibilities'. The telegrams informed the ambassadors that Wolf's formula might be made far more attractive to the Jews if it held out to them the prospect that when the colonists in Palestine 'grow strong enough to cope with the Arab population they may be allowed to take the management of the internal affairs of Palestine (with the exception of Jerusalem and the Holy Places) into their own hands'.[3] This was going far indeed. It was a leap in the direction of Zionism. The interests of the Arabs and their likely reactions were dismissed: they were to be 'coped with' by the Jews.

The Russians were sympathetic. The French were officially polite but unmistakably negative. From Petrograd Sykes reported that Picot, on hearing the gist of the telegrams, 'made loud exclamations and spoke of pogroms in Paris. He grew calmer but maintained that France would grow excited.' The French, Sykes informed London, were very touchy about the Levant; and 'any reference seems to excite memories of all grievances from Joan of Arc to Fashoda'.[4] In London, Edwin Montagu, hearing of Picot's reaction, complained to Lord Reading that the recrudescence of attempts to satisfy the Zionist movement would only 'stoke the fires of anti-Semitism just as he had warned a year before'.[5]

The French may have smelt a rat – the rat being that even while the Sykes–Picot agreement was awaiting ratification (it was not ratified by France until May 1916), the British were trying to improve their position in Palestine by supporting Zionism. Or, more likely, they felt scant sympathy with the Jews and took a poor view of Zionism, thinking that it could only lead to trouble with the Arabs, whose cause they felt was more important. Whatever the truth of the matter, Grey's extraordinary diplomatic foray in aid of Zionism came to a halt. By the time another initiative was launched a year later, Balfour had succeeded Grey at the Foreign Office.

Weizmann and his fellow Zionists knew nothing of these moves. It was ironic that those whose very purpose was to establish a Jewish settlement in Palestine knew nothing of what was being planned in furtherance of their cause. Wolf did not tell Weizmann anything about his 'formula' until a meeting between the two was arranged by James de Rothschild in deference to the wishes of his father, Baron Edmond, in August 1916. The Baron wanted the English Jews and the Zionists to cooperate in putting forward proposals about Palestine, and considered that divisions within Jewry, particularly if publicized, would do no one any good. At the meeting Wolf outlined the formula to Weizmann, but he did not disclose that he had submitted it to the Foreign Office. Despite the efforts of the Rothschilds there was no meeting of minds between Wolf and Weizmann.[6]

There were two stumbling blocks. One was the idea of Jewish nationality. It was at the core of Weizmann's Zionism, but the very thought was abhorrent to Wolf. Weizmann thought the central problem of Jewry was homelessness: the Jews were the scattered fragments of a nation without the concrete expressions of nationality. Only a national home – in the Holy Land – could provide what was missing. Wolf was unable to think of himself and his fellow Anglo-Jews as homeless: they were nonconformist British nationals.

The other difficulty for Wolf was the Zionist demand for preferential treatment for the Jewish population of Palestine over the other inhabitants. He thought this was unnecessary and would inevitably cause trouble with the Arabs. The outcome of the meeting, as Wolf saw it, was that 'Dr Weizmann showed no disposition to come to terms with us either on the subject of nationality or special rights'. What Weizmann objected to was not so much the opposition of men who thought as Wolf did, but that they tried their utmost to hamper the Zionists in their work. He wrote indignantly to Gaster:

They had no right to prevent other people from acting as nationalist Jews, especially as they are a small minority living in the West, detached from the masses in the East, from the joys and sorrows of those masses, from their aspirations and ideals.[7]

The dispute grumbled on until it erupted in public in the summer of 1917.

One of the objects of the Sykes–Picot agreement was to clear the ground for an Arab state or states to be set up in the Middle East. At the same time Britain was actively promoting a Jewish settlement in Palestine. To put it at its lowest, the two policies were going to be difficult to reconcile; and at no time did any British minister or official even try to do so.

Meanwhile Sykes had worked himself up to a high pitch of enthusiasm for Zionism and its potential. It opened up the prospect of a British stake in Palestine, something that he had been steadily advocating since his time on the de Bunsen committee. The Zionists were now Sykes' key to the entire Middle East situation. From his hotel in Petrograd he painted an alarming picture for the cautious Sir Arthur Nicolson in London of what might happen if the Germans captured the Zionists.

With 'Great Jewry' against us [he wrote breathlessly in a hand-written scrawl] there is no possible chance of getting the thing through – it means optimism in Berlin – dumps in London – unease in Paris – resistance to the last ditch in C'ople – dissension in Cairo – Arabs all squabbling among themselves – as Shakespeare says 'Untune that string and hark what discord follows' – Assume Zionists satisfied, the contrary is the case, of that I am positive . . . I am afraid this sounds rather odd and fantastic but when we bump into a thing like Zionism, which is atmospheric, international, cosmopolitan, subconscious, and unwritten, nay often unspoken, it is not possible to work and think on ordinary lines . . .[8]

On his return from Petrograd Sykes' mind was teeming with schemes for Palestine and he set about learning as much as he could of Zionism. In April 1916 Samuel introduced him to Moses Gaster. Gaster was a colourful figure with an impressive presence, but he had no official position in the Zionist movement. Sykes afterwards credited Gaster with opening his eyes as to what the Zionist movement really meant. They discussed Palestine and Gaster's diary for 2 May 1916 shows that he warned Sykes off the idea of a condominium of Britain and France in Palestine.

After long wrangle got his French colleague, Georges–Picot, to see the point of Jewish help. He first dead against. Then agreed condominium. I put the case clearly. Put the case against France and even preferred to have German condominium, as latter's interests not in Egypt . . . I advise a fait accompli. He answers: to occupy Jerusalem? – I: *not* by Jews, but by *English* soldiers . . .'[9]

Sykes' dislike of the kind of Jew who, in Leonard Stein's phrase, seemed to him to sail under false colours, led him to a natural affinity with the Zionists. They were intellectuals, idealists, nationalists and profound believers in their own separate destiny. Herbert Samuel and Moses Gaster were men of a sort he had never met before. Sykes' speech to a gathering of Manchester Zionists in December 1917, in the euphoria that followed the Balfour Declaration, showed how far he had travelled in eighteen months.

It may be your destiny to be a bridge between Asia and Europe, to bring the spirituality of Asia to Europe, and the vitality of Europe to Asia . . . your time of probation has been long, you are schooled in adversity, you can look to difficulties with calm, and you will overcome them . . . I hope you are going to set up a power that is not a domination of blood, not the domination of gold, but the domination of a great intellectual force. I believe you will see Palestine the great centre of ideals, radiating out to every country in the world where your people are . . . I look to see the return of Israel, with its majesty and tolerance, hushing mockery and dispelling doubt . . .'[10]

It was fortunate for Zionism that Sykes had his eyes opened to its cause just then in the spring of 1916, because the British government was pressed with other things. Asquith, who was always sceptical about British involvement in Palestine, was to be in power for another nine months. During almost all that time, from July until November 1916, the battle of the Somme was raging. It would eventually claim a million and a quarter lives. The winnings from this unimaginable slaughter were a few miles of Flanders soil. This most pointless of all battles in trench warfare claimed the almost constant attention of the cabinet.

Those in favour of opening up a diversion in the eastern theatre could hardly get a hearing. Of the principal 'Easterners', Balfour was at the Admiralty, his interest in Zionism apparently muted; Lloyd George was preoccupied with the Easter rebellion in Ireland and with his own heavy duties at the Ministry of Munitions; and Kitchener, the leading 'Easterner' in the government, was drowned in June when HMS *Hampshire*, carrying him on a visit to Russia, struck a mine off the

Orkneys. Neither Grey nor Samuel, who were both actively interested in the fate of Palestine, was in a position to give the government a strong lead. Only Sykes, perennially absorbed in eastern affairs, kept the flame alive. He was not a member of the government, but with the help of Hankey he had begun his climb to the highest sources of power, where his knowledge of the Middle East was to give him an unusual influence.

There were other agents at work to maintain the forward momentum of Zionism. In November 1915 the *Manchester Guardian* carried an editorial contending that the defence of Egypt needed a friendly neighbouring state in Palestine.[11] Two thousand years before the Suez Canal was built, it was argued, the defence of Egypt on its north-eastern land boundary was strengthened by the old Jewish nation acting as a buffer against the powerful empires in the north. Now the situation was a parallel one. Britain's sea-empire could not be attacked by land except at that self-same point. An enemy had only to invade Egypt from the north and occupy the canal, and the road to India would be closed. It would greatly benefit Britain if the Jews were allowed to settle in Palestine and form a similar buffer state. This was the argument, adopted by the Foreign Office a few months later, that for Britain to sponsor Zionism was only enlightened self-interest.

The author was Herbert Sidebotham, but the content must have been approved by the editor, C. P. Scott. Sidebotham, the *Manchester Guardian*'s highly respected military commentator, became an important ally of the Zionists. One of his colleagues on the newspaper was Harry Sacher, an early and close friend of Weizmann's and a friend also of Simon Marks and Israel Sieff. Sacher introduced Sidebotham to Marks and Sieff, and together they formed the British Palestine Committee whose purpose was to work for British political sponsorship of Zionism.

During the summer of 1916, the Zionists themselves began a campaign to make the movement better known by the British public. A collection of articles by different hands, edited by Sacher, was published under the title *Zionism and the Jewish Future*. Weizmann contributed an introduction. The purpose of the book was to draw attention to the aims and achievements of Zionism rather than to suggest what should be the political future of Palestine. But certain passages caused offence among Anglo-Jewry. Weizmann wrote that assimilation and anti-Semitism went hand in hand, and thus 'the position of the emancipated Jew, though he does not realise it himself, is even more tragic than that of his oppressed brother'. Gaster went further. In arguing that no one can be a Jew who does not belong to the Jewish faith, he said, 'the claim to be Englishmen of the Jewish persuasion – that is, English by nationality and Jewish by faith – is an absolute self-delusion'. It would have been better not to offend sensibilities when matters were approaching the time of decision.

The book sold well and it attracted a sympathetic review in *The Spectator* by no less a person than Lord Cromer. He had well understood the differing hopes and fears of the western and eastern Jews, and said of Zionism, 'it is rapidly becoming a practical issue, and . . . before long politicians will be unable to brush it aside as the fantastic dream of a few idealists'.[12]

Opinion among American Jews was also swinging towards Zionism. At the outbreak of war in 1914 there were about three million Jews in the United States. Of these some two million had poured into the country since the 1880s as refugees from eastern Europe. But surprisingly only a small fraction were active Zionists.[13] There were many reasons for this, but the most important was that the immigrant Jews were busy making their way in a new and intensely competitive environment. A national home in Palestine seemed to them a faraway abstraction, if not an embarrassment. Nevertheless, Zionism began to take hold of the imagination of American Jews.

The coming of war had crippled the Berlin headquarters of international Zionism, and it was not clear from where the lead was to come. Consequently, within weeks of the start of the war, a congress of American Zionists set up a provisional committee under the chairmanship of Louis Brandeis to act until an international organization could be revived. In what he described as 'the present strained relations, with a fierce life-and-death struggle going on', Weizmann welcomed the move unqualifiedly.[14]

Brandeis had been born in the United States as a child of Jewish immigrants. Although he later told Arthur Balfour that he had come to Zionism 'wholly as an American' and that his whole life had been 'free from Jewish contacts and traditions', in fact he had been interested in Zionism since about 1910 and he had joined the Federation of American Zionists in 1912.[15] In that year he was considered for office (but later dropped) by Woodrow Wilson, with whom he nonetheless developed a close association as the President's informal adviser on Jewish affairs. In 1916 Wilson nominated Brandeis to fill a vacancy on the

Supreme Court, where he served with the greatest distinction. Brandeis was convinced that Zionism was the answer to the Jewish question. He told Balfour when the two met in 1919 that as an American he had first-hand experience of the contribution that the Russian Jewish immigrants could make; and he felt sure they would do the same in their own national home. With his influence on Wilson, Brandeis was a force for Zionism in the United States.

Chaim Weizmann's wartime work in biochemistry was the greatest vindication of Vera Weizmann's advice to her husband many years earlier that he must run his political and scientific work together in double harness because each would benefit the other. In his war memoirs Lloyd George says flatly that the Balfour Declaration was a reward for Weizmann's work in biochemistry for the Admiralty. According to this account, Lloyd George told Weizmann that he had rendered great service to the state and that he would like to recommend him for some honour. Weizmann replied that he wanted nothing for himself, but he would like something to be done for his people; and he described the aspirations of the Jews to return to the sacred land of their forefathers. That, wrote Lloyd George, 'was the fount and origin of the famous declaration about the National Home for Jews in Palestine . . . So that Dr Weizmann with his discovery not only helped us to win the war, but made a permanent mark upon the map of the world.'[16]

The story has been repeated countless times, and it has been widely accepted as the rationale for the Balfour Declaration, but it was a product of Lloyd George's imagination. Weizmann's own ironic comment was, 'I almost wish that it had been as simple as that, and that I had never known the heartbreaks, the drudgery which preceded the Declaration. But history does not deal in Aladdin's lamps.'[17] However, the story does reflect an essential truth. The spectacular nature of Weizmann's discoveries and the British government's vital need for them gave their author a standing and credibility to which none of his fellow Zionists could aspire. Society in Britain was acutely class- and status-conscious. Weizmann had been disappointed in his expectation of a professorial chair at Manchester and a Fellowship of the Royal Society. Although he was naturalized, he was still liable to be seen as a Jew, a foreigner and an outsider. Although he had good social connections, including members of the Rothschild family, it was his inventions that made him an insider. The war cabinet knew that the man who was advocating Zionism with such persuasive force was also the chemist who was making a major contribution to the war effort. Weizmann himself was well aware of the connection. As early as July 1915, he wrote to Mrs James de Rothschild about his chemical experiments. 'If all that succeeds,' he wrote, 'it would help our Palestinian work very considerably and perhaps our Jewish star will bring us luck this time.'[18]

His most important discovery during the early part of the war was the method of making acetone in large quantities by bacterial fermentation. Acetone is a solvent used in the production of cordite, an explosive propellant which has the unusual property of being virtually smokeless. The discovery of cordite changed the nature of battle. When exploded there is no flash and it leaves only a faint haze, so that both naval and land-based artillery could conceal their position and could fire at a more rapid rate. Before 1914 acetone was produced mainly in the United States from the distillation of wood pulp. When war came the demand for acetone rose sharply and it became an indispensable and urgently needed ingredient in making cordite. The importance of Weizmann's discovery was that, by the isolation of a natural bacillus, acetone could also be produced through the fermentation of maize.

In early 1915, a colleague of Weizmann's at Manchester University suggested to him that he inform Nobel, the explosives manufacturer, of his discovery. The response was the sudden appearance of Nobel's chief chemist, William Rintoul, in Weizmann's laboratory to examine the process for himself. All went well and Weizmann reported the event to Mrs James de Rothschild: 'The "insect" [i.e. the bacillus used in the fermentation process] behaved very well; now I hope Nobel's will behave.'[19] Nobel made him a handsome offer, but the contract could not be proceeded with because there was an explosion at the factory in Scotland, and the building where the development work was to be carried out was destroyed. But Rintoul had already informed the Admiralty of Weizmann's work; and in April he received an invitation from the Admiralty to see Sir Frederick Nathan, a former works manager at Nobel and then adviser to the Admiralty on the supply of cordite. Nathan realized at once that Weizmann's process was the only acetone source capable of producing in large quantities in England.

Weizmann agreed to carry out trials for the Navy and in April he was taken to see Winston Churchill, the First Lord of the Admiralty. Churchill was then aged forty and at a low point in his political fortunes. He was widely regarded as being responsible for the disaster at the Dardanelles, and he left the Admiralty within days of his interview with Weizmann. But although he was under threat Churchill retained his characteristic panache. Weizmann found him 'brisk, fascinating, charming and energetic'. We need thirty thousand tons of acetone, Churchill demanded, can you make it? Weizmann was terrified by this 'lordly request' and explained that he was a research chemist with no experience of making commercial quantities of anything: he had made only a few cubic centimetres of acetone in the laboratory. Once the bacteriology was established in laboratory tests, he said, it became a question of brewing technique in order to make commercial quantities.[20]

He was given carte blanche. His first pilot plant was set up in July in the Nicholson gin factory in Bromley-by-Bow, a new plant was built by the Admiralty at its factory near Poole in Dorset and a large number of distilleries were also taken over and adapted. At the first trials completed early in 1916 Weizmann had to oversee the whole process. There were many technical difficulties. He had to train a group of chemists in this branch of chemistry. Maize had to be transported by sea from the United States, and the German submarines patrolling the Atlantic made supplies uncertain. There was even an attempt to replace maize with horse chestnuts, and collections were organized with parties of schoolchildren. 'It was particularly difficult', Weizmann wrote afterwards, 'to overcome the prejudice which existed among distillers against the process, which differed in many essentials from the ancient art of whisky distilling. Here was an outsider trying to convert good grain into a mysterious substance about which one thing only was clear – it was certainly not whisky!'[21]

The war was assuming unprecedented proportions. A coalition government was formed in May 1915 and Lloyd George, the most forceful personality in the new administration, was appointed to the vital post of Minister of Munitions. His time there transformed the war economy and with it his own standing in the country. As soon as Lloyd George was installed in his new post C. P. Scott brought Weizmann's process to his attention; and arrangements were made for Weizmann's development work to be made available to the Ministry of Munitions as well as the Admiralty.

Weizmann was beset with unlooked-for difficulties in his work. He became embroiled in time-consuming patent litigation, and there was obstruction from within the government. Lord Moulton, a former law lord and director of Explosives Supply, seemed to have decided to block Weizmann at all points. His motive was probably jealousy. It was galling that this foreigner seemed able to get anything done by the simple expedient of mobilizing the editor of the *Manchester Guardian*. By mid-September 1915, Weizmann was given leave of absence from Manchester University and moved to London. The strain of travelling constantly between the two cities had become more than he could bear. He thought the move was temporary but it turned out to be permanent. His wife joined him and they took a small house in Kensington. There she became, for the first time in her life, a political and social hostess, as her husband furthered the Zionist cause by cultivating his contacts in the government and higher social circles.

By January 1916, notwithstanding his difficulties, Weizmann had achieved complete success in large-scale production of acetone and was working on other problems. The value of his work was well understood by the government but he was never properly paid for it. When he started to work for the Admiralty, he volunteered that he would postpone any remuneration for his work until after the end of the crisis, except the payment of expenses. It was an impulsive and in the result, unwise, gesture. The Treasury and the Admiralty dragged their feet. Scott thought little of Balfour's part (at the Admiralty) in the miserable saga, and recorded in his diary that he 'was timid and did not like to act except on the advice of his officials'. Scott acted as a gadfly. His diaries show that he prompted Ministers and officials without cease. He fumed that Weizmann, 'who is much the most essential man in his department, who has worked so far practically for nothing, whose inventive genius has not only saved the country nine or ten millions in money but has secured it essential munitions in quantities otherwise unobtainable at any price', could not get security and 'at least some modest recompense'. The Weizmanns recognized what their friend had tried to do. 'It will remain always as *the* great comfort and pride of our life', Weizmann wrote, 'to have the privilege of your friendship, whatever else may happen.'[22]

In the end the question was settled in July 1917, when it was agreed that Weizmann should receive royalties which amounted in total to only £10,000.[23] It was a poor return for inventions which were not only vital in the war effort, but were also ground-breaking in their industrial applications. In the opinion of one commentator they were 'the decisive step in the transformation of micro-organisms into humanly controlled industrial agents', and the forerunner of all modern industrial fermentations such as those of antibiotics and vitamins.[24]

Weizmann's scientific work gave him easy access to Lloyd George; and each time he saw Lloyd George he had the opportunity to discuss Palestine. One meeting in November 1915, before the Sykes–Picot agreement had been signed and with Scott and Samuel present, is particularly revealing. There is a full account in Scott's diaries. Lloyd George was arguing that there might be objection to Palestine being under British protection.

> George remarked that France would probably object and wanted Palestine for herself ... moreover there would be an objection in this country to such an extension of our responsibilities. I [Scott] suggested that ... we already had the responsibility of defending Egypt and that it was only a question of how that could best be done ... George thought a condominium of the three powers might be proposed, but Samuel and Weizmann agreed that from their point of view this would be the worst solution, and it seemed to me not good from ours. George asked how many colonists the Jews expected to be able to supply and Weizmann said he thought half a million in fifty years. George evidently thought this a very small number, but W pointed out that this kind of colonisation was extremely expensive ... George thought there might have been a rapid immigration from Russia encouraged by the Russian government, but W said Palestine could offer no solution to the Jewish question in Russia with its six million Jews, and Samuel pointed out that the country, though a very fine one, was small and could not support more than about two and a half millions of a population – the Jews at present constituted about one tenth of the population.[25]

It is surprising that Weizmann projected so slow a pace of settlement. It was only realistic of him to recognize that Palestine could never absorb the millions of Jews waiting in subjection in Russia; but taking into account that Palestine then included the modern Jordan (it was only after the war that the land on the east bank of the Jordan was shorn off to form the new Arab kingdom of Transjordan) his figure of only half a million settlers in fifty years was very low – as Lloyd George was quick to question. Weizmann was later to revise upwards the estimate of settlers that could be absorbed into Palestine but, even so, in his thinking the Zionist dream could be realized for only a small fraction of world Jewry. Weizmann dissociated Palestine in his mind from the plight of Russian Jewry. In his view, no satisfactory result could be brought about in Russia by outside interference. The Land of Israel was first and foremost not a haven for refugees but a nation in which the Jewish people could shake off the debilitating influence of assimilation.

His dispute with Lucien Wolf showed that. What Wolf and Anglo-Jewry were striving for was 'assimilation, disintegration, dissolution'. He wrote to Mrs James de Rothschild in September 1916 about the hopelessness of her husband's attempts to arrange a compromise between the two men. No paper formula could bridge a gulf which was always widening. 'It is impossible for me to be enthusiastic about something in which I have no faith,' he wrote. 'This concession will lead to another one, and to a third and at the end we shall have a Zionism in conformity with the wishes of Mr Wolf and his friends, a "reasonable" tame movement, good for the digestion and fit for this climate.' The letter went on in a mood of depression. Perhaps it would be better, he wrote, to curtail Zionist ambitions, maintain what little had been created in Palestine, guard it jealously, and then take up the work again after the war and try to build on it.[26]

But things were astir which, had he known, would have given him cause to be more optimistic. In November 1915 Lloyd George had not made up his mind about Britain and Palestine. By the time he became Prime Minister a year later, he no longer had doubts. Scott's diary for 26 January 1917 describes a breakfast meeting he had with Lloyd George and Neil Primrose, the chief whip, which makes this graphically clear.

> I mentioned Weizmann. G sd there were several things he wanted to talk to him about – Later Primrose: 'What about Palestine?' G with a smile, 'Oh! We must grab that; we have made a beginning.'

11

The Turning Point

In the first four months of 1917 the tide began to set decisively in favour of Zionism. But this had little to do with the efforts of the Zionists, who were not expecting tangible support from Britain until the war was over. A year earlier, in March 1916, it had been Sir Edward Grey and the Foreign Office who had taken the initiative and suggested to Russia and France that there should be a home for the Jewish people in Palestine. However, the role of the Foreign Office in the ultimate success of Zionism can be exaggerated. Mayir Vereté's provocative article, 'The Balfour Declaration and its Makers', written in 1970, suggests that Britain was like the lady who was willing and only wanted to be seduced. 'Weizmann', he wrote, 'happened to come her way, talked to her to have the Zionists and go with them to Palestine, as only her they desired and to her they would be faithful. Britain was seduced.'[1]

It is an appealing picture but it is a caricature. In December 1916 and the first months of 1917, events for which the Zionists were in no sense responsible, and the Foreign Office was only tangentially involved, began to crowd in and give impetus to the converging courses of British interest and Zionist opportunity. There was a change of government in Britain, revolution broke out in Russia, the United States entered the war and Britain invaded Palestine.

Asquith's long spell as Prime Minister came to an end in December 1916, when a coup led by Lloyd George brought him down. Balfour had no part in the coup but he was in favour of giving the new Prime Minister a free hand. He thought Lloyd George was the best man to win the war. When he was told that Lloyd George planned to become a dictator, he replied, 'Let him be. If he thinks he can win the war, I am all for him having a try.'[2] With the advent of Lloyd George everything changed for the better. There was a new adventurousness and determination to win the war. Lloyd George had a small war cabinet of five over which he presided with Curzon and Milner, the two Tory peers and former proconsuls, Bonar Law, the Conservative leader, and Arthur Henderson, the Labour leader. Only Bonar Law as Chancellor of the Exchequer had outside departmental responsibilities. The rest were free to give their undivided attention to winning the war.

The new war cabinet was backed by a strongly staffed secretariat. This was an innovation which was so successful that it became a permanent part of the machinery of government. At its head as cabinet secretary was Sir Maurice Hankey, the supremely efficient bureaucrat, with assistant secretaries who included Mark Sykes, by now an ardent Zionist, and Leopold Amery, also strongly sympathetic. Sykes was Hankey's choice. Milner nominated Amery who had been a member of the coterie of young men whom he had gathered round him in South Africa. Balfour went to the Foreign Office and inherited his cousin, Lord Robert Cecil, as his junior Minister. These changes were all fortunate ones for Weizmann whose strategy was to place all his hopes in Britain, and who in the next crucial months became the de facto leader of world Zionism.

Weizmann did not know quite how fortunate he was. In Hankey's recommendations to Lloyd George, his first choice for chief political assistant to the new war cabinet was Edwin Montagu, and failing him he 'tentatively' suggested Sykes, whom he nonetheless praised for breadth of vision and 'a most extraordinary knowledge of foreign policy'.[3] The fortunes of Zionism would have been far different if Montagu, the most violent anti-Zionist in public life, had been appointed in Sykes' place.

The new war cabinet was dominated by Lloyd George and Milner both of whom were 'Easterners' and forceful advocates of the Jewish settlement in Palestine. Milner was a political outsider whose life and passion was the British empire. He had no previous ministerial experience, but he was a first-class administrator with long experience in Egypt and South Africa, and he proved to be an outstanding success. Although very well disposed to Jews he had not much interest in the Zionist movement until he joined the war cabinet. He was a close friend of Claude Montefiore but he did not allow the friendship to affect his view of Zionism. Weizmann's judgement was that Milner came to understand that only the Jews were capable of rebuilding Palestine and giving it a place in the family of nations.[4] But Milner was hard-headed. He was strongly influenced by strategic calculations about Palestine; and he was free of any pricking sense of guilt about the treatment by Christendom of the Jewish people. Milner exemplified what Weizmann admired about the British statesmen of his day. They were not 'realists' in the opportunist sense that the word has acquired. They had moral stamina. They did not live from hand to mouth. And the concept of the Return appealed to their traditional values. In Weizmann's view, such men included, as well as Milner and his disciple Leopold Amery, Robert Cecil, Mark Sykes and, pre-eminently, Arthur Balfour.

Balfour's translation from the Admiralty to the Foreign Office was particularly important. He emerged at last to take charge of British policy in the Middle East after having remained silent on the future of Palestine during the eighteen months since he joined the government. It was strange for someone of whom it was once said that he never cared for anything but Zionism.[5] But at the first meeting of the Imperial War Cabinet on 22 March 1917, he suddenly blurted out, 'I am a Zionist, but I do not know whether anybody else is.' No one responded to the implied question except Milner who said abruptly: 'It is impossible to go into that now.'[6] It was a tiny incident but a telling one.

The Revolution in Russia came at the end of February and the Tsar abdicated within days. One of the provisional government's first decrees was to free the Jews and all other national and religious minorities from their disabilities. The Russian Zionists could at last come into the open. The number of those enrolled in Zionist organizations rose sharply. But their atheistic Socialist opponents were also gathering strength. The desperate struggle for the soul of the Russian Jews between the Zionists and the revolutionaries, which had begun in Switzerland in furious debates nearly twenty years before by Weizmann and his friends against Trotsky and Plekhanov, now occupied centre stage in Russia, and with infinitely higher stakes. It was an open question whether the outcome would be favourable to the Zionists.

In its Palestine policy the Foreign Office had pinned its hopes on recruiting the support of the Jews of Russia and America. The Russian Jews, it was wrongly thought, were all Zionists and could help to stop the leftward drift set in motion by the February revolution, and so keep Russia in the war. The Foreign Office was still bemused by the supposed power of world Jewry. In February 1916 Lord Robert Cecil had said, 'I do not think that it is easy to exaggerate the international power of the Jews.'[7] He did not waver in his view, first as Grey's, then as Balfour's deputy at the Foreign Office; but it was a view which events were to test. Would a public promise of a home for Jews in Palestine persuade Russia to stay in the war, and influence the United States to give up its cherished neutrality and come in?

It was not pressure from her Jewish population which at last brought the United States into the war. Many of the American Jews had been refugees from Russia and eastern Europe and supported President Wilson's policy of neutrality. They wanted only to turn their backs on Europe and forget their painful memories. In February 1917 Germany launched an indiscriminate submarine campaign. Its aim was to strangle Britain and its target was neutral shipping. In spite of the sinking of some American ships, Wilson continued to haver, but a German plot was uncovered which gave him no option. Arthur Zimmerman, the German Foreign Minister, was found to be planning to bring Mexico into the war on the promise of regaining the 'lost' territories of Arizona, New Mexico and Texas. American public opinion was inflamed. On 6 April the United States was at war with Germany. There was, however, no declaration of war against Turkey.

President Wilson entered the war with a mission. At the Peace he would put an end to secret treaties and the greed which was inseparable from empire. This posed problems for Britain. How could Wilson be reconciled to the secret plans of Britain, France and Russia to divide the Ottoman empire between themselves, and to Britain's emerging policy, unknown even to her allies, of annexing Palestine on trust for the Jews? But the most important result of the United States coming into the war on the allies' side was that their chances of victory were greatly increased. And an allied victory was now the precondition for Zionist success.

By the beginning of 1917 the British Army had cleared Egypt of Turks and the Suez canal was safe. A month later it crossed the frontier with Palestine. 'Now is the moment for pressing the matter [Zionism] when British troops are actually on Palestinian soil', wrote Scott in his diary on 27 January. Of all the circumstances which conspired to advance the Zionist cause in the first months of 1917, Britain's determination to occupy Palestine was the crucial one.

The new government pressed ahead with the Palestine campaign in spite of objections from the General Staff that it was an expensive diversion that Britain could not afford. The army was held up by reverses at Gaza in March and April but Lloyd George was undeterred. He relieved Archibald Murray of the Palestine command and replaced him by the more decisive, if circumspect, Allenby. Taking

Jerusalem appealed to the new Prime Minister on historical grounds and fired his imagination. It would give Britain a badly needed decisive victory; and he told Scott and Weizmann that the campaign was 'the one really interesting part of the war'.[8] On 20 April, Lloyd George called on the British ambassador in Paris on his way back from a conference with the French and Italians. The French will have to accept our protectorate in Palestine, he lectured the ambassador. 'We shall be there by conquest and shall remain, we being of no particular faith and the only Power fit to rule Mohammedans, Jews, Roman Catholics and all religions.'[9]

It was against this background that negotiations started between the British government and the Zionists. During the autumn of 1916 Weizmann and Sokolow had been preparing a memorandum of Zionist aims to be held in readiness. This document proved difficult to draft and it was not seen by anyone in the government until February 1917, when Sir Mark Sykes asked to see a statement of the Zionist position.

The circumstances in which Sykes started discussions with the Zionists were unusual. When he came back from Petrograd in April 1916 he was eager to learn as much as he could about Zionism. He was introduced to Moses Gaster by Herbert Samuel, but by early 1917 he was doubting whether Gaster was the right contact. Sykes was now political adviser to the war cabinet on the Middle East and he wanted to be sure that his Zionist contacts could speak with the authority of their movement. But he did not make use of the resources of the Foreign Office to make further enquiries. Nor did he ask Gaster for fear of hurting his feelings. Instead he employed as a go-between an Armenian called James Malcolm, whom Sokolow described as a 'brasseur des affaires' and Scott dismissed as 'a self-important busybody'.[10] However that might be, Malcolm, through the good offices of Leopold Greenberg, the editor of the *Jewish Chronicle*, made introductions for Sykes with Weizmann and Sokolow. In that way Weizmann first met Sykes on 28 January 1917.

It seems that Sykes wanted to keep what he was doing to himself. The entry in Scott's diary for 27 January reads: 'Saw Weizmann in morning about Palestine question – Sir Mark Sykes deputed by the FO to deal with it – he and Ld. Rothschild and James Rothschild to see him – Memorial was being prepared on whole question.' This is the only evidence that Sykes had official backing for what he did; but whatever the truth of the matter, he intended it to be understood by the Zionists that he was meeting them as a private person. As usual Scott kept himself well informed. The same afternoon, he met James de Rothschild and heard the oft-repeated Zionist refrain: France was competing hard for Palestine, but she was the very last power whom the Zionists would wish to see in possession. 'She carried her civilisation everywhere', de Rothschild said, 'and would make the development of a Jewish type impossible.'[11]

The Rothschild family, the most famous name in Jewry and who, in Leonard Stein's phrase, stood 'at the summit of the Jewish aristoplutocracy', was not at one in its attitude towards Zionism. The French branch was headed by Baron Edmond, who supported the early settlements in Palestine with lavish and somewhat paternal munificence, but never whole-heartedly embraced Zionism. His son, James de Rothschild, who was settled in England, and his wife, Dorothy, were committed to Zionism and friendly to Weizmann personally. 'Both of them instantly became his allies', writes Stein, 'and from that time forth placed their contacts and social prestige at the disposal of the Zionist cause.'[12] In the English branch, Leopold, the younger brother of the first Lord Rothschild, was strongly opposed to Zionism and was a member of the Conjoint Committee. The second Lord (Walter) Rothschild, to whom the Balfour Declaration was addressed, came late to Zionism and it was not until May 1917 that British Jews learned with either pleasurable surprise or dismay, according to their own views, that he was committed fully to the cause.

It was the second Lord Rothschild who in February sought a meeting with Sykes, and agreed that Sykes should have an outline of the Zionists' proposals before they met. Sykes was accordingly supplied with a lengthy and eloquent memorandum which expounded the nature and origins of the 'Jewish Problem' and the various attempts at its solution.[13] It dealt in turn with assimilation, emigration and emancipation and explained why none met the problem squarely. The conclusion was that the only solution was the establishment of a national home in Palestine for the Jewish people, 'whose longings and aspirations have been directed for two thousand years towards the Promised Land of their ancestors'.

The soil of the country, the memorandum argued, was of great fertility and the climate mild, but the population was too poor and apathetic to cultivate it. The agriculture of the country was in a primitive state, manufacture and industry were almost entirely unknown, trade and commerce were very limited. At the root of these evils was the maladministration of the Turk. Under the Ottomans there was no continuity of agricultural tenure and much land had no permanent owner; law was debased by corruption and tax was imposed by an oppressive and unpredictable regime. The memorandum asked whether the regeneration of the country could be achieved by the present population through reform, and answered the question in the negative. Reforms in government, it averred, could never be effective without the introduction of a new element into the population.

Out of a population of some 600,000 souls in western Palestine (presumably meaning west of the river Jordan) about 120,000 were Jews (probably an overestimate), a larger percentage of the inhabitants than in any other country. Most were poor and dependent on charity. Palestine can and must be regenerated, the memorandum declared, as other countries have been by the introduction of an industrious population, with the necessary capital, organization and education. 'And these factors can be obtained only by the creation of conditions favourable to the colonisation of Palestine by the Jews; in a word by the recognition of Palestine as the home of the Jewish people.' The memorandum concluded by touching lightly on the unique suitability of Britain as sponsor of the Jewish people in the enterprise, and the advantages which would accrue to Britain from undertaking the role.

It was arranged that the meeting with Sykes should take place at Gaster's house and under his chairmanship. So on 7 February 1917 there gathered at no. 193, Maida Vale, Gaster himself, Herbert Samuel (who had retired from the government with the departure of Asquith), Lord Rothschild, James de Rothschild, Chaim Weizmann, Nahum Sokolow, Joseph Cowen and Herbert Bentwich (both prominent English Zionists), Harry Sacher and Sir Mark Sykes. A note of the meeting was kept, apparently by Sokolow, but it was not a verbatim record.[14]

The Zionists went into the meeting unaware of the Sykes–Picot agreement, so that they did not know that Britain, France and Russia had agreed that Palestine should be under international control. There were rumours of some agreement with the French but they knew nothing for certain. They guessed that Sykes' aim was an Anglo-French condominium. For them that would be the worst possible solution. They therefore concentrated their efforts on making the case for British annexation of the country. Samuel said that if there were a condominium the suzerain powers would soon get at loggerheads and the system would break down. James de Rothschild made the point that Brandeis, the head of the American Zionists, was strongly in favour of British annexation of Palestine and opposed to the idea of a condominium; Sokolow said that the Jews of the whole world had for generations looked up to England as the traditional benefactor of the Jewish people and the home of liberty.

The Zionists argued for a Jewish 'nation' in Palestine, although there were differences between them as to what that chameleon word meant. Two speakers referred to 'a Jewish *state* in Palestine'. Lord Rothschild said that he sympathized fully with the development of a Jewish state in Palestine; and Sacher said that 'Jews in Palestine would be members of the Jewish state and owe it political obligation'. Could it be inferred from these brief references that that was the Zionist aim at this stage? They are directly contradicted by a letter from Nahum Sokolow to Brandeis of 7 March:

> I think we all agree that we don't want Palestine to be handed over to us as an independent state. The responsibilities are too great and the risk of failure too terrible. The country is, or will be, too important strategically for a small race to depend on unless backed in some way by stronger powers. It would hardly be favourable for unprotected Jewish national aspirations, were Palestine to become the battlefield of the world.[15]

Weizmann spoke in similar terms of the eventual emergence of a Jewish State as a distant dream when he addressed the London Zionist Conference in May. 'States must be built up slowly, gradually, systematically and patiently'.[16] This was more representative of Zionist thinking in the spring of 1917. However, Weizmann's view may have reflected a tactical awareness of the danger at this early stage of asking for too much and frightening the sponsor. Whether that was so or not, Weizmann's way of putting it was almost identical with Balfour's later in the year. At the meeting of the war cabinet on 31 October, when the Declaration was finally approved, Balfour said in reference to the meaning of 'national home': 'It did not necessarily involve the early establishment of an independent Jewish state, which was a matter for gradual development in accordance with the ordinary laws of political evolution.'[17]

The Zionist view about a Jewish state fitted with what they said about immigration into Palestine and equal rights. The Zionists were never content with mere equality with the other inhabitants of Palestine. They argued that the situation of Jewry was exceptional, calling for an exceptional solution. The point was implicit in Weizmann's statement that no restriction should be put on Jewish immigration into Palestine. 'That would smack of Alien Bills and it would be deeply resented.' If immigration was unrestricted there would be no hindrance to the gradual building up of a Jewish state.

Sykes replied to the Zionists by listing the difficulties facing a Jewish Palestine. Chief among them were the Arabs and the French. 'One would have to go very carefully with the Arabs.' But, he said, the Arabs 'could be managed, particularly if they received Jewish support in other matters'. With that delphic utterance, he passed on. No one on the Zionist side had any questions to ask. Both an Arab nationalist and a Zionist, Sykes had never faced up to the question of how the two could be reconciled.

He named the French as the most serious difficulty of all. He did not understand them, he said. Was their motive in wanting a say in Palestine as well as having all Syria, sentimental, clerical or pure colonial ambition? The whole matter should be discussed very frankly with them. No pledge had been given them about Palestine. James de Rothschild pressed him for assurances on this last point, as he had been informed differently. Sykes suggested that the Zionists should approach Picot, the French delegate in London, and convince him of their case. The Zionists replied, with some justification, that it was the business of the British government to convince its allies. The note states that at this point Sykes became vague. After an argument over boundaries, James de Rothschild asked again whether any pledge had been given about Palestine. The embarrassment was almost palpable. Sykes suggested that Mr Samuel might say what had taken place. Samuel declined, saying that he could not reveal what had been done by the cabinet. Sykes then said that with great difficulty the government had managed to keep the question of Palestine open. He asked that the Zionists appoint someone to put the Jewish views before Picot, and Sokolow was chosen to do so. Sykes would introduce the two the next day.

Sykes had been given a hard time. But he could not help being disingenuous about the Anglo-French problem, since the agreement he had himself come to with Picot was a secret treaty, and somehow it was going to have to be reopened. The discussion about the Arab difficulty was another matter. Both Sykes and the Jews treated it with blithe unconcern. It deserved better. This meeting was, however, crucial to the Zionist cause. Sykes might insist, as he did, that he was acting privately, but the Zionists knew that at this juncture he was the man, the British expert advising the cabinet on the Middle East, on whom their hopes hung. Although the government might not have specifically authorized the negotiations, it could not afterwards forswear them. There was to be no going back.

Sokolow's meeting with Picot the next day was a fencing match conducted with elaborate courtesy but without result.[18] Sokolow would have to go to Paris to plead his case if he was to make any headway with the French. He made clear, however, what his position was about Jewish rights in Palestine. He told Picot that the granting of rights which were merely equal to those of the other inhabitants of Palestine would not do. That would not make the country flourish. Equal rights would be the correct approach in an already developed country, but Palestine was not such a country. The chief need, he said, was to attract capable and devoted settlers and only the Jews could provide them. From now on it was clear to the British that equal rights with the Palestinian Arabs and the other inhabitants would not satisfy the Zionists.

Sokolow was a patient and forbearing man. He lobbied the government in Paris, but before committing themselves the French said that he should go to Italy and speak to the Italian government. This he did at the end of April. Sykes had been before him and smoothed his path. When he arrived in Rome he found that arrangements had been made for him to visit the Vatican. On 29 April and 1 May he had interviews with Monsignor Pacelli, who later as Pope Pius XII became notorious for his failure to speak out against the Holocaust, and Cardinal Gasparri, Papal Secretary of State. The discussion was mainly about the reservation of the Holy Places. On 4 May Sokolow had an audience with Pope Benedict XV. He was kindly received.

It was in contrast to Herzl's audience thirteen years earlier with Pius X. Herzl had found 'an honest, rough-hewn village priest, to whom Christianity was a living thing – even in the Vatican'. But he went away empty-handed. Pius told him that the Jews who should have been the first to acknowledge Jesus Christ had not done so to that day. He could not prevent the Jews from going to Jerusalem, he said, but 'we could never sanction it'.[19]

During Sokolow's audience with Benedict in 1917 the Pope asked what the Vatican could do to help the Jews. Sokolow replied that the Pope should be assured of the loyalty of the Zionists and that they desired only that he accord them moral support. To which the Pope said, 'Yes, yes – I believe that we shall be good neighbours.'[20] It was nothing tangible and the sympathy of the Vatican was short-lived. But there was something surreal about the moment when the supreme Pontiff welcomed the deicides back to the Holy Land.

Sokolow returned to Paris optimistic. He was received by Alexandre Ribot, the Prime Minister, and Jules Cambon, the Foreign Minister. On 4 June he obtained a letter signed by Cambon, cast in those sonorous periods for which the French language seems to be specially designed.[21] You have been good enough, it read, to explain the project for the Jewish colonization of Palestine. You consider that, provided the independence of the Holy Places is safeguarded, it would be a work of justice and reparation to assist in the renaissance of the Jewish people in the land from which they were driven so many centuries ago. The French government entered the war to defend a people wrongly attacked. It could not but feel sympathy for the Zionist cause, the triumph of which was bound up with that of the Allies; and it was happy to give the assurance which was sought.

Sokolow was pleased with the results of his patient diplomacy, but Weizmann was more sceptical – and more nervous. From all he knew of French attitudes to the Jews he doubted the genuineness of French sympathy. In any case, French sympathy for Zionism did not touch the question of the sovereignty of Palestine. His fear was that Sokolow's journey might be interpreted as a Zionist move in favour of a French alternative. But whatever the significance of Cambon's letter, the progress thus far could not be gainsaid. At the beginning of April Weizmann told Sokolow that practically every London newspaper was writing about a Jewish Palestine under a British protectorate.[22] The Zionists had achieved an almost official status in London. Permission had been given them to communicate with fellow Zionists in Russia and the United States by means of British diplomatic channels.[23] Sokolow's mission was assisted by Sykes and blessed by the Foreign Office. The Zionists were being treated in Whitehall as a quasi-national power.

While Weizmann was worrying about French designs on Palestine and their habit of imposing 'l'esprit français' wherever they went, the British were making sure that Palestine would be theirs. Weizmann's worst fears seemed to be realized when in mid-April he learnt for the first time from Scott (who apparently had it from a French journalist) of the Sykes–Picot agreement. He need not have alarmed himself. Events were moving rapidly in his direction.

On 3 April Lloyd George found time to have breakfast with Weizmann and Scott.[24] The Prime Minister wanted to have Weizmann's views about the various possibilities for Palestine. Lloyd George altogether opposed a condominium with France and asked, what about international control? A shade worse, said Weizmann, it would be mere confusion and intrigue; but joint control with America would be acceptable. They then discussed the Russian Jews in London who were still Russian citizens. Weizmann said that he could recruit a couple of thousand volunteers for service in the British army. They ought to fight and would fight well. He mentioned Jabotinsky's Mule Corps which had been at Gallipoli. They wanted now to fight in Palestine. The Prime Minister became excited and said they were the very men he wanted. They would be precious too for 'spying out the land, as in Joshua's day'.

On 4 April Scott met Sykes for the first time and was favourably impressed. Sykes was leaving for the East the next day to act as political adviser to the British Palestine Expeditionary Force; and Weizmann was asked to hold himself in readiness to join him a little later. On 12 April the war cabinet appointed a committee, under the chairmanship of Lord Curzon, to consider 'the territorial desiderata in Asia in the terms of peace'. On 28 April the committee recommended that, in order to safeguard communication through the Suez Canal to the Far East, both Palestine and Mesopotamia should be under exclusive British control. The committee advised that the Sykes–Picot agreement should be modified in such a way 'as would give Great Britain definite and exclusive control over Palestine and would take the frontier of the British sphere of control to the River Leontes and north of the Hauran. Turkish rule should never be restored in Palestine . . .'[25] The much-criticized Sykes–Picot agreement was doomed. Weizmann called it 'the single greatest obstacle to our progress', and it was to be removed. But its legacy was lasting French bitterness.

Weizmann remained in London in command of the Zionist campaign. He did not think he could be of use in Palestine until the British got beyond Gaza and were on the road to Jerusalem. The reverses in Gaza in March and April aborted the plan for his visit, and Allenby, who prepared the ground carefully before launching his attack, did not make his celebrated entry into Jerusalem until after the Balfour Declaration had been promulgated.

On 25 April Weizmann had a lengthy interview with Lord Robert Cecil.[26]

Weizmann was still anxious about the French. Emphasizing the supreme importance of a British annexation of Palestine, he explained the disadvantages of any
other form of administration, particularly one in which the French had any part.
He said that he would go out to Palestine only on the basis that he work for a
Jewish Palestine under a British protectorate. They discussed the Sykes–Picot
agreement, apparently openly. Weizmann said that by its separation of Galilee
from Judea it effectively cut Palestine in half. 'There is little doubt', he said, 'that
the suggested division of Palestine would raise an outcry which will ring through
from one end of the world to the other as it is contrary to all the principles which
have been proclaimed by the Allies since the beginning of the war . . .'

Cecil made no comment. He did not say that Sykes–Picot would have to be
reopened. He remarked only that it would strengthen the position if the Jews of
the world would express themselves in favour of a British protectorate. Weizmann
therefore understood that he would have to work on the American and Russian
Jews to bring them into harmony with his own conception of Britain as the sole
sponsor and protecting power for a Jewish Palestine. Using British diplomatic
channels, he wrote to Brandeis and Yehiel Tschlenow (now back in Russia) to
keep them informed and to urge them to back a British protectorate in Palestine.
With Brandeis he was preaching to the converted, but it was less clear what was
the attitude of the Russian Jews. There was to be a conference of Russian Zionists
in June. It would then be seen what their aspirations were in their new-found
freedom from the oppressive rule of the Tsars.

While these critical events were taking place, Balfour maintained his silence
on the Zionist issue. He had a talk with Weizmann on 22 March, on which
Weizmann reported to Scott that Balfour 'did not at first see the importance of
the Zionist claim from the British point of view'.[27] Balfour suggested that it might
be advisable to bring the Americans into a joint Anglo-American protectorate.
The United States was then on the verge of declaring war and he was planning
to go there in April and May.

During his visit to America Balfour had two meetings with Brandeis, on 7 and
10 May. The meetings mark Balfour's first positive intervention in the Zionist
cause as Foreign Secretary. Unfortunately, there is no contemporary account of
the discussions. Felix Frankfurter, the future Supreme Court Justice and a close
friend of Brandeis, was present at the meetings and made a note many years later

for Mrs Dugdale's biography of Balfour.[28] Frankfurter's note says that Balfour was 'powerfully struck with the intellectual and moral distinction' of the great judge, and Brandeis, on his side, was impressed by Balfour's keen understanding of the Jewish problem. Balfour told Brandeis that he was a Zionist and would do all he could for the cause. From this moment he applied his long experience and prestige within the British government to that end.

Balfour said that he favoured joint Anglo-American sovereignty in Palestine. Brandeis replied that there could be no question of American participation: it would be contrary to the President's policy of avoiding any such commitments. He was in favour of British sovereignty, but any declaration by Britain would have to be 'so qualified as to express less than their desires and intentions'. What this obscure remark meant was veiled from view. More importantly though, the President had apparently told Brandeis on 6 May, just before the first meeting between Brandeis and Balfour, that he was 'in agreement with the policy, under England's protectorate, for a Jewish homeland'.[29] Brandeis believed that he and his American Zionist colleagues had secured the President's agreement to the Zionist idea long before he was prepared to make his agreement public.[30] Balfour must have had the impression that the Americans were ready to support a Declaration by Britain.

By the end of April the British government was virtually committed. If the Foreign Office was dismayed by what it had done, there is no evidence for it. It had been achieved by ruthlessness on the part of both the government and the Zionists. The British ministers, with the exception of Balfour, were actuated first and foremost by imperialist ambition. They could not be acquitted of duplicity towards the French and, to a lesser extent, to the Jews. The Zionists were ruthless too, with the ruthlessness of a militant idealism.

At this crucial point only Weizmann had anything to say about the Palestinian Arabs. Writing to Scott at the end of March, he conceded that the Arabs might be more important to the government than the Jews from the point of view of immediate war aims, but, he added, 'it makes our work very difficult if in all the present negotiations with the Arabs, the Jewish interests are not well defined'. He felt that the negotiations between the government and the Zionists 'must be placed very soon on a more definite practical basis'. His plan, he said, was to accompany Sykes to the East, enter into negotiations with the leading Arabs from

Palestine, and see what could be done to acquire land in the Palestinian territory already occupied by the British. 'It is of the utmost importance', he concluded, 'that we should *be there* as soon as possible, that the Palestinian people and Jews at large should realise that we mean business and mean to carry it out at once.'[31]

12

It's a Boy!

During Balfour's American visit he learned that the United States wanted to explore the possibility of detaching Turkey from the Central Powers and taking her out of the war. Weizmann too got to hear of this in early June 1917. He discovered that plans were well advanced for Henry Morgenthau, a former United States ambassador to Turkey, to lead a delegation for talks with unidentified intermediaries, and that he would be leaving New York shortly. Weizmann understood that representatives of Britain and France were to join Morgenthau in Switzerland. This was alarming. He knew that Morgenthau, although a Jew, was no Zionist and he did not trust him. He feared that the negotiations might result in a peace with Turkey in which her empire would be left intact. He knew that there was a soft, pro-Turkish group in the Foreign Office who might encourage such a result – with possibly fatal results for Zionism. He therefore made an urgent appointment to see Sir Ronald Graham, the head of the Eastern Department at the Foreign Office.

Weizmann could not have hoped for a more sympathetic official than Graham. He was an enthusiast for Zionism and at their meeting on 11 June he assured Weizmann that it was 'axiomatic' that no arrangement with Turkey could be arrived at unless Armenia, Syria and Arabia were severed from the Turkish empire. Weizmann understood this to include Palestine. He seized the occasion. He painted a lurid picture of the machinations of the German government which he said were designed to seduce the Zionists away from the Allies. (This proved to be a story without much foundation, but it was nonetheless both durable and influential.) Weizmann assured Graham that the great majority of the Jewish people was Zionist. Only a small 'oligarchy of Jewish haute finance', as he called it, and a small number of Jewish Socialists were against. 'Les extrêmes se touchent', he exclaimed, but this petty alliance would disappear as soon as the public realized that Zionism was a political reality. Accordingly, he pressed the

British government to move now and make a public declaration of its support for the aims of Zionism. Graham promised to submit the request to the proper quarter.[1]

Graham minuted Balfour and suggested that 'the moment has come when we might meet the wishes of the Zionists . . .'. He pointed out that important political advantages could be expected from a pro-Zionist declaration, especially in Russia, where he reported the vast majority of Jews were Zionists. Balfour was at first cautious. 'How can HMG announce their intention of "protecting" Palestine without consulting our Allies?' he noted. 'And how can we publicly discuss dismembering the Turkish empire before the Turks are beaten?' He was also uncomfortable about Britain taking sole responsibility for Palestine and he was still pondering American involvement in a protectorate. But on receiving Graham's explanation that there was no intention of raising the question of the sovereignty of Palestine, Balfour was satisfied. He wrote, 'I have asked Ld Rothschild and Professor Weizmann to submit a formula.'[2]

On 19 June Balfour saw Rothschild and Weizmann and, as Weizmann told Harry Sacher, they 'put it to him that the time has arrived for the British government to give us a definite declaration of support and encouragement. Mr Balfour promised to do so and he has asked me to submit to him a declaration which would be satisfactory to us which he would try and put before the war cabinet for sanction.'[3]

In this way the final act began. There were continuing misapprehensions on the part of the Foreign Office about both the power of world Jewry and the convictions of the Russian Jews, which Weizmann did nothing to dispel. Global Jewish power was always an illusion and in the spring of 1917 the Russian Jews were far from uniformly Zionist. Moreover, those that were Zionists were not ready to agree that Britain should be their sponsor. Although the wind now appeared to be set fair for a public affirmation by Britain of support for a Jewish national home in Palestine, there was an awkward passage that remained to be negotiated. The most intransigent opponents of Zionism proved to be Jews themselves.

Readers of *The Times* were surprised to read on 24 May a long statement under the heading 'The Future of the Jews: Palestine and Zionism: Views of Anglo-Jewry', signed by David Alexander, President of the Board of Deputies of British Jews, and Claude Montefiore, President of the Anglo-Jewish Association, writing on behalf of the Conjoint Foreign Committee. The statement noted that Zionist leaders were now favouring an 'essentially political scheme' for the Jewish home in Palestine, and were claiming 'all the Jewish communities of the world as constituting one homeless nationality'. The writers earnestly protested. The Zionist programme, they contended, must have the effect of stamping the Jews as strangers in their native lands, and of undermining their hard-won position as citizens and nationals of those lands. In their view, the only certain test of a Jew was the Jewish religion. The Zionist plan for Palestine was not only wrong, they argued, but dangerous, in that it claimed special rights for the Jewish settlers in excess of those enjoyed by the rest of the population. The Jews were in a minority in Palestine and the scheme might well involve them in bitter feuds with their neighbours.

What had provoked this venture into public controversy was the fear in the minds of the conjoint committee that the new government in Britain was becoming more pro-Zionist by the day, and that time was not on their side. Montefiore had seen Milner only a week before the bombshell in *The Times* and had pressed on him the dangers of Zionism. Milner told Montefiore that his fears were exaggerated, but the crisis had unbalanced Montefiore's judgement. He sent Milner a note of their conversation and added a postscript which betrayed his overwrought feelings. 'I would beg of you to trust your own fellow citizens', he wrote

> who at all events are Englishmen through and through, and whose sons are serving in England's armies, rather than foreigners who have no love for England, and who, if the fortunes of war went wrong, would throw her over in a trice, and hurry over to Berlin to join the majority of their colleagues. In old days they puffed up Turkey no end; now of course Turkey for the time being is run down.[4]

Public polemics which set Jew against Jew were ill-judged and would serve only to embarrass the British government. In the days following the publication of the statement by Alexander and Montefiore, *The Times* published letters from Lord Rothschild, the Chief Rabbi and Weizmann. All condemned the statement. The Chief Rabbi's letter was the most damaging. He denied that the views expressed in it were representative of those of Anglo-Jewry as a whole; and he said that the statement had not been properly authorized or even considered by the bodies of which the two signatories were the Presidents.

The *Jewish Chronicle* described the action of the conjoint committee as 'a grave betrayal' and on 29 May *The Times* published an editorial throwing its weight on the side of the Zionists. 'The truth is', it said, 'that the Jewish question cannot be exhaustively defined either in terms of religion or of race. It has important social, economic, financial and political sides.' And it dismissed out of hand 'the imaginary nervousness' which suggested that the realization of territorial Zionism would cause Christendom to round on the Jews and say, 'Now you have a land of your own, go to it!'

The nature of the so-called Jewish Question was being debated in the columns of the morning papers. What is a Jew? Is he to be defined by his religion, his blood, his social behaviour or by a combination of all his attributes? What is an English Jew? Is that different from a Jewish Englishman? Are they both contradictions in terms? These questions could be debated quietly and calmly. But not now. The two sides of Jewry in England were angry with each other. The conjoint committee, which had for so long enjoyed warm relations with the British political establishment, had overreached itself. British Jews were scandalized by a crude attempt, as it appeared, to discredit the Zionist movement.

The parent bodies met to consider what amounted to a vote of censure of the conjoint committee. On 8 June at a meeting of the Anglo-Jewish Association the motion was withdrawn only out of personal regard for Montefiore. Two weeks later the Board of Deputies carried the motion. A Foreign Office minute reported that Lucien Wolf was 'howled down each time he attempted to speak' and concluded, 'In any case this vote means the dissolution of the conjoint committee and it will no longer be necessary to consult that body . . .'[5]

In the middle of May Henry Morgenthau told Robert Lansing, the American Secretary of State, that he thought the time was ripe for a secret approach to be made to Turkey. Lansing proposed that Weizmann should meet Morgenthau at Gibraltar. The motive for suggesting Weizmann is obscure. It may perhaps have been to give colour to the ostensible purpose of the mission, which was for the relief of Jews already settled in Palestine who were then being persecuted by the Turks. In London the Foreign Office could not find a unified voice to react to the Morgenthau mission. To some officials the attempt to make peace with Turkey was attractive – as Weizmann feared. To others, including Sykes and his deputy, William Ormsby-Gore, the initiative was highly dangerous and threatened all their plans for Palestine and Arabia. On his return from the East in the middle of June, Sykes launched a vigorous campaign against 'the Foreign Office pro-Turk gang'. This was the sort of thing he enjoyed: 'Such worms do not take much dealing with, a few rights and lefts, a breakfast with the Prime Minister . . . laid them low, and I found myself again.'[6]

The Sykes faction won easily. It had the Foreign Secretary on its side. The Morgenthau intiative had to be snuffed out, but care must be taken not to upset the Americans. Weizmann thought that Sykes was the man to do it, and he was surprised when the choice fell on himself. According to Weizmann's recollection, Balfour asked him to undertake the task so that the affair would not have 'an official character'. He was to obtain leave of absence from his research work at the Admiralty and meet the Morgenthau party in Gibraltar. His instructions were to talk to Mr Morgenthau, and keep on talking until he had talked him out of the mission.[7] It was a tribute to Weizmann's standing with the government that he should be asked to undertake this delicate mission, even if it did turn out to be more like comic opera than serious diplomacy.

Weizmann travelled to Gibraltar via Paris and Madrid by boat, train and car. He had for companion an intelligence officer who happened to be Kennerley Rumford, the husband of Clara Butt and a fine singer himself. The party was joined at the Spanish frontier by another intelligence officer, this time a lady, 'very smart and exceedingly well dressed; she arrived in a big luxury car. From that point on we moved, as it were, with a cortège of German spies'. Fortunately the spies were easily shaken off. The party reached Gibraltar on 3 July. Morgenthau arrived shortly afterwards with his wife. A French representative, Colonel Weyl, also joined the talks. Although Weizmann's view of the whole business was that it was a *canard*, it was clear that the French were taking the possibility of a separate peace with Turkey seriously. The meetings were held in one of the casemates in the Rock. Inside the heat was stifling. The talking lasted for two whole days. 'The Tommies on guard marched up and down outside,' Weizmann recalled, 'no doubt convinced that we were a pack of spies who had been lured into a trap . . .'[8]

Weizmann followed his instructions to the letter and was entirely successful. He asked Morgenthau whether he thought that the time was ripe for negotiations, in other words whether Turkey knew she was beaten; and if he had a clear idea about the conditions under which the Turks would be prepared to detach themselves from their German masters. Weyl was anxious to have precise answers. After some changes of mind, Morgenthau eventually agreed that he was unable to answer either question affirmatively. The meeting closed and the plans were abandoned. Weizmann's conclusion was that he had little to do to persuade Morgenthau to drop his project. He simply persuaded himself. Weizmann described Morgenthau to his wife: 'He has a great deal of ambition and this is not commensurate with his abilities and knowledge. His wife, who is much cleverer than he is, encourages him to undertake glorious exploits.'[9]

Meanwhile, as he saw the dream of the Return under British sponsorship becoming a tangible reality during the spring of 1917, Weizmann had been urging the Russian Jews to support his plan. At the end of April he wrote a long letter to Tschlenow in Moscow spelling out his reasons.

> England is not aiming at annexing Palestine and, were she not co-operating with us, it would be doubtful whether she would have fought against internationalising the country. On the contrary, it is feared here that with the present mood in Russia and America it will be difficult to work for a British Protectorate except under one condition, *that the Jews themselves want it* . . . It is very important that Russian Jewry should voice its views and that this question in its present form and its significance should be explained to the Russian government.[10]

Russia still held more than half the Jews in the world and the mood among them was cool about the British plan. The provisional government, which had been in power since the February revolution, was inclined to seek peace; and any policy favouring the Tsar's former allies was not popular with Russian Jews. Tschlenow had to consider the precarious position of the Jews already in Palestine (the great majority were Russian) who were being terrorized by the Turks. He was against doing anything which might further inflame Constantinople.

In all these circumstances, the Russian Jews would be hard to persuade. Sokolow had planned to continue his proselytizing journey from France to Russia, but he was delayed by the diversion to Rome. He therefore missed the all-Russia Zionist conference called in Petrograd for 6 June. On the eve of the conference Weizmann sent a further message to Tschlenow. It betrayed his anxiety – and somewhat overstated his case. A British protectorate is best, he urged. 'This will save us from Arab domination, from internationalisation, and from French domination . . .' He feared that in the present state of feeling in Russia some traces of English imperialism might be discerned in the plan for a British Protectorate. That, he declared 'categorically and solemnly', would be a cruel injustice. 'England does not seek Palestine. It is of value to her only if we are to be strong there.'[11]

He was disappointed. The conference passed only bland resolutions in favour of 'the re-settlement and re-birth of Palestine as a national centre', and omitted any reference to Britain or any other possible sponsoring power. The Russians voted for neutrality, preserving the international character of Zionism, and taking care to avoid being identified with Britain or any other combatant power. Weizmann would have to wait for the Balfour Declaration – and the chaos attending the Bolshevik coup in November – before he was to see wild demonstrations of gratitude to Britain among the Russian Jewish masses. Even then Tschlenow was reluctant to join in the cheering. The outcome of the war was still uncertain and he wanted to be sure. 'Everybody is enthusiastic', wrote Vera Weizmann in her diary rather harshly, 'except Tschlenow, who still advocates Jewish neutrality and the policy of sitting on the fence'.[12]

In the feverish atmosphere of the last months leading to the Balfour Declaration, one idea threatened the unity of the English Zionists and would cost the movement Weizmann's leadership. This was the idea of a Jewish Legion for service in Palestine alongside British troops. The prime mover was Vladimir Jabotinsky, a Russian Jew and close friend of Weizmann with whom he had shared a London flat for a time. Weizmann agreed with him. He had been impressed when Lloyd George said to him that if the Jews wanted a national home in Palestine, public opinion would expect them to be ready to fight for it. Jabotinsky was a romantic figure. Courageous and energetic, he was impatient of others who were more cautious, but he lacked judgement. Lord Rothschild's view was that he was a dangerous adviser. Weizmann and Jabotinsky were to drift apart after the war, but although Weizmann recognized that his friend was obsessed with the idea of a Jewish legion, he supported him in his campaign.

There were some thirty thousand Russians living in the Jewish East End who had not been naturalized British. They had been given asylum, but very few volunteered for military service and they could not be conscripted under the new law for compulsory military service passed in July 1917. This anomaly was intolerable to British public opinion, and eventually the able-bodied were given the choice of serving in the British Army or being deported to Russia. Jabotinsky proposed to recruit his legion from this group. He went down to Whitechapel to harangue them and was pelted with vegetables. The War Office disliked the idea. It was opposed to 'fancy' regiments and it did not believe in the Jew as a fighting soldier. The concept was intensely unpopular among the anti-Zionist members of the Jewish community. They argued, predictably, if a Jewish regiment, why not a Roman Catholic or a Methodist one?

It was also just as unpopular among many of the Zionists. Some thought it would seal the fate of the Jews who were living in Palestine and were already being persecuted by the Turks. Ahad Ha'am considered that it was right to have Jewish soldiers in the Palestine campaign, but they should be in British units and not in a separate regiment. He thought Jabotinsky's idea would be 'an empty demonstration' and might prove disastrous both to Palestinian and Turkish Jewry.[13]

Many of Weizmann's friends and colleagues thought the same. He felt isolated and imagined a conspiracy. He imagined 'Soviet tactics' against himself. He told Sokolow that the atmosphere surrounding him was 'full of suspicion, envy and a certain fanaticism, in the presence of which any fruitful work is impossible for me.'[14] He placed his resignation from the Presidency of the English Zionist Federation in the hands of the Council. Those who admired him most were appalled. Ahad Ha'am said that his departure would undermine the British government's confidence in the Zionist leadership and be 'tantamount to treason'. Scott wrote: 'So far as I can judge and my experience goes, you are the only statesman among them.'[15]

In the end the idea of the Jewish Legion died a natural death. Although the War Office at one time seriously contemplated a Jewish infantry regiment with its own cap badge of King David's shield, the idea was dropped. The Jewish recruits were enlisted in a separate battalion of the Royal Fusiliers and saw active service in the Jordan valley. Weizmann withdrew his resignation. But the episode showed how fragile unity was. It showed too that Weizmann could become overexcited in a crisis and incapable of accommodating other views than his own.

He was under great strain. On the eve of the October revolution Russia was descending into chaos while he watched. He confided his fears about his native country to Scott: 'The Soviets are the real government', he wrote, 'and possess executive power without responsibility. The elements constituting the Soviets are not constructive, they are narrow-minded and fanatical. The misfortune of Russia is that it possesses a small group of intellectuals inexperienced in statecraft and a huge inert mass of peasants who can be swayed by political demagogues.'[16]

More immediately Weizmann was anxious about the British government dragging its feet. On 19 June Balfour had asked Lord Rothschild and Weizmann to submit a draft declaration for him to put before the war cabinet. Weizmann was away on his errand to Gibraltar between the end of June and 22 July, but in his absence a draft was prepared and submitted to Balfour on 18 July. The drafting presented some difficulty. The Zionists were divided about how much they should ask for. Sacher thought that they should be bold and come out for a Jewish state in Palestine. But he was overruled by the more cautious Sokolow who took the view that if they were moderate they would be more likely to gain sympathy. The process was further complicated by consultation with the Foreign Office during drafting. For this Mark Sykes was deputed, assisted by two junior officials, one of whom was Harold Nicolson.

Many years later Nicolson recalled the days spent at this work in a dark basement of the Foreign Office.[17] The room was used as an air raid shelter. There was an old harmonium in the corner. On occasions when Lloyd George took refuge there it was said that he used it to play Welsh hymns. The slow and solemn Sokolow came in to consult. Sykes was 'full of energy, imagination, zest and knowledge'. He had none of the bureaucrat's obsession with files and minutes, and preferred to while away the time producing irreverent sketches of the dramatis personae.

This unlikely team eventually produced a draft declaration for Lord Rothschild to send to Balfour. In the form in which it went to the Foreign Secretary on 18 July it read:

1. His Majesty's Government accepts the principle that Palestine shall be reconstituted as the National Home of the Jewish people.
2. His Majesty's Government will use its best endeavours to secure the achievement of this object and will discuss the necessary methods and means with the Zionist Organisation.

It was now clear what the Zionists were asking for. Palestine was to be *reconstit-uted* (that is, reorganized or reconstructed) as *the* (not *a*) national home for the Jews. What would be the future of the population that was not Jewish? The draft was silent. It was to be Milner's role to face the question and attempt to deal with it by words of qualification.

Balfour passed on the draft to the war cabinet with some slight amendments, but it was not considered until 3 September. By then the composition of the war cabinet had changed somewhat from its original membership. Lloyd George and Milner remained the dominant figures; Bonar Law and Curzon were still members; George Barnes had replaced Arthur Henderson as the representative of the Labour Party; and the numbers had been increased by the addition of Edward Carson and Jan Smuts. Balfour continued as Foreign Secretary outside the war cabinet.

Smuts had turned down the offer of the Palestine command (which went instead to Allenby) but rather than returning to his native South Africa, he accepted an invitation to join the war cabinet. Like Milner, he was an unusual choice, having no experience of Westminster, but he added great strength and wisdom. He was an exceptionally tolerant man, both racially and religiously, and a lifelong friend of the Jews. In spite of their having been enemies in the South African war Smuts and Milner were natural allies in the war cabinet. They had a common belief in the beneficent effects of empire and the strategic importance of Palestine. Smuts became a committed sympathizer with the aims of Zionism. 'As for me', he later said, 'a Boer with vivid memories of the recent past, the Jewish case appealed with peculiar force. I believed with all my heart in historic justice, however long delayed.'[18]

With the war cabinet composed as it now was, the Zionists hoped that the declaration might go through quickly and smoothly. But it was not to be. Both Lloyd George and Balfour (who would have attended for the item on the agenda concerning Zionism) were absent on 3 September. Lloyd George was taking a rest enforced by his doctors, and Balfour was on holiday in Scotland. Moreover, Edwin Montagu, who represented the single most dangerous threat to the safe passage of the declaration, had joined the government as India Secretary on 17 July. The Zionists did not underestimate the threat he posed. Lord Rothschild wrote to Weizmann, 'I said to you in London, as soon as I saw the announcement in the paper of Montagu's appointment, that I was afraid we were done.'[19]

Montagu had been out of government since the fall of Asquith in December 1916. The Asquithian Liberals were sulking in their tents on the back benches. They were outraged that Montagu, their former intimate, should accept office from the hand of the traitorous Lloyd George, and they treated him like a leper. Montagu's peace of mind was easily disturbed. He was haunted by the feeling that anti-Semitism had been pursuing him all his life like a vengeful beast. The thought of Zionism induced a sort of claustrophobia in him. Just how personal were his nightmares about its possible consequences would become clear in the final stages of the drama.

When the war cabinet met on 3 September, it had not only the form of draft declaration submitted in July by Lord Rothschild to Balfour, the text of which has already been quoted, but also one revised by Milner.* The Milner revisions had the effect of weakening the simple force of the original; and correspondingly, because the obligation was expressed with more vagueness, it made it the more acceptable to a government that did not quite know where the policy of the declaration was leading.

Montagu was invited to attend. He had submitted a paper characteristically entitled 'The Anti-Semitism of the present Government' and he proceeded to elaborate its arguments in vehement terms. The war cabinet was taken aback by the ferocity of Montagu's assault. No decision was made and instead it was agreed to seek President Wilson's view. The war cabinet's tentativeness was betrayed by the form of request that Cecil was instructed to send to Colonel House, the President's personal adviser and confidant. 'We are being much pressed here', it ran, 'for a declaration of sympathy with the Zionist movement and I should be very grateful if you felt able to ascertain unofficially if the President favours such a declaration.'[20] There was no mention of the British government's own disposition in favour of a declaration, and no draft wording was submitted for the President to consider.

The President's response came on 10 September. His view was that 'the time is not opportune for any definite statement further perhaps than one of sympathy provided it can be made without conveying any real commitment'.[21]

---

* The versions before the war cabinet on 3 September, together with the two later ones, including the Balfour Declaration in its final form, are set out in the Appendix.

This disheartening reply is difficult to explain as it is at variance with Wilson's known views. When he heard, Weizmann was astonished and dismayed. He wired Brandeis begging him to intervene.[22] In his telegram he set out the wording of the draft declaration sent by Lord Rothschild to Balfour on 18 July, saying that it had been approved by the Foreign Office and submitted to the war cabinet. On 24 September Brandeis telegraphed Weizmann that from talks he had had with the President, 'I feel sure I can answer that he is in entire sympathy with the declaration quoted in yours of nineteenth'.[23]

The mystery of President Wilson's mind became more impenetrable. But the situation in London was the main worry. Zionism was off the war cabinet's agenda. Weizmann thought he knew who was responsible and continued his frantic efforts to reactivate Ministers. He fulminated against the obstructions of a handful of 'Englishmen of the Jewish persuasion', and belaboured Philip Kerr, the Prime Minister's private secretary. In a barely veiled attack on Montagu he wrote:

> The 'dark forces' in English Jewry have again been at work and this time they have mobilised their great champion who although a great Hindu nationalist now, thought it his duty to combat Jewish nationalism … This declaration of Palestinian policy has been approved by Mr Balfour and the PM. Still it is hung up owing to opposition of a few Jews, whose only claim to Judaism is that they are working for its disappearance.[24]

Balfour was back in London by 19 September and Weizmann saw him that day. Balfour promised him that he would go and see the Prime Minister as soon as the latter returned to London. But Lord Rothschild and Weizmann were leaving nothing to chance. Montagu had succeeded in kicking the question into the long grass once and might do so again. Understanding that the war cabinet were to consider the Zionist issue afresh on 4 October, they sent Balfour a strongly worded memorandum. They could not ignore rumours, they said, that the anti-Zionist view would be urged at the meeting by 'a prominent Englishman of the Jewish faith who does not belong to the war cabinet'; they were reluctant to believe that the war cabinet would allow the divergence of views on Zionism existing in Jewry to be presented to them 'in so strikingly a one-sided manner'.[25]

The war cabinet met again on 4 October and this time both Lloyd George and Balfour were there. Montagu was in attendance as well. He had submitted another memorandum. Like the first, it was eloquent and not without its pathos. He argued that by taking up the cause of Zionism the war cabinet was betraying

British Jews, and the Prime Minister was being misled by 'a foreigner, a dreamer, an idealist'. Curzon, while arguing on different grounds, was also opposed to a declaration. He was no philo-Semite and, looking back afterwards, he told Scott that Palestine was 'the worst of our recent commitments . . . He was dead against the whole Zionist arrangement. The Zionists were very grasping and arrogant . . .'[26]

But Balfour, who had been growing steadily in conviction, was now in charge. He refuted Montagu's points one by one, arguing that, although opposed by a number of wealthy Jews in Britain, the Zionist movement was supported by the vast majority of world Jewry. He saw nothing inconsistent between the establishment of a Jewish national focus in Palestine and the complete assimilation and absorption of Jews into the nationality of other countries. He went on:

> What was at the back of the Zionist Movement was the intense national consciousness held by certain members of the Jewish race. They regarded themselves as one of the great historic races of the world, whose original home was Palestine, and these Jews had a passionate longing to regain once more this ancient national home.[27]

He continued by reading the sympathetic letter which Sokolow had obtained from the French government in June, and saying that he knew that President Wilson was also 'extremely favourable to the movement'. Finally, he told his cabinet colleagues, 'the German government were making great efforts to capture the sympathy of the Zionist movement'. The delusion of German fishing in Zionist waters, encouraged by Weizmann, continued to loom in the minds of Ministers and their officials. They might, however, have asked themselves what the Germans could do for the Zionists at that juncture. Palestine was Turkish, the Turks were fighting for it, and Turkey was Germany's ally. How could they interfere? In any case, the British offensive in Palestine under Allenby was now under way in force.

Montagu must have realized that the game was almost up. He would soon be on the boat to India and unable to carry on the battle. Out of something like desperation, as soon as the war cabinet was over, he wrote an extraordinary personal plea to Lloyd George. He told the Prime Minister that he was in great distress. The situation in India, for which he was responsible, was critical and its population had pinned its faith in him. During the coming year India would decide whether to acquiesce in, or rebel against, British rule. He continued:

I believe firmly that if you make a statement about Palestine as the national home for Jews, every anti-Semitic organisation and newspaper will ask what right a Jewish Englishman, with the status at best of a naturalised foreigner, has to take a foremost part in the Government of the British empire . . . The country for which I have worked ever since I left the University – England – the country for which my family has fought, tells me that my national home, if I desire to go there, therefore my natural home, is Palestine. How can I maintain my position?[28]

The war cabinet was given pause by Montagu's anguish. Once more no decision was taken. It was agreed to make quite sure of President Wilson's view and this time he was given a form of words to approve. This was the draft submitted by Milner in September, but revised again by Milner with the assistance of Leopold Amery. The latest revision contained two new provisos. The first made clear that the rights of all non-Jews in Palestine were not to be prejudiced; and the second, that the rights and political status of Jews in all other countries would remain unaffected. The latter was to give some comfort to the unhappy Montagu. To Weizmann the provisos emasculated the text and were 'a bitter pill to swallow'. It made him wonder if he should have stood out for something stronger.[29] But be that as it may, on 16 October the British embassy in Washington informed London that the President had approved the latest draft.

As a result of Montagu's determined opposition, it was also decided to give both sides of Jewry a last opportunity to state their case. A list of ten representative Jewish leaders was made up by Hankey in consultation with Montagu and Weizmann. The list comprised the Chief Rabbi, Lord Rothschild, Herbert Samuel, Claude Montefiore, Sir Stuart Samuel (the President of the Board of Deputies), Sir Philip Magnus, Leonard Cohen (the President of the Jewish Board of Guardians), Weizmann, Sokolow and Montagu. All had Milner's latest version for comment. Six of those consulted were in favour of the declaration, and four opposed. The replies were collected in a cabinet paper.[30] The Chief Rabbi's response spoke of the profoundest gratitude which he personally felt to the British government for lending its support to the re-establishment of a national home for the Jewish people. It was fortunate for the Zionists that the spiritual head of British Jewry brought his dignity and authority to their cause.

Now it remained only to get the subject back on the war cabinet's agenda. Weizmann was engaged all day and every day in furious activity. He organized over three hundred synagogues and Jewish organizations to pass resolutions supporting the declaration and sent the list to the Foreign Office. He wrote to Hankey, Kerr and Graham. On 25 October Graham was provoked to minute Balfour that further delay might lose the cooperation of Zionist masses in Russia and throw them into the arms of the Germans. Balfour at once sent the minute on to Lloyd George with a covering note saying that, in view of the fact that it was now more than three months since the Zionists had sent their draft of the declaration to him, they now had reasonable grounds for complaining of delay.[31]

Then at the very last minute Curzon intervened. He submitted a memorandum for the war cabinet headed 'The Future of Palestine'.[32] Although pompous almost beyond endurance (Sykes called him 'Alabaster') no one could doubt Curzon's ability, informed as it was by long experience. His memorandum was closely argued. It disclaimed altogether any part or interest in the dispute between Zionist and anti-Zionist Jews, and dealt instead with practicalities. Palestine (which Curzon had in fact not seen for twenty years) was, he wrote, a very poor country. It could never support a population swollen by a large influx of Jews. The land of milk and honey was a mirage. In any case, what was to become of the existing inhabitants? They and their forefathers had occupied the land for fifteen hundred years and owned the soil. They would not be content either to be expropriated for Jewish immigrants or to act merely as hewers of wood and drawers of water.

But persuasive and even prophetic as Curzon's arguments were, they did not deflect his colleagues. Their author's weakness, as Winston Churchill identified in his sketch of Curzon in *Great Contemporaries*, was that he thought too much about stating his case, and too little about getting things done. 'When he had written his cogent dispatch, or brought a question before the cabinet in full and careful form with all his force and knowledge, he was inclined to feel that his function was fulfilled. Events must now take their course.' In any case, Curzon was never a match for Lloyd George.

The war cabinet met for the third time on 31 October. Balfour put as the main advantage of the declaration its 'extremely useful propaganda' value in Russia and America. He understood, he said, that the remaining arguments against Zionism that were still being persisted in were that Palestine could not support a home for the Jewish people, and the difficulty felt about the future of Jews in western countries. He dealt shortly with both points, and the minutes record that Curzon admitted the force of the diplomatic arguments in favour of an expression of sympathy for Zionism. The cabinet then at last approved the latest Milner draft of the Declaration, with only minor alterations.[33]

The situation of the Palestinian Arabs had not been discussed on any of the three occasions when Zionism had been on the war cabinet's agenda, although it had been part of both Montagu's and, particularly, Curzon's objections. The war cabinet had added Milner's two provisos, one of which was designed to protect non-Jewish interests in Palestine. But that suffered from the weakness of all proviso drafting – it sought to take away with one hand what was being given with the other – as Weizmann realized immediately. The Balfour Declaration was pregnant with ambiguity and a seed-bed of confusion. It reflected its authors' attempt to ride the two horses of Arab and Jewish nationalism at once.

On 2 November Balfour wrote the letter to Lord Rothschild which has become known as the Balfour Declaration.

> His Majesty's government view with favour the establishment in Palestine of a National Home for the Jewish people, and will use their best endeavours to facilitate the achievement of this object, it being clearly understood that nothing shall be done which may prejudice the civil and religious rights of existing non-Jewish communities in Palestine, or the rights and political status enjoyed by Jews in any other country.

Weizmann waited in an ante-room while the war cabinet was in session on 31 October. As soon as it was over Sykes rushed the Declaration out to him in a state of high excitement. 'Dr Weizmann, it's a boy!' 'Well', wrote Weizmann afterwards, 'I did not like the boy at first. He was not the one I had expected. But I knew that this was a great event. I telephoned my wife, and went to see Ahad Ha'am.'[34]

13

At the Threshold

The Balfour Declaration was published on 9 November 1917. A surge of pent-up relief, elation and gratitude swept through the Jewish world. An eyewitness reported that the news was received in Cracow with indescribable joy and Jews ran amok in the streets; in Odessa, the British Consul told London, a procession two miles long marched past the Consulate playing the Jewish and British national anthems again and again. It was the same in countless Jewish communities all over the world.

In London on 2 December a great thanksgiving demonstration was held in the Opera House in Kingsway. Lord Rothschild presided and the speakers included the Chief Rabbi, Dr Gaster, Chaim Weizmann, Lord Robert Cecil, Sir Herbert Samuel, Sir Mark Sykes and leaders of the Arab and Armenian national movements. In the audience was a large contingent from the Jewish East End, and they heard Samuel, a figure from an incomprehensibly different world, recite in the Hebrew language the time-honoured words, 'Next year in Jerusalem'. Buoyed on the tide of excitement, Cecil declared, 'Our wish is that Arabian countries shall be for the Arabs, Armenia for the Armenians, and Judaea for the Jews.' The London press, too, assumed too much. 'Palestine for the Jews' was the headline in *The Times*, *Morning Post* and *Daily News*; and the *Manchester Guardian*, *Spectator* and *Observer* all spoke of a Jewish state, the *Observer* saying, 'It is no idle dream that by the close of another generation the new Zion may become a State.'

As if it were a sign, Gaza fell to British forces the day before the Declaration was announced and the road to Jerusalem lay open. Other omens, however, were not so favourable. A Zionist mission was supposed to leave England for Russia, but the Bolshevik coup put a brutal end to the plan. Lenin's seizure of power occurred at almost the same time as Gaza fell. It would lead swiftly to civil war, Russia's withdrawal from the anti-German alliance and renewed isolation and tribulation for her Jewish population. The Jewish socialists who took part in the revolution were triumphant. They were Weizmann's old enemies and bitterly opposed to Zionism.

Britain's remaining allies were unenthusiastic about the Balfour Declaration. The French oscillated between sullen silence and grudging approval. As seen from Paris, Britain's designs on Palestine were already menacing with her army advancing inside the country. The Declaration could only strengthen Britain's position. In the words of a report laid before the French Senate in December, Zionism could be summed up as 'une utopie dangereuse'.[1] In Washington too there was a tepid reaction. Although the American Zionists greeted the Declaration enthusiastically, President Wilson had spoken with more than one voice when asked for his approval. The United States had never been at war with Turkey and was not prepared to sanction any disposition of Turkish territory before the terms of peace had been fully worked out.

Altogether, the international power of the Jews, to which the Foreign Office had attached so much importance and which Cecil had once described as 'not easy to exaggerate' was found to be imaginary when put to the test. Worldwide Jewry did not weigh with those governing Russia and the United States, nor did it have any serious effect on the remaining course of the war. But these doubts and disappointments paled beside the Palestinian reaction to the Declaration. While their country was being forcibly occupied by the greatest empire in the world, the news broke of Balfour's letter to Lord Rothschild. Allenby's celebrated entry into Jerusalem followed only weeks afterwards. At the same time it was revealed by the Bolshevik government in Russia that Britain had, by the Sykes–Picot agreement, made a secret treaty with France for the disposition of Palestine. The cumulative effect was profound resentment and dismay. Palestinians felt that alone among the Arab peoples they were not to have their freedom and nationhood. Instead, their country was to become home to unknown numbers of foreign Jews.

One immediate consequence of the Balfour Declaration was that it put at rest any doubt about Chaim Weizmann's personal ascendancy in the Zionist movement. He was the one indispensable leader who had achieved Herzl's lifelong ambition – to harness a great power as sponsor of the Return. The source of his influence over British policy was described by Felix Frankfurter in a letter to Louis Brandeis in 1919:

He is one of the significant figures in English public life. He has a sway over English public men and over English permanent officials who will continue to govern England when Lloyd George and Balfour will be no more – such as no other Jew in England or on the continent has or can easily acquire.[2]

On 12 November 1917, only ten days after Balfour had written his letter to Lord Rothschild, Weizmann wrote to Brandeis to confirm the good news. He added, 'We shall also have to think about sending out a commission to Egypt and Palestine very soon. I shall write fully to you about the scope and purpose . . .'[3] The Commission's immediate purpose was to protect Zionist interests in a dangerous period of vacuum in Palestine. The British army was clearing the country, there was a temporary military administration in power and Arab opposition to Zionism was growing. It was essential to lose no time in building the foundations of the Jewish national home.

The idea of the Commission went back to the summer of 1917, but its prime mover was Weizmann. He would be its first chairman and it would have representatives of the main Zionist communities in worldwide Jewry. The Commission was to be a permanent body. Whether it was in Weizmann's mind at the time or not, it would eventually become transmuted into the Jewish Agency and form the embryonic Jewish government.

The terms of reference of the Commission were agreed with the Foreign Office. It was to be attached to Allenby's army and its first responsibility was to form a link between the Jewish community in Palestine and the military. Weizmann had an audience with the King and set off for Palestine in March 1918. Major William Ormsby-Gore, an assistant cabinet secretary and later the Colonial Secretary, was attached as political officer to maintain liaison with the military. His enthusiasm for Zionism and his value to the Commission, Weizmann told Brandeis, could not be overestimated. The more so as on Weizmann's arrival he found that Allenby was preoccupied with the campaign and his staff were barely aware of the Balfour Declaration.

Before leaving London Weizmann had been able to secure Balfour's agreement to the laying of the foundation stones of the Hebrew University on Mount Scopus in Jerusalem. When he broached the subject with Allenby, the Commander-in-Chief was incredulous, telling Weizmann that he could not have chosen a worse moment in the war. The front line then was static and lay on an east–west axis just north of Jerusalem. Mount Scopus was almost within sight of the guns. Moreover, the final German offensive in the West had rapidly gained ground and almost reached Paris. But the ceremony went ahead on 24 July in Allenby's presence as well as that of representatives of the Moslem, Christian and Jewish communities.

The atmosphere between the military administration and the Zionist Commission was uncomfortable. Vladimir Jabotinsky, who became the political officer of the Zionist Commission after Weizmann went back to England, put his finger precisely on the attitude of the soldiers who were then governing Palestine. It was not a simple matter of anti-Semitism, although the members of the Commission were shocked by the prejudice and ignorance of many British officers. The administration treated Palestine as a colony, Jabotinsky wrote to Weizmann in November 1918.

> Arabs are just the same old 'natives' whom the Englishman has ruled and led for centuries, nothing new, no problems, but the Zionist was a problem from top to toe, bristling with difficulties in every way . . . My dear friend, it will grieve you, but I must say that the whole official attitude here is one of apologising to the Arabs for Mr Balfour's *lapsus linguae*, of endeavours to atone for it by putting Jews always in the background.[4]

In a conversation with General Wyndham Deedes, one of the most understanding of British soldiers, Weizmann learned soon after he arrived in Palestine of one of the sources of the Zionists' tribulations. Deedes handed him some typewritten pages and advised him to read them carefully. It was an extract from the 'Protocols of the Elders of Zion', the notorious forgery purporting to describe secret Jewish plans for acquiring world power by undermining the morals and health of the non-Jewish world. The 'Protocols' were exposed as a forgery in 1921 by Philip Graves, *The Times* correspondent in the Near East. Deedes warned Weizmann that copies could be found in the haversacks of many British officers in Palestine who believed what they read. The Foreign Office, too, had been infected with these poisonous falsehoods. A minute from one official in 1919 contained the view that 'Jewish aspirations . . . are unlimited, and the Jew will control his controller, not only in Palestine but in every quarter of the globe.'[5]

Allenby and a few of his staff did their best to be even-handed, but Allenby himself thought there was no future in Palestine for the Jews: it was simply not a practical proposition. Later on he was inclined to give Zionism the benefit of the doubt and considered Weizmann's plans 'bold and progressive' if not hurried through. He admired Weizmann and paid him what was in the circumstances a very high tribute when writing to Lloyd George. 'Dr Weizmann has been of great assistance to my administration,' he wrote, 'his moderate views having gone a long way to ameliorate the political conditions in Palestine and restore the confidence of the Arab in the Jew.'[6]

When Weizmann had been in Palestine for some weeks he wrote Balfour a long letter giving him his own impressions.[7] There is a tone of complaint about the military administration running through the letter as he elaborated a long list of mistakes and obstacles to what he took British policy to be. He pointed out that the principle of preserving the status quo in Palestine was being treated as sacrosanct by the administration. The Commander-in-Chief, in trying to be fair and just, was applying 'the democratic principle' which reckoned only with the relative numerical strengths of five Arabs to one Jew. Both principles were handicapping the Zionist plans for the country. Balfour's only comment (in the margin of the letter) was: 'It is very interesting but hardly optimistic.'[8] Underlying Weizmann's complaints there was an assumption that the Jews were entitled to special treatment that amounted to something more than equality with the other inhabitants of Palestine. He had always held that view.

Ormsby-Gore gave his own assessment of the situation on the ground in Palestine in a letter to Sykes in April 1918. He noticed a tendency among the Englishmen who had lived in India or the Sudan (who represented a fair proportion of the senior officers in the military administration at the time) to unconsciously favour the Moslem against both Christian and Jew. The Arabs, he thought, were showing 'their old tendency to corrupt methods and backsheesh and are endeavouring to "steal a march" on the Jews'. It was his conviction that 'the Zionists are the one sound, firmly pro-British, constructive element in the whole show'.[9]

Ormsby-Gore was a committed Zionist. Clayton, the Chief Political Officer, and Storrs, the military governor of Jerusalem, both of whom Ormsby-Gore thought were doing well under difficult circumstances, were more even-handed. Clayton, writing to Sykes in December 1917, did not think that Sykes' idea of an 'Arab-Jew-Armenian combine' had much chance of success. 'It is an attempt to change in a few weeks the traditional sentiment of centuries.' The Arab cared nothing for the Armenian and either despised or feared the Jew. He summed up: 'We have therefore to consider whether the situation demands out and out support of Zionism at the risk of alienating the Arabs at a critical moment.'

Storrs had some sympathy for the Arabs. He told Sykes that 'the Moslems are, as you have doubtless heard, in a state of highly charged apprehension and anxiety. They hear a voice in every wind . . .' He thought they had reason to be worried. 'The C in C comes up from GHQ and drives through the Jewish quarters under a rain of flowers, side by side with Dr Weizmann to receive a copy of the Tora in Hebrew. The air is filled with vague rumours of a Zionist University dominating the city . . . trafficking for the possession of the ground in front of the Wailing Wall . . .'[10]

Reading these contemporary views of officers on the spot, it is as easy to understand the frustration of the Zionists as it is to sympathize with Arab fears about the situation that had been created by the Balfour Declaration.

Within days of his arrival in Palestine Weizmann wrote to his wife that the Arab problem cut across every explanation he gave of the Zionist programme. He wrote again after he had made a conciliatory speech in Jerusalem calling for peace with mutual respect between Arab and Jew. The Arabs responded politely, he told Vera, but it was difficult to trust them. 'I feel I do not need to concern myself with the Arabs any more; we have done everything that was required of us, we have explained our point of view publicly and openly: *c'est à prendre ou à laisser*. If the government were to undertake to arrange matters with the Arabs, that would be the only thing required.'[11]

He may here have used language to his wife in a moment of frustration which he would not have used to, say, Balfour, but he was in quite a different mood when describing a meeting in June with Feisal, the son of the Sherif Hussein. Weizmann travelled with Ormsby-Gore to Feisal's camp with the Anglo-Arab army in the south of the country near Aqaba. There was a group of British officers there among whom was T. E. Lawrence, who was engaged at the time in disrupting the Turkish supply lines by blowing up the Hejaz railway. It was the first time that Weizmann had met either Feisal or Lawrence and the meeting was highly successful. He found Lawrence's personality complex and difficult, his manner 'whimsical . . . and much given to the Oxford type of sardonic humour. But when one did manage to get him into a serious vein he was frank and friendly.'[12] Feisal cast a spell over him. He told Vera:

He is the first real Arab nationalist I have met. He is a leader! He's quite intelligent and a very honest man, handsome as a picture! He is not interested in Palestine, but on the other hand he wants Damascus and the whole of northern Syria. He talked with great animosity against the French, who want to get their hands on Syria. He expects a great deal from collaboration with the Jews! He is contemptuous of the Palestinian Arabs whom he doesn't even regard as Arabs![13]

The Hashemites, Hussein and his sons, particularly Feisal, were regarded by the British as spokesmen for the Arab world, and the meeting between Feisal and Weizmann had been arranged by Allenby as part of a propaganda campaign to promote good relations between the Zionists and the Arabs. The campaign had started in January 1918 with a mission to Hussein in Jeddah by Commander D. G. Hogarth. Hogarth, the head of the Arab Bureau (the British intelligence agency in Cairo concerned with Arab affairs) was an archaeologist and Arabist, and he carried a carefully worded message for Hussein. It confirmed that the Allies would ensure that the Arab race should be given a full opportunity of forming a nation, and it went on to commend warmly to Hussein the advantages of friendship and cooperation of the Zionists. The British government, Hussein was told, was 'determined that, in so far as is compatible with the freedom of the existing population, no obstacle should be put in the way of the return of the Jews to Palestine'. On his return from Jeddah Hogarth reported that Hussein was agreeable in principle but, he warned, he would not accept a Jewish state in Palestine.[14]

This line of policy was confirmed by Weizmann at his meeting with Feisal when he emphasized that the Jews would not be a threat and did not intend to set up their own government: their wish was to work under British protection to colonize Palestine without encroaching upon Arab interests. Weizmann's assessment of the Hashemites' ambitions, as reported to his wife, was accurate. Hussein wanted to unite the Arab world under his own monarchy in preparation for assuming the Caliphate. The restoration of an Arab Caliphate from the usurping Turkish Sultans would carry with it not only spiritual supremacy, but also a political power comparable to that of the Ottoman empire.[15] Although it was not clear beyond a peradventure, the impression given by Feisal was that Palestine was not part of his ambition except as a bargaining counter for Syria. He would use his British comrades-in-arms to help him to establish an independent

Syrian monarchy, free of the hated French, with himself, Feisal, as King, in return for giving the British and their Zionist clients a free hand in Palestine.

Weizmann and Feisal were at one in holding a low opinion of the Palestinian Arabs. They had not helped in the Arab revolt against the Turks and had shown no sign of understanding the benefits the Jews could bring to their country. For their part the Palestinians mistrusted the Hashemites who they were sure would never give them independence. Weizmann had told Balfour that he thought the Hejaz and its Hashemite rulers were the centre of Arab gravity, and Allenby had encouraged him to think of Sherif Hussein and Feisal as having influence with all Arab peoples. But to assume that the Palestinian Arabs could be left out of account in the reordering of the Middle East was worse than a miscalculation. It was an opportunity lost with tragic consequences.

The story of Weizmann and Feisal continued. The conversations between the two led to a lasting personal friendship and they signed a treaty of co-operation on the eve of the Peace Conference convened in Paris in 1919. The agreement provided for the carrying into effect of the Balfour Declaration, the encouragement of large-scale Jewish immigration into Palestine and expert help to be given by the Jews to the Arabs in developing the country. It was subject to the condition that the Arabs should obtain their independence as set out in a memorandum submitted simultaneously to the Foreign Office.[16]

The agreement was intended to strengthen the interests of the British in the Levant, and to weaken those of the French, and so serve the political interests of both Arabs and Jews. It was always an improbable arrangement, but it showed how far Feisal was prepared to go towards Arab-Jewish cooperation at the end of the war, if Arab independence and freedom could be guaranteed. But it was fated never to have any effect. It disappeared in the widening rift between Hussein and his son, Feisal, on the one hand, and the British on the other, over the extent of the territory promised to the Arabs in the McMahon–Hussein correspondence.

In November 1918, on the eve of the armistice on the western front, the British and French governments made a public declaration about the aims of the war in the Middle East. These were the liberation of Syria, Palestine and Mesopotamia from the oppressive rule of the Turks, and the setting up of national governments which would 'derive their authority from the free exercise of the initiative and choice of the indigenous populations'.[17] The declaration was regarded by Feisal, with good reason, as a promise to the Arab peoples of representative govern-ment which would reflect their own choice. The promise was not made good. Having occupied northern Syria in 1920, the French expelled Feisal from Damascus by force.

The Peace Conference opened in Paris on 18 January 1919. It was the greatest assembly of statesmen ever convened and it opened with high hopes. Justice between nations was to be done, and sovereign states were to subject themselves to a new international order. The horrors of war would never be allowed to visit Europe again, and people would choose for themselves who should rule them. The achievements of the Congress fell pitifully short of these expectations. The unmanageable number of delegates and hangers-on who converged on Paris (the British delegation alone was four hundred strong) and the complexity of the issues which had to be resolved were among the reasons. More important were the vindictiveness and greed of Britain and France. An anachronistic idea of empire more fitted for the nineteenth century than the twentieth which was persisted in by the European powers was the main obstacle to any fair and final disposition of the Turkish empire.

The peoples freed from the defeated Habsburg and Ottoman empires were to decide their own fate. That was a principle adopted by Woodrow Wilson with missionary zeal and accepted at least by lip service by the victorious European powers. If any of these former peoples of the Austrian or Ottoman empires were not ready for autonomous statehood, one of the victorious powers would be appointed by the League of Nations to act as trustee. The trustee was to be appointed under a system of 'Mandates' and had the duty of bringing the country in its care to the degree of political maturity judged necessary for independent statehood. A permanent 'Mandates Commission' was to be appointed by the League to supervise the work of the mandatory powers. Syria, Palestine and Mesopotamia were all to be subject to the scheme of mandates.

Lloyd George and Clemenceau had met in London at the end of 1918. Their intention was to arrange matters between themselves so that they could form a united front when they faced Woodrow Wilson in Paris. Clemenceau agreed to change the Sykes–Picot agreement. Mosul, the oil town in northern Mesopotamia, was to be transferred from the French to the British sphere of influence, and Palestine was to come under British instead of international

control. Nothing was said about what Clemenceau obtained from the British
in return for these important concessions. The variation of Sykes–Picot was
not recorded in writing and is only mentioned in an inconspicuous note in
the official record.[18] The Sykes–Picot agreement died unmourned – although
France made several resentful attempts to resuscitate it. It had been Lloyd
George's intention throughout that this inconvenient agreement should be swept
away. Balfour agreed. He had never understood the basis on which the French
claim to Syria was supposed to rest. But C. P. Scott thought the British Prime
Minister was cynical. He wrote to Weizmann a few days before the Anglo-French
meeting, contrasting the characters of Woodrow Wilson and Lloyd George, and
told him that 'Ll.G. doesn't know (it is an intellectual defect) what principle
means'.[19]

Balfour did not agree entirely with Lloyd George about Palestine. He was still
reluctant for Britain to take on the mandate alone and was concerned about
the entanglements to which it might lead. He persisted in the idea of a joint
arrangement with the United States, but it was a lost cause. America had no wish
to assume any lasting responsibilities in the Middle East. Balfour considered
that it would be impolitic to make any public statement about Palestine until
the whole eastern situation had 'cooled down'. 'The weak point in our position'
he wrote to Lloyd George early in the Peace Conference, 'of course is that in
the case of Palestine we deliberately and rightly decline to accept the principle
of self-determination. If the present inhabitants were consulted they would
unquestionably give an anti-Jewish verdict.' The words 'and rightly' were added
in manuscript.[20]

Lloyd George was unlikely to have been troubled by such logical inconsistencies,
but Balfour returned to the point in a long memorandum on Syria, Palestine and
Mesopotamia written in August 1919.[21] By then the victorious allies gathered in
Paris had accepted the policy of the Balfour Declaration. This was plainly at odds
with the wishes of the inhabitants of Palestine, and therefore with the principle
of self-determination enshrined in the Covenant of the League of Nations. It
offended Balfour's intellectual honesty to evade the issue. He embraced it and
added a dose of irony. The language of the Covenant, he wrote, might suit the
longitude of Washington, Paris or Prague but in the longitude of Damascus it
would probably get us into trouble, unless we treated it with a very wide latitude

of interpretation. He summarized the position of the victorious Powers towards Palestine in a phrase which was embarrassing but true: 'In short, so far as Palestine is concerned, the Powers have made no statement of fact which is not admittedly wrong, and no declaration of policy which, at least in the letter, they have not always intended to violate.'

The contradiction between the Covenant and British Palestine policy could only be resolved by giving primacy to one or the other. Balfour had no doubt which should be preferred; and he gave the reasons for his choice in a single sentence. No other contemporary British statesman could or would have used such language.

> The four great powers are committed to Zionism. And Zionism, be it right or wrong, good or bad, is rooted in age-long traditions, in present needs, in future hopes, of far profounder import than the desires and prejudices of the 700,000 Arabs who now inhabit that ancient land.

A Zionist delegation had been in Paris since December 1918 to prepare for the presentation of their case before the Council of Ten. It was headed by Sokolow with Weizmann following later. The first draft, a document of more than forty pages and putting forward extravagant claims to reconstitute Palestine as a Jewish commonwealth, was submitted to the British delegation in January 1919. Balfour observed mildly to Lloyd George that as far as he knew Weizmann had never put forward a claim for a Jewish government of Palestine, and that such a claim would be inadmissible. Ormsby-Gore was blunter. He told Weizmann that he did not like such phrases as 'Jewish Commonwealth' or 'Jewish Palestine': they would excite fears and opposition.[22] The document was returned and a shorter, anodyne substitute was prepared and delivered to the Conference secretariat at the beginning of February.

What should the Zionists ask for? There was no unanimity or even clarity among them. The same disparities persisted from the time when the Declaration was being drafted in the summer of 1917. Hotheads like Sacher argued that now was the time to seek Jewish sovereignty over the Land of Israel. He complained that the Jews had helped give England Palestine and their usefulness was now exhausted; things would be worse under the English than the Turks; the Jews would be ruled by anti-Semitic public schoolboys with a pro-Moslem bias.

Weizmann had more of a sense of what was politically possible, and Balfour was right in saying that he had never put forward a claim to a Jewish government in Palestine. His final aim was a Jewish state but it was a question of tactics how to achieve it. Writing to a colleague in 1918, he put it this way.

> We need an evolutionary tactic, for example: we ought not to ask the British government if we will enter Palestine as masters or equals to the Arabs . . . The Declaration implies that we have been given the opportunity to become masters . . . There is a British proverb about the camel and the tent: at first the camel sticks one leg in the tent, and eventually it slips into it. This must be our policy.[23]

Balfour, like Weizmann, thought that a Jewish state would emerge by a gradual evolutionary process. But he did not use the language of master and subject. In 1922, in a debate on the Mandate in the House of Lords, he had to meet the direct contention that it was an essential consequence of the establishment of a Jewish national home that the Jews would exercise some sort of dominion over the Arabs. He answered by denying that it followed. To suppose, he said, that one section of the population would ever be allowed to dominate another was a very poor compliment to the British government and to the Mandates Commission. He acknowledged that tact, good judgement and sympathetic goodwill would be required on the part of both Jew and Arab. But in the last resort he hoped that the Arabs would remember that they owed their independence and autonomy in the Hejaz and Mesopotamia to the British, and would not 'grudge that small notch in what are now Arab territories being given to the people who for all these hundreds of years have been separated from it'.[24] These arguments do not read well with the advantage of nearly one hundred years of hindsight.

The Zionists were summoned to appear before the Council of Ten at the end of February. A few days earlier Mark Sykes died suddenly of an attack of influenza a month short of his fortieth birthday. Hogarth, who often could not accept Sykes' idealistic vision, paid him a rueful tribute. Sykes, he wrote

> was full of gorgeous all-embracing ideas, amazingly incongruous with the Near East of the past or present, as we knew it, or with any future within hail, and he drummed them into us with an exuberant emphasis on single features of men or groups, and single aspects of history or present politics which often ended in his snatching at a pencil and dashing off a whole series of caricatures. But as there is always a serious element in caricature, so there was in his talk, and the more he caricatured men and things, the

more he convinced himself. We used to watch with sympathy, admiration and some amusement his courageous efforts to turn native minds to his own paths of idealism ... Had he lived longer, he would have reconstructed something of a more lasting sort; in any case one cannot but think that some of the shifts, some of the surrenders, some of the pretences and some of the casuistry which have marked our peace policy in the Near East, would not have been, or not have been so disastrous.[25]

With Mark Sykes gone, Zionism had lost an influential friend and a loveable human being. It was a cruel blow. He had acted as the midwife for the Balfour Declaration, but his conception of a Middle East of independent Arab, Jewish and Armenian states living together in harmony died with him.

The tribunal before which the Zionists were to plead their case was not one composed of all the belligerents, as many, particularly the Russian Jews among them, had envisaged. It was made up only of the victors: the United States, Britain, France, Italy and Japan. Their purpose was to dictate the terms of the new world order. Balfour and Milner represented Great Britain. The proceedings were formal and the Jews were invited to state their case one by one. Sokolow was first. He spoke, said Weizmann, as if the centuries of suffering rested on his shoulders, and of this moment for which the Jewish people had waited eighteen centuries.[26] Weizmann was next. His statement dealt with the failure of all solutions to the Jewish question except that one which would end its homelessness and weakness. Ussishkin, the leader of the Russian Zionists, followed speaking in Hebrew.

The last speaker was Sylvain Lévi, who had been chosen to speak for French Jewry at the insistence of Baron Edmond de Rothschild. To the horror of the others, he began to take the Zionist case to pieces as they listened. He spoke of Palestine as being no more than the home of a philanthropic venture. He dwelt on the poverty of the land, and how Zionism would lead to the Arab farmers being dispossessed by the Jews who, he said, were mainly Russians of explosive tendencies. Under the influence of Zionism, the country might be likened to a concentration camp of Jewish refugees.[27] Help came from an unexpected quarter. Lansing, the American Secretary of State, said there was some confusion about what was meant by a 'Jewish national home': did it mean an autonomous Jewish government? Weizmann seized the opportunity and set about Lévi. The Zionists did not want an autonomous government, he said in answer to Lansing. That might come later. For now they wanted to build up a nationality gradually by sending to Palestine 70,000 to 80,000 Jews annually, 'and so make Palestine as Jewish as America is American or England English'. Weizmann was congratulated there and then by Balfour. He wrote to Vera that it was a marvellous moment, the most triumphant of his life.[28] The day was saved but Weizmann's words about a Jewish Palestine were not forgotten.

The Zionists had a good press in Paris after the hearing. Only *Le Matin* struck a discordant note. It published an unfriendly interview with Feisal. Afterwards Feisal repudiated what had been published and wrote a warm letter to Felix Frankfurter about Weizmann and his fellow-Zionists. We feel, he said, that the Arabs and Jews are cousins in race. 'We Arabs, especially the educated among us, look with the deepest sympathy on the Zionist movement . . . we will wish the Jews a most hearty welcome home.'[29]

The Council of Ten, which had sat in judgement, gave no verdict. The victorious Powers accepted the policy of the Balfour Declaration but no peace treaty with Turkey was signed in Paris. So the consequent questions of the grant of the Mandate for Palestine and what should be its borders were held in abeyance. It took another year. The delay was caused by the hesitation and ambiguous attitude of the United States. In the end the Americans washed their hands of the Turkish treaty, and Britain, France and Italy proceeded without them. Another conference was convened in London in February 1920. By this time Balfour, who was exhausted, had left the Foreign Office for the less demanding office of Lord President, and had been replaced by Curzon. Curzon loyally defended the Zionist policy of his predecessor, but his personal views on the subject were a great deal less warm than those of Balfour. Britain continued to press for the Palestine Mandate and the acceptance of responsibility for implementing the Balfour Declaration.

There were angry differences between Britain and France at the London conference. The old arguments were revived about the extent of France's historic sphere of influence in Syria, and the French fear that Britain was trying to extend her empire with a solid block of territory from the Persian Gulf to the Mediterranean. Another conference was held in San Remo in April 1920. Britain and France at last agreed: France was to have the Mandate for Syria and Britain for Palestine and Mesopotamia. It was a good agreement for the policy of the Balfour Declaration. Britain gained Palestine and the Zionists secured the Mandatory that they wanted. But it was a compromise not without cynicism. As Curzon said in August 1920, each Mandatory was given a free hand in the territory for which it was responsible. Referring to the French occupation of Damascus and the forcible expulsion of Feisal, he confessed that he was completely ignorant of what had actually happened but, he said, 'the action of the French has been accepted by the British, who made no representation at all to the French in regard to that action'.[30]

While these matters of state were being debated by the politicians in Paris, London and San Remo with little apparent sense of urgency, the situation on the ground in Palestine was worsening. The British army had cleared Palestine of the Turks by the end of 1918 and the country was governed by the military, until a civil administration under Sir Herbert Samuel was established in June 1920. The military government was faced with a sharply deteriorating situation between Arab and Jew. The Jews living in Palestine adopted an aggressive attitude towards the administration and made public pronouncements about a Jewish state. On the Arab side there was much anti-Jewish propaganda with outbreaks of violence. A minority of officers like Clayton, the Chief Political Officer, tried to hold the ring fairly. But the majority thought the Balfour Declaration just an additional, and explosive, burden heaped on the soldiers by faraway politicians. Jabotinsky had been right. The administration did show bias against the Jews and there were unfortunately many instances of ugly anti-Semitism. The failure of nerve on the part of the military culminated in May 1919 with a telegram from Clayton to the Foreign Office reporting the view of the Chief Administrator, General Money. The General in effect wanted to cancel the Balfour Declaration. If the Zionist pro-gramme were a necessary adjunct to a mandate, General Money said, the people of Palestine would rather have the United States or France as their protector.

> The idea that Great Britain is the main upholder of the Zionist programme will preclude any local request for a British mandate and no mandatory power can carry through the Zionist programme except by force and in opposition to the wishes of the large majority of the people of Palestine.[31]

It is not the business of soldiers to make policy and the generals were firmly put in their place. Balfour suggested that Clayton should remind himself that France, the United States and Italy had all approved the policy of the Declaration. When the hapless Clayton persisted that unity among the allied governments would not affect local opinion, Curzon summarily ended the correspondence by sending a telegram 'for the information and guidance of all heads of administration'. It stated in plain words that Britain was to have the Palestine Mandate, that its terms would embody the Balfour Declaration, and that it should be impressed on Arab leaders that the matter was 'a *chose jugée*'.[32]

Weizmann shuttled between London, Paris and Palestine with many cares on his shoulders. There were disputes between the Palestinian Jews and the Zionist Commission as the latter tried to curb the excesses of the former. Weizmann had to meet criticism from those among his colleagues who thought he was placing too much reliance on Britain, and those who opposed his determined policy of accommodation with Feisal and the Arabs. A damaging split opened between himself and Brandeis. His worries were increased by the situation of the Jews in eastern Europe. There were pogroms in the Ukraine, Galicia and Poland which increased the pressure on immigration into Palestine. He was much involved in the drafting of the terms of the Palestine Mandate and the negotiation of its borders. And in the British government his old friends were departing: not only Sykes, but also Graham, Ormsby-Gore and then Balfour himself.

In September 1919 he wrote to Vera from Paris and told her that Balfour was going home, he feared for good. 'He'd become tired and fed up, which is not good for us.'[33] Balfour had not quite given up. Although he relinquished the Foreign Office in October he returned for San Remo the following April to see the Mandate agreed. By his patience, unvarying courtesy and determination he had achieved the Declaration and, when he was at last persuaded that the Americans would not join, the sole Mandate for Palestine which was the indispensable condition for carrying the Declaration into effect. Lloyd George was no more than just when he wrote to Balfour in August 1918 and described the Declaration as 'your' policy.[34]

Curzon's strong affirmation of the policy of the Balfour Declaration in August 1919 did not arrest the worsening situation in Palestine. Colonel Richard Meinertzhagen who was Chief Political Officer from September 1919 wrote a report to the Foreign Secretary within days of his arrival in Palestine. He was, he confessed, strongly prejudiced in favour of Zionism, although he had no Jewish blood in him. He was nonetheless fair-minded. He told Curzon that there was strong local opposition to Zionism. This was 'mainly traceable to a deliberate misunderstanding of the Jew and everything Jewish'. All anti-Zionist feeling viewed with alarm the question of immigration which was regarded as 'the unlimited dumping of undesirable Jews from eastern Europe'. On the other side, the local Zionists' eagerness and pressure to get on with the Zionist programme before the Mandate was established caused friction with the administration. It was not easy for those governing the country, said Meinertzhagen, but the work of the officials had been doubly difficult 'as their personal views, no matter how anxious they are to conceal them, incline towards the exclusion of Zionism in Palestine'.[35] Meinertzhagen's studied language of warning lost nothing by its understatement.

As the politicians were gathering in San Remo in April 1920, three days of anti-Jewish rioting in Jerusalem left six Jews dead and over two hundred injured. The army stood by without intervening. Weizmann was in Palestine to spend Passover with his mother. He was incensed by the behaviour of the military administration. It reminded him of the worst days in Tsarist Russia. He wrote to Vera, '*tout comme chez nous*. Verochka, my child, don't pay any attention to the newspaper reports: they lie.' The letter was written in the train from Genoa to San Remo where he arrived in a wild, dishevelled state. A few days later he wired her, 'Mandate granted. Boundary discussion favourable. Prime Minister gave definite assurances change administration.' After all that he had seen and experienced, he wanted only to sleep; but he was able to write once more to his wife and tell her 'Ll. G. took leave of us before his departure in a touching manner, and said: "Now you have got your start, it all depends on you."'[36]

14

Epilogue

The British Mandate for Palestine lasted until 1948 when it slid to an ignominious end and Britain washed its hands of the country and handed it back to the United Nations. It was probably always unworkable. Expectations were too high among the Jews and those like Balfour who were supporters of the Zionist ideal. Those who tried to govern the country – British officials, police and soldiers – disliked the policy of the Balfour Declaration from the start, treated Palestine as a colony and, at best, tried to deal with all sections of the population equally. But the Zionists had never believed in equality for the Arabs. The predominant British aims in seeking the Palestine Mandate and supporting Zionism were to secure the Suez Canal and the road to India against France, Russia and all other interlopers, and to expand Britain's interests in the oil-rich states of the Arab world. These were imperialistic aims and they proved to be impossible of achievement in any but the short term. Lloyd George and his colleagues did not foresee that the days of Empire were numbered.

Above all, considerations of strategic advantage could not displace the awkward fact that a large majority of those who lived in Palestine was unalterably opposed to the establishment of a Jewish state there. Milner's juggling with words in the last stages of drafting the Declaration were of no use against actual bitterness and violence. A crescendo of anger and bloodshed marked the history of the Mandate. There were anti-Jewish riots in 1920, 1921 and 1929, and a full-scale Arab revolt in 1936. The British government reacted predictably with a series of Commissions, Enquiries, Conferences and White Papers. The result of each successive step was to whittle away Jewish hopes without placating the Arabs. The plight of the German Jews in the thirties made the feeling of despair throughout Jewry only more intense.

Arthur Balfour died in 1930 and did not live to see the tragic outcome of his Declaration for the Middle East, or how Zionism could do nothing to ward off the Holocaust. But he was under no illusion that the Declaration had 'solved' the 'Jewish Problem'. Even when in 1919 Britain's allies had accepted that there should be a national home for the Jews in Palestine, he still thought it 'as perplexing a question as any that confronts the statesmanship of Europe'. Palestine was only a fragment of the difficulty, and he remained 'exceedingly distressed and harassed by difficulties'.[1]

He continued in public life until almost the end, serving as Lord President in Stanley Baldwin's government until it fell in 1929. His belief in Zionism never waned, nor his tendency to dismiss as inconsequential the increasing force of Arab nationalism. But his interest became less active. In Ramsay MacDonald's phrase, he viewed it from afar. In 1925, however, he accepted an invitation from the Zionist Organization to visit Palestine. It took place against a background of Arab protest and some thought it a mistake. But Balfour was greatly moved by the visit. He told his friend, Chaim Weizmann, that he was particularly impressed by the Jewish settlements, one of which had been named 'Balfouria' in his honour. The centrepiece of his tour was his opening, in the presence of ten thousand, of the Hebrew University on Mount Scopus in Jerusalem. It was the realization of Weizmann's most precious idea. Everywhere he was greeted by crowds of enthusiastic Jews. The Arabs were kept away.

Chaim Weizmann was the last person outside Balfour's immediate family to see the old statesman alive. The farewell between the two men, so diverse yet joined by a deep understanding of the cause they had each worked for, was witnessed by Balfour's niece, Blanche Dugdale, herself a passionate Zionist. Balfour never liked goodbyes. The meeting was brief and no word was spoken. But there was an emotional sympathy between the two men. Balfour moved his hand and in a simple gesture touched Weizmann's bowed head.[2]

Was the personal bond between Balfour and Weizmann as powerful an instrument in the history and ultimate success of Zionism as Blanche Dugdale thought? Balfour's personal contribution to the policy of the Declaration which bears his name has been doubted. It has been argued that his reasons for embracing Zionism do not much matter. Nor was it of much consequence if they were different from those which appealed to his ministerial colleagues. It was the cabinet and the Foreign Office, not Balfour, who really made the Declaration; and it is unlikely that Balfour's advocacy would have carried the cabinet if it had not been buttressed by the strategic arguments which were so important to his colleagues. It was therefore little more than fortuitous that it was Balfour, as Foreign Secretary, who wrote the letter to Lord Rothschild.[3]

The short answer to these arguments is that the Jews knew whom to thank. The millions of Jews in the ghettos of eastern Europe and the slums of New York who mourned the death of Balfour did not know him and had never seen his face. To Weizmann he was the first spiritual leader and teacher whom Israel had received from the Gentiles. 'We mourn him', Weizmann wrote, 'as we have never mourned a Gentile.'[4]

For Chaim Weizmann the all-excluding preoccupation of the Mandate period was the relation between Jew and Arab. Everything that the Zionists attempted in Palestine or London was affected by it, and it was the root cause of the paralysis in British Palestine policy. It was imperative for Weizmann to do all he could to bring about some accommodation with the Arabs. But he was confronted by Arab neighbours who were leaderless and could not agree among themselves, and he was constantly sniped at by his own disputatious constituency. His fellow-Zionists accused him of being soft on the Arabs and in the pocket of the British. The truth was that the existence of the Palestinian Arabs had never entered the consciousness of Zionism. He finally turned on his critics at the 1923 Zionist Convention in Baltimore and told them the unpalatable facts. 'For years', he said, 'we have drafted political resolutions that we Jews want to live in peace with the Arabs.'

> We have passed resolutions which have the character of a pledge. But as soon as it comes to taking decisive and effective steps to carry out those resolutions, because the realisation of all these problems is a question of the life or death of our work in Palestine, one is attacked on all sides . . . whatever the National Home will ultimately become, even if it absorbs millions of Jews . . . it will nevertheless remain an island in the Arab sea. We have to come to an understanding with this people which is akin to us and with which we have lived in concord in the past.

He brought his mordant wit to bear. Of course, he said, it would have been better if it had been the Nile, and not the Jordan, that had watered Palestine; better still if Moses had led the Jews to America; better yet if the Jews had to deal with Englishmen instead of themselves. But in Eretz Israel [the sacred land] there was the Jordan and there was a people who resisted the coming of the Jews and who encircled Palestine. 'We have to deal with these realities with reason and with political honesty; for these are the strongest weapons a man possesses'.[5]

It was a lonely furrow. In 1931 it cost him the Presidency of the World Zionist Organization which he did not regain for five years. It meant accepting Winston Churchill's White Paper of 1922 which removed the land east of the Jordan from the Jewish national home. In 1937 it meant accepting the recommendation of Lord Peel's Royal Commission for the partition of Palestine. Weizmann's reasons for accepting the attenuation of the borders of Israel are revealing:

> I know that God promised Palestine to the children of Israel, but I do not know what boundaries He set. I believe they were wider than the ones now proposed and may have included Transjordan. Still, we have forgone the eastern part and are now asked to forgo some of the western part. If God will keep His promise to His people in His own time, our business as poor humans who live in a difficult age is to save as much as we can of the remnants of Israel.[6]

Weizmann believed that God had always chosen small countries to reveal His purposes to humanity: Judea and Greece, not Carthage or Babylonia. He saw partition and its consequence – the end of the Mandate and the formation of a small Jewish state – as a real opportunity for coming to terms with the Arabs. Although the Peel Commission's scheme gave the Jews only twenty per cent of Palestine, it was a basis for negotiation. But it was not to be. The Arabs rejected it out of hand and the British allowed the chance to slip.

Although the way was strewn with frustration and danger, important gains were made by the Zionists under Weizmann's leadership. Churchill's White Paper of 1922 permitted Jewish immigration into Palestine up to the 'economic absorptive capacity' of the country. When the Mandate ended there were half a million Jews in Palestine, approaching one third of the population. Nothing could have been more important for the future state of Israel.

But against a darkening European background in the thirties, the British government continued to take the line of least resistance and to eat away at the policy of its own Balfour Declaration. In 1938 Weizmann had a visit from Jan Masaryk, the Czech leader, just after the betrayal of his country at Munich. 'When he arrived at our house that evening he was almost unrecognisable. The gaiety and high spirits which we always associated with him were gone.' Masaryk pointed to the little dog he had brought with him while he was pacing the London streets in despair: 'That's all I have left,' he said, 'and, believe me, I am ashamed to look him in the eye.' Neither the Czechs nor the Jews, wrote Weizmann, could forget Neville Chamberlain's words: why should England risk war with Hitler for the sake of 'a far-away country of which we know little'? If this was the way the Czechs were spoken of, what could the Jews expect from a government of that kind?[7]

There was not long to wait. A White Paper of May 1939, issued on the eve of the Second World War and at a time when many Jews were desperate to get out of Germany, effectively repudiated the Balfour Declaration. It declared that it 'could not have intended that Palestine should be converted into a Jewish state against the will of the Arab population of the country'. It proposed that a further 75,000 Jews should be allowed to enter Palestine during the next five years, and after that immigration would not be permitted without the consent of the Arabs of Palestine.[8]

Nearly six years of war followed. The Zionist programme was at a standstill and the Palestinian Jews were in a precarious position as the German armies stood at the gates of Egypt. The Weizmanns lost their son, Michael, on active service in the Royal Air Force. In the summer of 1944 Weizmann begged the British government to bomb Auschwitz. It would mean, he said, that the allies were waging war on the Nazi extermination policies; and he added that it would give the lie to the often-repeated Nazi propaganda that the Allies were not really displeased with the Nazis' ridding Europe of Jews.[9] Nothing was done.

As soon as the war in Europe was ended Weizmann sent Churchill a letter recalling Churchill's attack on the 1939 White Paper, and making a personal plea in which he summed up all the things he had been working for.

> We remember with gratitude how in the debate of May 23rd, 1939 the voice of British conscience spoke through you. We have noted how, during the years of war, you have never let yourself be drawn into saying anything which could be interpreted as an accept-ance of the White Paper. This has enabled me to urge upon my people patience . . . The position of the Jews in liberated countries is desperate. The political position in Palestine is becoming untenable, and so is my personal position . . . This is the hour to eliminate the White Paper, to open the doors of Palestine and to proclaim the Jewish State.'[10]

During the war Churchill had continued to hold out hope that the White Paper could be withdrawn and that Palestine could be partitioned. But he now replied that there could be no possibility of these matters being considered until the allies were seated at the Peace Table. In July he was decisively defeated at the polls and replaced by a new Labour government under Clement Attlee.

At first the Labour Party promised new hope for the Zionists. Only months before the election they had said at their party conference that after the atrocities committed by the Nazis there was an irresistible case for allowing Jewish immigration into Palestine. Perhaps incautiously, but in the relief and euphoria of victory, Hugh Dalton, who was expected to be Foreign Secretary in the new government, had proposed an exchange of populations: 'Let the Arabs be encouraged to move out as the Jews move in.' But Ernest Bevin, not Dalton, became Foreign Secretary.

'Mr Bevin', wrote Abba Eban, a future Foreign Minister of Israel, 'was destined to be Israel's George III, the perverse and unwilling agent of her independence.'[11] Bevin's coarse-grained and somewhat brutal style grated on Weizmann, but it was not only a matter of style. Bevin quickly showed that he had no enthusiasm for a Jewish national home in the post-war world. When President Truman proposed that 100,000 European Jews should be admitted to Palestine at once, Bevin told Weizmann that that was not 'the right way to set about the business', and he proposed another Committee of Enquiry. He refused to cancel the 1939 White Paper and he repudiated the statements made by Dalton. It seemed incredible to Weizmann that the British should break their promises, or that anyone could be playing fast and loose with the Jews at a time when they were so battered and exhausted. It was a sad end to Weizmann's lifelong love affair with England.

Events moved to a bitter climax. Disenchantment with Britain turned to anger and the Jews began to use terror as a weapon. In 1944 Lord Moyne, the Colonial Secretary, was murdered. In 1946, the King David Hotel in Jerusalem, which served as the offices of the Mandate secretariat, was blown up by the Irgun, a terrorist organization, with the loss of many innocent lives. Finally, in 1947, opinion was outraged by the Irgun's hanging of two British Sergeants in a eucalyptus grove. Weizmann had always detested terror as an instrument of policy. He considered that Zionism was a movement that was ethical as well as political. He thought the Irgun and Stern gangs were destructive, retrograde and, above all, un-Jewish. He understood the motives that had led some young Jews in Palestine to violence: they felt that it was the only way left them to draw the attention of the world to Palestine. It was a familiar argument but it was a fallacy, a short cut which could prove fatal to Zionism. The Jews came to Palestine to build, not destroy. Weizmann warned that the Jews had many hostages all over the world; although Palestine was the primary consideration, the path taken by Zionism must never rekindle anti-Semitism or endanger Jews elsewhere.[12]

By 1946 Weizmann was exhausted. He was ill and half-blind with glaucoma. Driven from office as President of the Zionist Organization, he left London for Palestine to retreat to his beloved Weizmann Institute of Science at Rehovot. In February 1947 the British government announced that it had no power to award Palestine either to the Jews or to the Arabs, and no power to divide the country between the two. It would therefore submit the problem to the United Nations. In that way Britain, tired and worn down by the inhuman experience of six years of total war, decided to make an end of its adventure in Palestine. The project of a Jewish national home, which had been moored in the shelter of British waters for thirty years, was adrift.

A United Nations committee was given the task of solving the Palestine problem. While it was in the country the Jewish refugee ship *Exodus*, filled with 'displaced persons' from a stricken Europe, was boarded and her passengers transhipped first to France and then, of all destinations, to Germany. It was a pitiful symbol of Britain's exhaustion. The United Nations committee, however, was impressed by the Peel Commission's proposal of partition and recommended a similar solution, more generous to the Jews. Weizmann was persuaded to leave Rehovot and go to New York to take part in the submissions to the General Assembly of the United Nations. The vote, in November 1947, was in favour of partition. But it was soon apparent that the Arabs would reject the decision. There were bloody clashes and Arab 'liberation' forces entered Palestine from all sides. The Arabs had started the war in which Israel was born. The partition plan was in jeopardy and in a rapidly worsening situation there was talk of a United Nations trusteeship.

Weizmann summoned up one more effort: to ward off the trusteeship, and to save the plan of partition, or if that were not possible, to declare the state of Israel and get the United States to recognize it. That would require a personal approach to the President. Harry Truman was a very different proposition from Balfour. He lacked the subtlety and speculative character of Balfour's mind. He liked to reduce things to the simple and straightforward, and he expected the same of others. Weizmann had been seriously ill in New York, but rising from his sickbed, he went down to Washington for a long private interview with the President at the White House. Truman recalled the meeting in his memoirs:

> Dr Weizmann was a man of remarkable achievements and personality. His life had been dedicated to two ideals, that of science and that of the Zionist movement. He was past seventy now and in ill health. He had known many disappointments and had grown patient and wise in them . . . When he left my office I felt that he had reached a full understanding of my policy, and that I knew what it was he wanted.[13]

Weizmann told Truman that the choice for his people was either statehood or extermination; and the President gave him a specific commitment. He would work for the establishment and recognition of a Jewish state. In April 1948 Britain announced that the Mandate would end on 15 May. It was still uncertain what the United Nations would decide. David Ben-Gurion in Jerusalem asked Weizmann for advice. 'Proclaim the State, no matter what ensues', was the reply. On 14 May, in Tel Aviv, Ben-Gurion declared the state of Israel with himself as its first Prime Minister. Within hours the United States recognized the new state. Truman had kept his word. 'The old Doctor will believe me now', he said. The United States had taken the place of Britain as the friend and sponsor of Zionism and its consummation, the state of Israel.

It was a long way from the Vienna of Theodor Herzl and his formal, deferential diplomacy; even further from the Motol of Chaim Weizmann's upbringing in the desolate marshes of the Russian Pale of Settlement. Jews had been living in misery in the Diaspora, unable to stand erect and look the world straight in the eye, having to make do with a dream of Zion. Now they were free. The former time was also a time of innocence. With the birth of Israel in the midst of a war for survival the Jews tasted the fruit of the Tree of Good and Evil – as the history of the state over its first sixty years amply attests. Weizmann was invited to be the first President of Israel. He did not know that the office was intended to be honorific, and that for the last years of his life he would become a virtual prisoner in Rehovot, unable to influence events. The mantle of Moses had already passed to Joshua. But on the long journey no man had played a greater part.

Appendix

Drafts and Final Text of the Balfour Declaration

ZIONIST DRAFT (JULY 1917)

1. His Majesty's Government accepts the principle that Palestine should be reconstituted as the national home of the Jewish people.
2. His Majesty's Government will use its best endeavours to secure the achievement of this object and will discuss the necessary methods and means with the Zionist Organisation.

BALFOUR DRAFT (AUGUST 1917)

His Majesty's Government accepts the principle that Palestine should be reconstituted as the national home of the Jewish people and will use their best endeavours to secure the achievement of this object and will be ready to consider any suggestions on the subject which the Zionist Organisation may desire to lay before them.

MILNER DRAFT (3 SEPTEMBER 1917)

His Majesty's Government accepts the principle that every opportunity should be afforded for the establishment of a home for the Jewish people in Palestine and will use its best endeavours to facilitate the achievement of this object and will be ready to consider any suggestions on the subject which the Zionist Organisation may desire to lay before them.

MILNER DRAFT (4 OCTOBER 1917)

His Majesty's Government views with favour the establishment in Palestine of a national home for the Jewish race and will use its best endeavours to facilitate the achievement of this object, it being clearly understood that nothing shall be done which may prejudice the civil and religious rights of existing non-Jewish communities in Palestine or the rights and political status enjoyed in any other country by such Jews who are fully contented with their existing nationality.

FINAL TEXT OF THE BALFOUR DECLARATION
(31 OCTOBER 1917)

His Majesty's Government view with favour the establishment in Palestine of a national home for the Jewish people and will use their best endeavours to facilitate the achievement of this object, it being clearly understood that nothing shall be done which may prejudice the civil and religious rights of existing non-Jewish communities in Palestine or the rights and political status enjoyed by Jews in any other country.

Notes

ABBREVIATIONS

BL	British Library, London
CAB	British cabinet resolutions and papers, National Archives
CZA	Central Zionist Archives, Jerusalem
DBFP	Documents on British Foreign Policy
FO	British Foreign Office records, National Archives
IOLR	India Office Records, British Library
NA	National Archives, Kew
NAS	National Archives of Scotland, Edinburgh

Notes to Chapter 2: The Dream of Zion

1 Leonard Stein, *The Balfour Declaration* (London, 1961), p. 81. The author gives the number at the outbreak of war as 85,000 Jews and 600,000 Arabs.

2 *Weizmann Letters*, vii, no. 45. Weizmann to Mrs James de Rothschild, 22 November 1914.

3 Shindler, *What do Zionists Believe?* (London, 2007), p. 31.

4 *Herzl Diaries* (London, 1958), p. xix.

5 *Ibid.*, pp. 4, 69.

6 *Ibid.*, p. 9.

7 *Ibid.*, 23 August 1897, p. 220.

8 Cohen, *The Zionist Movement* (London, 1945), p. 76.

9 Selbie, 'The Influence of the Old Testament on Puritanism', in Bevan and Singer (eds) *The Legacy of Israel* (Oxford, 1927), pp. 407–31.

10 *Ibid.*

11 Webster, *The Foreign Policy of Palmerston* (London, 1951), ii, p. 761.

12 Hodder, *The Life and Work of the Seventh Earl of Shaftesbury* (London, 1886), i, p. 310.

13   *Herzl Diaries*, 7 June and 23 November 1895, pp. 34, 80.

14   *George Eliot Letters*, ed. Gordon Haight, (Oxford, 1956), vi, p. 301, 29 October 1876.

Notes to Chapter 3: Arthur Balfour

1   Balfour papers. NAS GD 433/2/145.

2   Balfour, *Chapters of an Autobiography* (London, 1930), pp. xii, 5.

3   Balfour Papers. BL Add. 49836, f. 83, Balfour to Mary Elcho, 10 August, 1911.

4   Balfour papers. NAS GD 433/2/214/1. 30 July 1898.

5   Egremont, *Balfour* (London, 1980), p. 26.

6   Dugdale, *Arthur James Balfour* (London, 1936), i, p. 27.

7   *Ibid.*, p. 29.

8   Balfour, *Chapters of an Autobiography*, p. 113.

9   Young, *Arthur James Balfour* (London, 1963) pp. 139, 319.

10   See Halévy, *A History of the English People in the Nineteenth Century* (London, 1929), v, pp. 372–5.

11   Cd. 1741.

12   *Ibid.*, paras. 91–8.

13   Parliamentary Debates, 4th Series, 145, col.795. 2 May 1905.

14   *Jewish Chronicle*, 5 May 1905.

15   Parliamentary Debates, 4th series, 149, col.155. 10 July 1905.

16   Leonard Stein, *The Balfour Declaration* (London, 1961), p. 165.

17   See Tomes, *Balfour and Foreign Policy* (Cambridge, 1997), pp. 34–7, 204.

18   Balfour, *Speeches on Zionism* (London, 1928), p. 28.

19   Balfour, Introduction to Sokolow, *Zionism* (London, 1919), p. xxxiv.

20   *Spectator*, 6 May 1939.

21   DBFP, 1st series, iv, p. 1276. Memorandum by Frankfurter of meeting on 24 June 1919.

22   *Weizmann Letters*, vii, no. 323. Weizmann to Scott, 23 March 1917; *The New Judaea*, March–April 1930, p. 110.

23   Balfour, *Speeches on Zionism* (London, 1928), p. 25; Meinertzhagen, *Middle East Diary* (London, 1959), p. 25; DBFP 1st series, iv, no.242. Balfour memorandum 11 August 1919, p. 345.

24   House of Lords Debates 5th series, 50, cols.1018–1019. 21 June 1922.

Notes to Chapter 4: Chaim Weizmann

1   Isaiah Berlin, *Personal Impressions* (London, 1980), p. 46.
2   *Weizmann Letters*, i, no.1. Weizmann to Sololovsky, summer 1885.
3   Weizmann, *Trial and Error* (London, 1949), p. 44.
4   *Weizmann Letters*, i, no.38. Weizmann to Herzl, 19 August 1899.
5   Weizmann, *Trial and Error*, p. 70.
6   *Weizmann Letters*, i, no. 144, Weizmann to Motzkin, 23 November 1901.
7   *Ibid.*, no.60. Weizmann to Motzkin, 3 March 1901.
8   Vera Weizmann, *The Impossible Takes Longer* (London, 1967), pp. 1, 9.
9   *Weizmann Letters*, i, no.104. Weizmann to Chatzman, 6–7 July 1901.
10 *Ibid.*, no.127. Weizmann to Chatzman, 8 September 1901.

Notes to Chapter 5: 'Uganda'

1   *Herzl Diaries* (London, 1958), 19 October 1898, p. 268.
2   *Ibid.*, 19 and 21 May 1901, pp. 338–43 and 350.
3   Stein, *The Balfour Declaration* (London, 1961), p. 18.
4   *Herzl Diaries*, 23 October 1902, p. 377.
5   *Ibid.*, 22 October 1902, p. 376.
6   *Ibid.*, p. 382.
7   Weizmann, *Trial and Error* (London, 1949), pp. 105–7.
8   *Weizmann Letters*, ii, no.316, 6 May 1903.
9   *Ibid.*, no.336, n.3. Herzl to Weizmann, 14 May 1903.
10 *Weizmann Letters*, ii, no.292. Weizmann to Chatzman, 15 March 1903; Weizmann, *Trial and Error*, p. 116.
11 *Herzl Diaries*, p. 387; Vital, *Zionism: The Crucial Phase* (Oxford, 1987), p. 47.
12 *Herzl Diaries*, 17 August 1903, p. 404.
13 Weizmann, *Trial and Error*, pp. 110–17.
14 *Weizmann Letters*, ii, no.423 n.1.
15 *Herzl Diaries*, p. 407.
16 Vera Weizmann, *The Impossible Takes Longer* (London, 1967), p. 20.
17 *Weizmann Letters*, iii, no.10, 16 September 1903.
18 *The Times*, 28 August 1903.
19 Stein, *The Balfour Declaration*, p. 31.
20 Weizmann, *Trial and Error*, p. 122.

Notes to Chapter 6: England

1 Weizmann, *Trial and Error* (London, 1949), p. 123.
2 *Weizmann Letters*, vii, no.176. Weizmann to Lady Crewe, 19 June 1915.
3 *Ibid.*, iii, no.253. 6 July 1904; no.224, 14 April 1904. In the United States an Immigration Act was passed in 1903; in England an Aliens Bill to restrict immigration was introduced in Parliament in March 1904.
4 Vera Weizmann, *The Impossible Takes Longer* (London, 1967), p. 17.
5 *Weizmann Letters*, iii, no. 44. Weizmann to Chatzman, 8 October 1903.
6 *Ibid.*, nos. 285 and 290, 1 and 5 August 1904.
7 *Ibid.*, iv, no.9. Weizmann to Chatzman, 23 January 1905; no.176. Weizmann to Gaster, 19 November 1905.
8 *Ibid.*, no.174. Weizmann to Chatzman, 13 November 1905.
9 *Ibid.*, no.195. Weizmann to Chatzman, 9 January 1906.
10 Dugdale, *Arthur James Balfour* (London, 1939), i, p. 327.
11 Weizmann, *Trial and Error*, p. 143.
12 Balfour, Introduction to Sokolow, *History of Zionism, 1600–1918* (London, 1919).
13 Weizmann, 'The Messenger of Grace', in *The New Judaea*, March–April 1930, p. 110.

Notes to Chapter 7: Palestine before the War

1 Weizmann, *Trial and Error* (London, 1949), p. 161.
2 *Ibid.*, p. 168; Herzl, *Diaries* (London, 1958), p. 284 (31 October 1898).
3 *Ibid.*, p. 167.
4 *Weizmann Letters*, v, no.56. Weizmann to Mrs Weizmann, 14 September 1907.
5 *Jewish Chronicle*, 25 October 1907.
6 Stein, *The Balfour Declaration* (London, 1961), p. 85, n.89.
7 CZA. H-III-D14. Khalidi to Kahn, 1 March 1899. See also Mandel, *The Arabs and Zionism before World War I* (Berkleley, CA, 1976), p. 47; and Rashid Khalidi, *Palestinian Identity* (New York, 1997), p. 74.
8 *Ibid.*, Herzl to Khalidi, 19 March 1899.
9 Mandel, *The Arabs and Zionism before World War I* (Berkeley, 1976), p. 28.
10 Herzl, *The Jewish State* (New York, 1988), p. 95.
11 Stein, *The Balfour Declaration*, pp. 90, 91.
12 Mandel, *The Arabs and Zionism before World War I*, pp. 214, 217.
13 *Ibid.*, p. 198.
14 *Ibid.*, p. 212.
15 *Weizmann Letters*, vi., no.187. Weizmann to Mrs Weizmann, 3 January 1914.

16 Weizmann, *Trial and Error*, p. 177.
17 *Ibid.*, p. 179.

Notes to Chapter 8: Messianic Times

1 *Weizmann Letters*, vii, no.65. Weizmann to Mrs Weizmann, 10 December 1914.
2 *Ibid.*, no.21. Weizmann to Levin, 18 October 1914.
3 A. G. Gardiner, *Prophets, Priests and Kings* (London, 1908), p. 247.
4 *Memoirs of Viscount Samuel* (London, 1945), p. 140.
5 *Ibid.*
6 Asquith, *Letters to Venetia Stanley* (Oxford, 1982), no.281, 28 January 1915.
7 The text is set out in Bowle, *Viscount Samuel* (London, 1957), pp. 172–7.
8 Asquith, *Letters to Venetia Stanley*, no.347, 13 March 1915.
9 Grigg, *The Young Lloyd George* (London, 1973), p. 34.
10 *Weizmann Letters*, vii, no.9. Weizmann to Greenberg, 16 September 1914.
11 Ayerst, *Guardian: Biography of a Newspaper* (London, 1971), p. 382.
12 *Weizmann Letters*, vii, no.95. Weizmann report to the Executive of the International Zionist Organization, 7 January 1915.
13 Weizmann, *Trial and Error* (London, 1949), p. 192.
14 Lloyd George papers. Parliamentary Archives. LG/C/25/14/1, 16 March 1915.
15 Asquith, *Letters to Venetia Stanley*, no.354, 17 March 1915.
16 *Weizmann Letters*, vii, no.68. Weizmann to Ahad Ha'am, 14 December 1915.
17 Weizmann, *Trial and Error*, p. 201.
18 *Weizmann Letters*, vii, no.68. Weizmann to Ahad Ha'am, 14 December 1914; and no.95. Weizmann to the executive of the International Zionist Organization, 7 January 1915.
19 Dugdale, *Arthur James Balfour* (London, 1939), ii, p. 165. An example of Weizmann's occasional lack of scruple about the truth is that he told Mrs de Rothschild in 1914 that he was in Kishinev at the time of the pogrom in 1903, whereas he was then in Geneva. See *Weizmann Letters*, vii, no.45, 22 November 1914. n.6.
20 *Weizmann Letters*, vii, no.95. Weizmann to the Executive of the International Zionist Organization, 7 January 1915.

Notes to Chapter 9: Placating the French, inciting the Arabs

1 Paléologue, *An Ambassador's Memoirs 1914–1917* (London, 1923), p. 175.
2 De Gaulle, *War Memoirs* (London, 1955), i, p. 188.

3   NA CAB 27/1. Committee report, paragraph 96, 30 June 1915.

4   Kedourie, *In the Anglo-Arab Labyrinth* (London, 1976), p. 34.

5   Storrs, *Orientations* (London, 1937), p. 143.

6   Kedourie, *In the Anglo-Arab Labyrinth*, p. 7.

7   *Ibid.*, p. 28.

8   Kedourie, *The Chatham House Version* (New York, 1970), p. 14.

9   Cmd. 5957.

10 Kedourie, *In the Anglo-Arab Labyrinth*, p. 78.

11 *Ibid.*, pp. 86 ff.; Fromkin, *A Peace to End All Peace* (London, 1989), pp. 178 ff.

12 Kedourie, *In the Anglo-Arab Labyrinth*, p. 106.

13 *Ibid.*, p. 121.

14 *Ibid.*, p. 108.

15 NA CAB 42(6) 9–10, 16 December 1915.

16 Lloyd George, *The Truth About the Peace Treaties* (London, 1938), ii, p. 1023.

17 Storrs papers. Pembroke College, Cambridge. Box ii, folder 4, 21 June 1916.

18 Kedourie, *Arab Political Memoirs* (London, 1974), p. 243.

19 *Weizmann Letters*, vii, no.143. Weizmann to Samuel, 21 March 1915.

20 NA CAB. 42/11/9. Hall to Nicolson, 12 January 1916.

Notes to Chapter 10: First Steps to the Balfour Declaration

1   *Weizmann Letters*, vii, no.147. Weizmann to Scott, 23 March 1915.

2   Stein, *The Balfour Declaration* (London, 1961), p. 222.

3   NA FO 800/96. Grey to Bertie and Buchanan, 11 March 1916.

4   *Ibid.*, Buchanan to Nicolson, 14 March 1916.

5   Reading Papers. BL IOLR Eur. Mss. F 118/95. Montagu to Reading, 17 March 1916.

6   *Weizmann Letters*, vii, no.271, headnote. Weizmann to Wolf, 3 September 1916.

7   Weizmann, *Trial and Error* (London, 1949), p. 202.

8   NA FO 800/381. Sykes to Nicolson, 18 March 1916.

9   Stein, *The Balfour Declaration*, p. 285, n.3.

10 *Jewish Chronicle*, 7 December 1917.

11 *Manchester Guardian*, 22 November 1915.

12 *Spectator*, 12 August 1916.

13 Stein, *The Balfour Declaration*, p. 188.

14 *Weizmann Letters*, vii, no.21. Weizmann to Levin, 18 October 1914.

15 DBFP 1st Series, iv, appendix ii, p. 1276.

16 Lloyd George, *War Memoirs* (London, 1938), i, p. 349.

17 Weizmann, *Trial and Error*, p. 191.

18 *Weizmann Letters*, vii, no.190. Weizmann to Mrs de Rothschild, 18 July 1915.

19 *Ibid.*, no.127. Weizmann to Mrs de Rothschild, 4 March 1915.

20 Weizmann, *Trial and Error*, p. 220.

21 Lloyd George papers. Parliamentary Archives. LG/G/19/18/6. Note prepared for Lloyd George's memoirs, 4 December 1932.

22 C. P. Scott diaries and letters. Cambridge University Library. Microfilm MS 9810, 22–4 March 1916; 8 May 1916; Weizmann to Scott, 26 May 1916.

23 *Weizmann Letters*, vii, no.289. n.2. Weizmann to Mrs James de Rothschild, 12 November 1916.

24 Reinharz, 'Science in the Service of Politics', *English Historical Review* (1985) p. 572.

25 Scott diaries, 26 November 1915.

26 *Weizmann Letters*, vii, no.276. Weizmann to Mrs James de Rothschild, 21 September 1916.

Notes to Chapter 11: The Turning Point

1 Vereté, 'The Balfour Declaration and its Makers', *Middle Eastern Studies*, vi, (1970) pp. 48, 67.

2 Egremont, *Balfour* (London, 1980), p. 281.

3 Lloyd George papers. Parliamentary Archives. LG/F/23/1/2. Hankey to Lloyd George, 14 December 1916.

4 Weizmann, *Trial and Error* (London, 1949), p. 226.

5 Bruce Lockhart, *Giants Cast Long Shadows* (London, 1960), p. 13.

6 Balfour papers. BL IOLR Eur. Mss. F112/134, 22 March 1917.

7 NA FO 372/2817, 11 February 1916.

8 Scott diaries. Cambridge University Library. Microfilm Ms 9810, 3 April 1917.

9 *Diary of Lord Bertie* (London, 1924), ii, p. 123.

10 Stein, *The Balfour Declaration* (London, 1961), p. 362.

11 Scott diaries, 27 January 1917.

12 Stein, *The Balfour Declaration*, p. 184.

13 Lothian Papers. NAS GD40/17/42.

14 *Ibid.*; Stein, *The Balfour Declaration*, p. 370 n.29.

15 Vital, *Zionism: The Crucial Phase* (Oxford, 1987), p. 268.

16 Stein, *The Balfour Declaration*, p. 523.

17 NA CAB 21/58. War Cabinet 261, 31 October 1917.

18 Lothian Papers, NAS GD 40/17/42.

19 *The Diaries of Theodor Herzl* (London, 1958), p. 428, 26 January 1904.

20 Stein, *The Balfour Declaration*, p. 408; Minerbi, *The Vatican and Zionism* (Oxford, 1990), p. 111.

21 NA FO 371/3058. Cambon to Sokolow, 4 June 1917.

22 *Weizmann Letters*, vii, no.329. Weizmann to Sokolow, 4 April 1917.

23 Lothian Papers. NAS GD 40/17/42/63.

24 Scott diaries, 3 April 1917.

25 NA CAB 21/77. 28 April 1917. The Leontes flows into the Mediterranean some distance north of the present northern boundary of Israel, between Tyre and Sidon. The Hauran is the upland plain lying to the east of the Jordan valley.

26 *Weizmann Letters*, vii, no.356. Note of interview with Lord Robert Cecil, 25 April 1917.

27 *Ibid.*, no.323. Weizmann to Scott, 23 March 1917.

28 *Ibid.*, no.382, n.6; and Stein, *The Balfour Declaration*, p. 427.

29 *Ibid.*

30 Strum, *Louis B. Brandeis* (Cambridge, MA, 1984), p. 272.

31 *Weizmann Letters*, vii, no.321. Weizmann to Scott, 20 March 1917.

Notes to Chapter 12: It's a Boy!

1 *Weizmann Letters*, vii, no. 432. Weizmann to Graham, 13 June 1917.

2 *Ibid.*, n.17.

3 *Ibid.*, no.435. Weizmann to Sacher, 20 June 1917.

4 CZA A77/3. Montefiore to Milner, 17 May 1917.

5 NA FO 371/3058. 18 June 1917.

6 Sykes papers. Hull University Archives DDSY2/11/61. Sykes to Clayton. 22 July 1917.

7 Weizmann, *Trial and Error* (London, 1949), p. 247.

8 *Ibid.*, pp. 247–50.

9 *Weizmann Letters*, vii, no. 453. Weizmann to Graham, 6 July 1917; no. 458. Weizmann to Mrs Weizmann, 13 July 1917.

10 *Ibid.*, no.364. Weizmann to Tschlenow, 29 April 1917.

11 *Ibid.*, no.413. Weizmann to Rosov and Tschlenow, 2 June 1917.

12 Stein, *The Balfour Declaration* (London, 1961), p. 441.

13 *Ibid.*, p. 494.

14 *Weizmann Letters*, vii, no. 490. Weizmann to Sokolow, 5 September 1917.

15 Stein, *The Balfour Declaration*, p. 496.

16 *Weizmann Letters*, vii, no. 501. Weizmann to Scott, 13 September 1917.

17 *Spectator*, 26 May, 1939 and 3 January 1947.

18 Stein, *The Balfour Declaration*, p. 481.

19 *Ibid.*, p. 497.

20 NA FO 800/204. Cecil to Bayley for House, 3 September 1917.

21 NA FO 371/3083. House to Drummond for Cecil, 10 September 1917.
22 *Weizmann Letters*, vii, no. 496. Weizmann to Brandeis. Date uncertain. It appears that Brandeis received it only on 19 September.
23 *Ibid.*, no. 5 to no. 496.
24 *Ibid.*, no. 502. Weizmann to Kerr, 16 September 1917.
25 *Ibid.*, no. 514. Rothschild and Weizmann to Balfour, 3 October 1916.
26 Scott diaries. Cambridge University Library. Microfilm Ms 9810, 12 August 1919.
27 NA CAB 21/58. War Cabinet 227, 4 October 1917.
28 Lloyd George papers. Parliamentary Archives. LG/F/39/3/30. Montagu to Lloyd George, 4 October 1917.
29 Weizmann, *Trial and Error*, p. 261.
30 NA CAB 21/58. 'The Zionist Movement', 17 October 1917.
31 Lloyd George papers. Parliamentary Archives. LG/F/3/2/34. Balfour to Lloyd George, 25 October 1917.
32 Curzon papers. BL IOLR Mss.Eur. F112/124. 'The Future of Palestine', 26 October 1917.
33 NA CAB 21/58. War Cabinet 261, 31 October 1917.
34 Weizmann, *Trial and Error*, p. 262.

Notes to Chapter 13: At the Threshold

1 Stein, *The Balfour Declaration* (London, 1961), p. 589.
2 Reinharz, *Chaim Weizmann: The Making of a Statesman* (Oxford, 1993), p. 304.
3 *Weizmann Letters*, viii, no.6. Weizmann to Brandeis, 12 November 1917.
4 Reinharz, *Chaim Weizmann: The Making of a Statesman*, p. 278.
5 Weizmann, *Trial and Error* (London, 1949), p. 273; Vital, *Zionism: The Crucial Phase* (Oxford, 1987), p. 369, n.11. Note by Kidston, 27 February 1919.
6 Lloyd George papers. Parliamentary Archives. LG/F/49/13/2. Allenby to Lloyd George, 24 December 1919 and 14 April 1920.
7 *Weizmann Letters*, viii, no. 208, 30 May 1918.
8 Vital, *Zionism: The Crucial Phase* (Oxford, 1987), p. 323, n.65.
9 Sykes papers. Hull University Archives. DDSY2/11/96. Ormsby-Gore to Sykes, 9 April 1918.
10 *Ibid.*, DDSY2/11/83. Clayton to Sykes, 15 December 1917; DDSY2/11/101. Storrs to Sykes, 17 July 1918.
11 *Weizmann Letters*, viii, nos.151 and 181. Weizmann to Mrs Weizmann, 6 and 30 April 1918.
12 Weizmann, *Trial and Error* (London, 1949), p. 295.
13 *Weizmann Letters*, viii, no.213. Weizmann to Mrs Weizmann, 17 June 1918.

14　Stein, *The Balfour Declaration*, pp. 632–3.

15　Kedourie, *In the Anglo-Arab Labyrinth* (London, 2000), p. 148.

16　The text of the treaty was reproduced in *The Times*, 10 June 1936, with a covering letter from Weizmann. Disturbances in Palestine at the time had given new currency to the argument that the Balfour Declaration was inconsistent with the promises made to the Arabs during the war. This prompted Weizmann to write to *The Times* about the cooperation between the Arabs and the Jews in 1919. The precise wording of the condition attached to the treaty was unclear. According to Antonius, *The Arab Awakening* (London, 1938), appendix F, p. 437, the condition was added in Arabic although the agreement was written in English; and the version of the condition appearing in *The Times*, in facsimile of Lawrence's handwriting, is only a rough summary translation of the Arabic original into English.

17　Antonius, *The Arab Awakening* (London,1938), Appendix E, p. 435.

18　DBFP, 1st series, iv, p. 251.

19　Scott diaries and letters, Cambridge University Library. Microfilm MS. 9810, 19 November 1918.

20　Lloyd George papers. Parliamentary Archives LG/F/3/4/2. Balfour to Lloyd George, 19 February 1919.

21　DBFP 1st series, iv, no.242, 11 August 1919.

22　Reinharz, *Chaim Weizmann: The Making of a Statesman*, pp. 294–5.

23　*Ibid.*, p. 219.

24　House of Lords Debates, 5th series, 50, col.1011, 21 June 1922; Balfour, *Speeches on Zionism* (London, 1928), p. 24.

25　Sykes papers. Hull University archives DDSY2/10/16. Note of Hogarth, undated.

26　Weizmann, *Trial and Error*, p. 304.

27　*Ibid.*

28　Vital, *Zionism: The Crucial Phase*, p. 355; *Weizmann Letters*, ix, no.123. Weizmann to Mrs Weizmann, 28 February 1919.

29　Weizmann, *Trial and Error*, p. 307.

30　DBFP 1st series, viii, no.83.

31　*Ibid.*, iv, no.183, n.1. Clayton to Curzon, 2 May 1919.

32　*Ibid.*, no.196, n.4. Balfour to Curzon, 19 May 1919; and no.236. Curzon to French, 4 August 1919.

33　*Weizmann Letters*, ix, no.214. Weizmann to Mrs Weizmann, 11 September 1919.

34　Lloyd George papers. Parliamentary Archives LG/F/3/3/30. Lloyd George to Balfour, 27 August 1918.

35　Meinertzhagen, *Middle East Diary* (London, 1959), pp. 49–53.

36　*Weizmann Letters*, ix, nos.306, 309 and 317. Weizmann to Mrs Weizmann, 19, 25 and 29 April 1919.

Notes to Chapter 14: Epilogue

1 DBFP 1st series, iv, appendix ii, p. 1276. Note by Frankfurter of meeting between Balfour and Brandeis in Paris on 24 June 1919.

2 Dugdale, *Arthur James Balfour* (London, 1936), ii, p. 301.

3 Tomes, *Balfour and Foreign Policy* (Cambridge, 1997), pp. 199, 209; Vereté, *The Balfour Declaration and its Makers*, in Middle East Studies, vi (1970), p. 50.

4 *The New Judaea*, March–April 1930, p. 110.

5 Weltsch, 'The Fabian Decade', in Weisgal and Carmichael, (eds), *Chaim Weizmann: A Biography by Several Hands* (London, 1962), p. 193.

6 Weizmann, *Trial and Error* (London, 1949), p. 474.

7 *Ibid.*, p. 501.

8 Cmd. 6019.

9 Eban, 'Tragedy and Triumph' in *Chaim Weizmann: A Biography by Several Hands*, pp. 272, 273.

10 *Weizmann Letters*, xxii, no.10. Weizmann to Churchill, 22 May 1945.

11 Eban, 'Tragedy and Triumph', p. 280.

12 Weizmann, *Trial and Error*, p. 556.

13 Truman, *Memoirs*, ii, *Years of Trial and Hope* (London, 1956), p. 172.

Bibliography

ARCHIVES

Balfour papers: British Library, London, and National Archives of Scotland, Edinburgh.

Cabinet and Foreign Office records: CAB and FO series, National Archives, Kew.

Curzon papers: India Office records, British Library, London.

Lloyd George papers: House of Lords Record Office, London.

Lothian (Philip Kerr) papers: National Archives of Scotland, Edinburgh.

Scott diaries and correspondence: John Rylands Library, Manchester University, and microfilm in Cambridge University Library.

Storrs papers: Pembroke College, Cambridge.

Sykes papers: Brynmor Jones Library, Hull University.

Weizmann papers: Weizmann Archives, Rehovot, Israel.

Zionist records: Central Zionist Archives, Jerusalem.

OFFICIAL PUBLICATIONS

1903. Cd. 1741. Report of the Royal Commission on Alien Immigration.

1937. Cmd. 5479. Report of the Palestine Royal Commission.

1939. Cmd. 5957. Correspondence between Sir Henry McMahon and The Sherif Hussein of Mecca between July 1915 and March 1916.

1939. Cmd. 6019. Palestine: Statement of Policy.

BOOKS AND PERIODICALS

Adams, R. J. Q. (2007), *Balfour: The Last Grandee*, London, John Murray.

Adelson, R. (1975), *Mark Sykes: Portrait of an Amateur*, London, Jonathan Cape.

Ahad Ha'am (Asher Ginsberg) (1962), *Selected Essays*, L. Simon (trans. and ed.) New York, Meridian Books.

Antonius, G. (1938), *The Arab Awakening: The Story of the Arab National Movement*, London, Hamish Hamilton.

Asquith, H. H. (1982), *Letters to Venetia Stanley*, M. and E. Brock (eds), Oxford, Oxford University Press.

Ayerst, D. (1971), *Guardian: Biography of a Newspaper*, London, Collins.

Balfour, A. J. (1928), *Speeches on Zionism*, I. Cohen, (ed.), London, Arrowsmith.

—— (1930), *Chapters of Autobiography*, Mrs E. Dugdale, (ed.), London, Cassell.

Bein, A. (1957), *Theodor Herzl: A Biography*, London, East and West Library.

Berlin, I. (1980), *Personal Impressions*, London, The Hogarth Press.

Bertie, Lord, of Thame (1924), *Diary*, G. Lennox, (ed.), London, Hodder and Stoughton.

Bowle, J. (1957), *Viscount Samuel*, London, Gollancz.

Bruce Lockhart, R. (1960), *Giants Cast Long Shadows*, London, Putnam.

Cohen, I. (1945), *The Zionist Movement*, London, Frederick Muller.

Dugdale, B. (1936), *Arthur James Balfour*, London, Hutchinson.

Egremont, M. (1980), *Balfour: A Life of Arthur James Balfour*, London, Collins.

Fromkin, D. (1989), *A Peace to End All Peace*, London, André Deutsch.

Gilbert, M. (2007), *Churchill and the Jews: A Lifelong Friendship*, New York, Henry Holt.

Green, J. R. (1874), *A Short History of the English People*, London, Macmillan.

Herzl, T. (1988), *The Jewish State*, trans. S. D'Avigdor, New York, Dover.

—— (1958), *Diaries*, M. Lowenthal (trans. and ed.), London, Gollancz.

Hodder, E. (1886), *The Life and Work of the Seventh Earl of Shaftesbury*, London, Collins.

Josephus, (1981), *The Jewish War*, trans. G. A. Williamson, rev. edn, London, Penguin Books.

Kedourie, E. (1974), *Arab Political Memoirs*, London, Frank Cass.

—— (1976), *In the Anglo-Arab Labyrinth: the McMahon–Husayn Correspondence and its Interpretations 1914–1939*, Cambridge, Cambridge University Press.

—— (2004), *The Chatham House Version and other Middle-Eastern Studies*, rev. edn, Chicago, Ivor Dee.

Khalidi, R. (1997), *Palestinian Identity: The Construction of Modern Consciousness*, New York, Columbia University Press.

—— (2006), *The Iron Cage: The Story of the Palestinian Struggle for Statehood*, Boston, Beacon Press.

Leslie, S. (1923), *Mark Sykes: His Life and Letters*, London, Cassell.

Lloyd George, D. (1938), *War Memoirs*, London, Oldhams.

—— (1938), *The Truth about the Peace Treaties*, London, Gollancz.

Mackay, R. (1985), *Balfour: Intellectual Statesman*, Oxford, Oxford University Press.

MacMillan, M. (2002), *Paris 1919: Six Months that Changed the World*, New York, Random House.

Mandel, N. (1976), *The Arabs and Zionism before World War I*, Berkeley, University of California Press.

Minerbi, S. (1990), *The Vatican and Zionism*, Oxford, Oxford University Press.

Meinertzhagen, R. (1959), *Middle East Diary 1917–1956*, London, The Cresset Press.

Paléologue, M. (1923), *An Ambassador's Memoirs 1914–1917*, London, Hutchinson.

Rabinowicz, O. K. (1960), *Winston Churchill on Jewish Problems*, New York, Yoseloff.

Reinharz, J. (1985), 'Science in the Service of Politics: The Case of Chaim Weizmann during the First World War', in *English Historical Review*, vol. 100, p. 572.

—— (1985), *Chaim Weizmann: The Making of a Zionist Leader*, Oxford, Oxford University Press.

—— (1993), *Chaim Weizmann: The Making of a Statesman*, Oxford, Oxford University Press.

Rogers, P. (2005), *Herzl's Nightmare: One Land, Two Peoples*, London, Constable.

Sacher, H. (ed.) (1916), *Zionism and the Jewish Future*, London, John Murray.

Samuel, H. (1945), *Memoirs*, London, Cresset Press.

Segev, T. (2000), *One Palestine, Complete*, trans. H. Watzman, London, Little, Brown.

Selbie, W. B. (1927), 'The Influence of the Old Testament on Puritanism', in Bevan and Singer (eds) *The Legacy of Israel*, Oxford, Clarendon Press.

Shindler, C. (2007), *What do Zionists Believe?*, London, Granta Books.

Shlaim, A. (2000), *The Iron Wall: Israel and the Arab World*, London, Allen Lane.

Short, W. M. (ed.) (1912), *Arthur James Balfour as Philosopher and Thinker: A Collection of the More Important and Interesting Passages in his Non-Political Writings, Speeches and Addresses 1879–1912*, London, Longman, Green.

Sokolow, N. (1919), *History of Zionism 1600–1918*, London, Longman, Green.

Stein, L. (1961), *The Balfour Declaration*, London, Valentine Mitchell.

Stein, L. and Weisgal, M. (eds) (1968), *The Letters and Papers of Chaim Weizmann*, series A (Letters), London, Oxford University Press.

Storrs, R. (1937), *Orientations*, London, Ivor Nicholson and Watson.

Strum, P. (1984), *Louis B. Brandeis: Justice for the People*, Cambridge, MA, Harvard University Press.

Sykes, C. (1953), *Two Studies in Virtue*, London, Collins.

Tomes, J. (1997), *Balfour and Foreign Policy: The International Thought of a Conservative Statesman*, Cambridge, Cambridge University Press.

Truman, H. S. (1956), *Memoirs*, ii, *Years of Trial and Hope: 1946–1953*. London, Hodder and Stoughton.

Tuchman, B. (1957), *Bible and Sword: How the British Came to Palestine*, London, Redman.

Vereté, M. (1970), 'The Balfour Declaration and its Makers', in *Middle East Studies*, vi, p. 48.

Vital, D. (1975), *The Origins of Zionism*, Oxford, Oxford University Press.

—— (1982), *Zionism: The Formative Years*, Oxford, Oxford University Press.

—— (1987), *Zionism: The Crucial Phase*, Oxford, Oxford University Press.

Webster, Sir C. (1951), *The Foreign Policy of Palmerston 1830–1841*, London, Bell.

Weisgal, M. W. and Carmichael, J. (eds) (1962), *Chaim Weizmann: A Biography by Several Hands*, London, Weidenfeld and Nicolson.

Weizmann, C. (1949), *Trial and Error*, London, Hamish Hamilton.

Weizmann, V. (1967), *The Impossible Takes Longer*, London, Hamish Hamilton.

Wheatcroft, G. (1996), *The Controversy of Zion: Jewish Nationalism, the Jewish State and the Unresolved Jewish Dilemma*, New York, Addison-Wesley.

Wilson, T. (ed.) (1970), *The Political Diaries of C. P. Scott 1911–1928*, London, Collins.

Woodward, E. and Butler, R. (eds) (1952), *Documents on British Foreign Policy 1919–1939*, First Series, vols. iv, viii., London, HMSO.

Young, K. (1963), *Arthur James Balfour: The Happy Life of the Politician, Prime Minister, Statesman and Philosopher 1848–1930*, London, G. Bell.

Index